THROUGH THE TEMPEST

Give ear to my prayer, O God;
and hide not thyself from my supplication!
Attend to me, and answer me;
I am overcome by my trouble. . . .
I would haste to find me a shelter
from the raging wind and tempest.

Psalm 55:1–2, 8

THROUGH THE TEMPEST

Theological Voyages in a
Pluralistic Culture

LANGDON GILKEY

Selected and edited by
JEFF B. POOL

Fortress Press   Minneapolis

THROUGH THE TEMPEST
Theological Voyages in a Pluralistic Culture

Scripture quotations unless otherwise noted are from the Revised Standard Version of the Bible, copyright © 1946, 1952, and 1971 by the Division of Christian Education of the National Council of Churches.

The following publishers have graciously given permission to adapt and publish from copyrighted works. Chapter 2: "Plurality: Christianity's New Situation" from *The Pastor as Servant,* ed. Earle Shelp and Ronald H. Sunderland, copyright © 1986 Pilgrim Press, New York. Chapter 3: "Theology: Interpretation of Faith for Church and World" from *The Vocation of the Theologian,* ed. Theodore W. Jennings, Jr., 87–103, copyright © 1985 Fortress Press. Chapter 4: "Symbols, Meaning, and the Divine Presence" from *Theological Studies* 35 (June 1974): 249–67. Chapter 5: "The Christian Understanding of God" from *Christian Theology: An Introduction to Its Traditions and Tasks,* ed. Peter C. Hodgson and Robert H. King, 62–87, copyright © 1985 Fortress Press. Chapter 6: "Creation: Being and Non-Being" by Langdon Gilkey from *God and Creation: An Ecumenical Symposium,* ed. David B. Burrell and Bernard McGinn, 226–41, copyright © 1990 University of Notre Dame Press, Notre Dame, Ind. Chapter 7: "The Meaning of Jesus the Christ" from *The Christ and the Bodhisattva,* ed. Donald S. Lopez, Jr., and Stephen C. Rockefeller, 193–207, copyright © 1987 State University of New York Press, Albany, N.Y. Chapter 9: "Theology of Culture and Christian Ethics" from *The Annual of the Society of Christian Ethics,* ed. Larry L. Rasmussen, 341–64, copyright © 1984 Society of Christian Ethics. Chapter 10: "Ethics in Christianity and Buddhism" from *Dialog* 28 (Winter 1989): 37–42. Chapter 11: "The Church and Public Policy" from *Religion and Public Life: The Role of Religious Bodies in Shaping Public Policy,* ed. Joseph A. Bracken, S.J., 29–42, copyright © 1986 Xavier University Press, Cincinnati, Ohio. Chapter 12: "Theodicy and Plurality" from *Archivio di Filosofia* 56 (1988): 707–20. Chapter 14: "The Christian Understanding of Suffering" from *Buddhist-Christian Studies* 5 (1985): 49–65. Chapter 15: "Death and Its Relation to Life" from *Archivio di Filosofia* 49 (1981): 19–32.

Interior design: Karen Buck
Cover design: Patricia Boman

Library of Congress Cataloging-in-Publication Data

Gilkey, Langdon Brown, 1919–
    Through the tempest: theological voyages in a pluralistic culture
    / Langdon Gilkey: selected and edited by Jeff B. Pool
        p. cm.
    ISBN: 0-8006-2484-X
    1. Theology. 2. Christianity—20th century. 3. Christianity—
United States. I. Pool, Jeff B., 1951– II. Title.
    BR85.G449 1991
    230—dc20   90-19764
                                                            CIP

The paper used in this publication meets the minimum requirements of American National Standard for Information Sciences—Permanence of Paper for Printed Library Materials, ANSI Z329.48-1984.   ∞™

Manufactured in the U.S.A.   AF 1-2484
95   94   93   92   91   1   2   3   4   5   6   7   8   9   10

With affection to the
Goldstein Family
Paul, Iris, Tom, Kaylin, Alexa, and Leigh

CONTENTS

PREFACE

As I have reread these chapters, written prior to the crucial year of 1989, I realize more clearly than before how unexpected to me, as apparently to everyone else, were the collapse of the Soviet empire and the concurrent re-appearance, at least initially, of democracy throughout the so-called Eastern Bloc. The assumptions that our time is one of a sharply and perhaps fatally divided world of competing ideologies, that democracy — at least ours — can squander its inheritance by supporting oppressive regimes, and that we face the possibility of another fatal and global war, lie heavily across these pages. To all of us the resurgence of devotion to and hope for democracy and the virtual end of Cold War conflict came as a welcome but totally unexpected new beginning. To read this book, therefore, is to celebrate anew the wonder, the mystery, inherent in the great and propitious events that have happened in the past years. History is unpredictable, its course contingent, its seemingly long-term trends suddenly reversible — thus it can usher in unexpected creative beginnings as well as unexpected terrors. Most of this century has seen more than its share of the latter; now, thank God, we have been blessed with new possibilities where none appeared before as well as with startling examples of the human courage and commitment capable of bringing these events about.

The crisis of Western society has, therefore, significantly eased since most of these chapters were written, and I wish to record this undoubted fact. I want also to recognize how much the renewed strength and obvious capa-bility of an almost united and now thoroughly resurrected Western Europe adds to this brighter picture. Despite these clear pluses in the current scene, however, this book's general assessment of our times is still, I think, sound. Ours remains a period of crises, a time of troubles, a duration of history facing exceedingly perilous possibilities, and hence one increasingly subject to severe testing, a veritable "tempest," as the title puts it.

With these exceedingly positive developments, new possibilities of instability and conflict have come and certain deep crises have continued. When the hand of tyranny is finally lifted, the sudden possibility of a new and nonoppressive order is a vast relief. But an oppressive order can long submerge old forms of anarchy; hence, with freedom long forbidden—ethnic, religious, class and national, even gender—rivalries are now able to surface politically and to create new and seemingly unresolvable conflicts. Despite its manifest new possibilities of justice and peace, our future remains unpredictable, still replete with heretofore unseen possibilities of destructive disorder as well as of creative order.

On a deeper level of crisis, moreover, the problem of the earth, the issue represented by ecology, has only increased since these chapters were written. I need not rehearse these dangers for our now near future; awareness of them is much sharper and more widespread than it was a decade ago. The intractable population problem also remains steadily with us. We seem fated to endanger, if not to eliminate, ourselves through our own destruction of our benevolent environment or fatally overcrowding it or both. Certainly we will be so fated unless we can be rational and self-disciplined enough to control our greed, to mitigate our anxieties, and to temper our wants. This requirement of self-control is not new in history; but modern civilization faces a more ultimate threat than ever before, and the demand on our self-discipline and our rationality—the two are interdependent—is more exacting than ever. On a multitude of fronts, therefore, our time of troubles is not over: Injustices remain everywhere, not least among us. Racial and gender discrimination are still present. The banality and the impersonality of a technological-industrial culture continue to spread. Thus, although these essays on current history would now be written differently, the challenge to us for courage, self-control, and love that they seek to embody remains the same.

I have dedicated this volume to a family long securely bonded to our own in affectionate ties of many sorts. Not often in two families have parents, sons, and daughters each and on their own been best friends from the beginnings of their respective family's life, nor do such close relations formed long ago usually remain as enriched after two decades as ours have. I hope that the fact that some of these chapters are theological in content, and most of them sober in tone, will not hide the happy and humorous memories or the affection and deep respect lying back of this dedication. All of this has the even happier prospect, now and in the next generation, of continuing in, even spreading to, Maine as well as in its point of origin, Hyde Park.

I would like to express my very great gratitude to Jeff Pool for all the care and work he has given to this project. Without him this collection of addresses, papers, and articles, written from the middle 1970s through the late 1980s and on a wide variety of themes, would never have come to publication. He has chosen these chapters, fitted them together into a thematic whole, and provided subtitles for the chapters and title for the entire work. For all this—and for the close bond of companionship it expresses—I cannot thank him enough.

Thanks also to Gwenn Barnes for typing most of these chapters in the original, and, as always, love and gratitude to my family for a love and support that is quite undeserved.

Langdon Gilkey
West Boothbay Harbor, Maine

EDITOR'S PREFACE

The common threads of both Christianity's encounter with the critical situation of the present and the prospects for the future to be found within it are woven throughout the chapters of this book. Langdon Gilkey characterizes our situation as a "time of troubles," on the one hand, and as an age of pluralism, on the other.

Three elements in Gilkey's thought typify his approach to understanding Christianity. First, his theology possesses a boldness, a willingness to explore the unknown and to chart new areas. A fitting metaphor for this aspect of his theology is a ship embarking for passage on the open sea. Second, his repeated description of our contemporary situation as a time of troubles qualifies our situation as a stormy sea through which Christian theology must pass. Third, his theology manifests a tempered but hopeful confidence that a successful, although perhaps perilous, passage will be made. The sailing vessel ventures boldly upon stormy seas, but with a confidence of fulfilling its mission even if the result means docking in a new port. The title chosen for this book, *Through the Tempest: Theological Voyages in a Pluralistic Culture,* reflects these three elements.

The first characteristic of Gilkey's theology — embarking — correlates with the nautical metaphor of voyages. Those who know Gilkey are familiar with his love for sailing. He has for many years spent part of his summer in Boothbay Harbor, where he sails with his family along that stretch of the coast of Maine. Interestingly, a connection between Gilkey's theological writings and his love for sailing signaled itself early in his career when he purchased his first sailboat with the royalties from his book, *Shangtung Compound.* So opportune was the book's success that Gilkey christened the vessel *Kairos!* In fact, some of Gilkey's ancestors were shipbuilders in Maine; in honor of them, he named his second sailboat after a ship built by one of them: *Royal Welcome!* Those familiar with his published works, and with his work as a teacher, are also well aware of his fondness for applying nautical metaphors to the obscurity of the essential structures of our finitude by our fallenness, to the exploratory theological efforts of others, and even to his own career.[1] Thus, this book of explorations in theology quite fittingly has been described as voyages. In fact, from Gilkey's life and work, one receives the distinct impression that he truly has found it to be joyful, if not exhilarating, to be sailing "above a depth of seventy thousand fathoms."[2]

The second characteristic—his assessment of our situation as a stormy sea—correlates with the metaphor of the tempest. Many people know Gilkey best for his whirlwind books.[3] These two books take their metaphorical titles from allusions to biblical passages: "Then answered the Lord unto Job out of the whirlwind, and said, 'Gird up thy loins now like a man: I will demand of thee, and declare thou unto me'" (Job 40:6-7), and, "Israel sows the wind and reaps the whirlwind" (Hos. 8:7).[4] Many of the themes, methodologies, and theological concepts found in these two books reappear in this present book. Because of this continuity, the metaphor of the tempest has been chosen. It too is a metaphor of wind and storm and has been taken from a biblical passage: "Give ear to my prayer, O God; and hide not thyself from my supplication! Attend to me, and answer me; I am overcome by my trouble . . . I would haste to find me a shelter from the raging wind and tempest" (Ps. 55:1-2, 8).[5] Thus, the use of tempest alludes to the presence in this book of many of the same concerns about the intense storm through

---

[1] For example, see his use of such metaphors in the following: Langdon Gilkey, *Message and Existence: An Introduction to Christian Theology* (New York: Seabury Press, 1981), 104-5; Langdon Gilkey, "A Theological Voyage with Wilfred Cantwell Smith," *Religious Studies Review* 7 (October 1981): 298, 306; and Langdon Gilkey, "A Retrospective Glance at My Work," in *The Whirlwind in Culture: Frontiers in Theology,* ed. Donald W. Musser and Joseph L. Price (Bloomington, Ind.: Meyer-Stone Books, 1988), 1. Many present and former theology students from the Ph.D. program of the University of Chicago Divinity School will remember a set of guidelines for writing dissertations in theology, written by Professor Gilkey, in which his sailing metaphor tempered with humor the utter seriousness of those academic requirements.

[2] Søren Kierkegaard, *Concluding Unscientific Postscript,* trans. David F. Swenson and Walter Lowrie (Princeton: Princeton University Press, 1941), 126. According to Frater Taciturnus, this is the realm of the religious, the right place to be joyful: "It is . . . in danger, above seventy thousand fathoms of water, many, many miles from all human help, there to be joyful—that is great! To swim in shallow water along with the bathers is not the religious" (Kierkegaard, *Stages on Life's Way,* trans. Walter Lowrie [Princeton: Princeton University Press, 1945], 425).

[3] Langdon Gilkey, *Naming the Whirlwind: The Renewal of God-Language* (Indianapolis: Bobbs-Merrill, 1969); Gilkey, *Reaping the Whirlwind: A Christian Interpretation of History* (New York: Seabury Press, 1976).

[4] In the case of *Naming the Whirlwind,* Professor Gilkey described in an interview the circumstances surrounding the choice of the title for that book. It arose out of discussions with the editorial staff of the Bobbs-Merrill Company. Professor Gilkey had originally entitled his book "The Renewal of God-Language." In that interview Gilkey said, "They called me on the phone and said, 'We've got a marvelous title.' I said, 'I don't want to hear it; you publishers are always changing my titles and I don't like what you do.' The guy called back and said, 'It's really a great title. Please listen to it: *Naming the Whirlwind.*' I said, 'That is a marvelous title. It's from Job, isn't it?' 'Yes,' he said. 'A member of the sales force read your book and came up with this title; he really understood it.' I said, 'He certainly did.' " "Namer and Tamer of the Whirlwind," interview by Kendig Brubaker Cully, *The New Review of Books and Religion* 2 (February 1978): 3.

[5] Professor Gilkey has described our period of history as "a stormy epoch" (Gilkey, "Retrospective Glance," 34).

which Christianity must pass and is even now already passing, such crises as dwindling religious authority, the meaningfulness of religious language, ecological threats, Western political dominance, the hegemony of industrial technology, economic instability, Third World social distress, and the new recognition of parity among religions. In the biblical inscription of *Naming the Whirlwind,* Yahweh spoke to the worshiper out of the whirlwind; in the biblical inscription of *Reaping the Whirlwind,* Yahweh's prophet spoke to God's chosen yet faithless people about the impending disaster of their encounter with the whirlwind. Here, in the biblical inscription of *Through the Tempest,* by contrast, the now humble worshiper speaks with urgency to that same God for deliverance from the present tempest. With this third biblical allusion, all the characters of the worshiping community have finally assembled, and all have spoken—God, the prophet, and the people. In this book also, the dynamism of the divine and human relationship has reached a hopeful denouement in the worshiper's humble plea to God. Consequently, many of the emphases in this book deviate from the two whirlwind books; some of the viewpoints have shifted in order to take into account the clarity provided by some of the crises, just as the direction of a boat shifts when the sails have been trimmed in accordance with tempestuous winds.

The third characteristic of Gilkey's theology—a tempered but hopeful confidence—is reflected in the preposition *through* in the book's title. Hope is a prominent element in his thought. Many of Gilkey's efforts have been devoted to unveiling the demonic aspects of the religious dimension of secular experience—one might call these the pretensions of secular culture such as, for example, its unarticulated pretensions to absoluteness—whether those of scientific inquiry or of politics and political theory. Further, with these same kinds of efforts, he has prophetically identified the crux of current crises and indicated their probable calamities should we not assume the required responsibilities in our situation. Nevertheless, despite the sometimes grim pictures of the objects of his analyses that he paints for us (whether they are aspects of the life of the Christian communities, the role of Western culture and politics, the new status of Christianity in relation to the religions of the world), he also offers a deep and abiding expectation of meeting these crises and overcoming them. A story by Kierkegaard illustrates some of the more profound facets of this characteristic: "It happened that a fire broke out backstage in a theatre. The clown came out to inform the public. They thought it was a jest and applauded. He repeated his warning, they shouted even louder. So I think the world will come to an end amid general applause from all the wits, who believe that it is a joke."[6] Our society and culture often value more highly the clown's antics than the prophet's warnings and, in so doing, ignore the prophet. Gilkey's profound writings constitute warnings to us all, warnings that the structure is on fire.

---

[6] Søren Kierkegaard, *Either/Or,* trans. David Swenson and Lillian Marvin Swenson (Garden City, N.Y.: Doubleday, 1959), 1:30.

Notwithstanding those serious and urgent pleas, Gilkey voices a healthy hope that our world will heed those warnings. In this sense, then, this book suggests that the destiny of our world is to enter a historical, ecological, and religious tempest — in fact, that our world has already entered that storm. Yet *Through the Tempest* also suggests an element of hope: that our world may pass through that tempest, that, having gone in on the one side, it will come out on the other.

CENTRAL FEATURES

This book has been conceived as an overview of some of the most recent theological efforts by one of the foremost North American theologians of the latter half of the twentieth century. Although some of the concepts and arguments may be difficult for the person unfamiliar with theological and philosophical language, their original form as lectures and addresses, and hence their more conversational style, makes them more readily accessible. Furthermore, several features draw the chapters of this book together.

Two Foci of Organization

As a first feature, two foci have served to organize this book. First, this book follows the order of the Christian narrative as it has been classically perceived, conceived, transmitted, and remembered. Second, the book reflects Gilkey's approach to Christian theology. It begins in Part One with two chapters in which the author discerns, analyzes, and interprets the major components of our contemporary situation and two chapters in which the author provides methodological perspectives on the task of theology (its dual task of interpreting both the contemporary situation and the Christian message) and a theory of religious symbols. Thus, by looking back at the situation described in chapters 1 and 2 and by utilizing the theory of religious symbols in chapter 4, chapter 3 has prepared the reader to consider the interpretations of Christian symbols that follow.

Consequently, Part Two, with its four chapters, engages Gilkey's actual interpretations of several aspects of the central symbols contained within the historic Christian creeds: God, creation, Jesus Christ, and the church. In Part Three, the author examines, in three chapters on the symbols of Christian and ecclesial existence, some broad perspectives on the questions of Christian ethics, both at the personal and the institutional or communal levels. Finally, in the four chapters of Part Four, Gilkey interprets the more negative Christian symbols of theodicy, original sin, suffering, and death. Thus, in addition to the author's assessment of the contemporary situation, his theory of religious symbols, and his proposal for the task of theology, this book moves within the logic of the Christian narrative: from protology (talk of first things: God and creation) through the historical in its ethical-political and

natural dimensions (God and providence) to eschatology (talk about last
things: God and the end).

TRANSMISSION OF CHRISTIAN SPIRITUALITY

An interest in spirituality describes a second feature and becomes an explicit
focus of Gilkey's analysis in chapters 1, 2, 4, 10, and 15. As he repeatedly
insists, authentic spirituality, and its transmission, have become urgent needs
in our time. He suggests that spiritual disciplines be developed or retrieved
from past Christian traditions or even learned and borrowed from other
religious traditions. He comments further that religious leaders need to take
up the difficult responsibility of transmitting traditions of spirituality to
those with whom they minister. Furthermore, he points out that our divinity
schools and seminaries once again need to attend to this area of religious
experience, an area that has largely been neglected in modern and post-
modern Western theological education.

PARITY OF RELIGIONS

A third feature of the chapters of this book may be described as the continued whisper of Christian dialogue with other religious traditions echoing
throughout this book. Many of these chapters were originally presented not
only in ecumenical Christian contexts (one might call these Catholic-
Protestant dialogues, in chapters 4, 6, and 11) but also in meetings intentionally focused on interreligious dialogue: chapter 1 at the Conference on
Confucian-Christian dialogue; chapter 7 at the Symposium on Christ and
the Bodhisattva; chapter 10 at the Third International Buddhist-Christian
Dialogue Conference; chapter 14 at the First International Buddhist-
Christian Dialogue Conference. In addition, some were delivered in cross-
cultural settings: chapter 1 in Hong Kong; chapters 12 and 15 in Rome; and
chapter 13, although not delivered, was scheduled for delivery in Germany.

Gilkey's interest in and dialogue with Asian religions has focused prin-
cipally on Buddhism. Because his wife, Sonja, became a member in the Sikh
Khalsa, he has also developed a personal dialogue with Sikhism.[7] In his

---

[7] Gilkey, "Retrospective Glance," 31. As Professor Gilkey himself has recognized, the
concern with interreligious dialogue, in the sense of parity between the religions, has not
always been his approach; in fact, this particular approach to the issue of interreligious dialogue
began to emerge in 1975, when he taught for four months at Kyoto University in Japan,
through the seminar on technology and religion that he taught with the Buddhist philosopher
Takeuchi Yoshinori (Gilkey, "Retrospective Glance," 30). Dialogue with other religions had
been present in Gilkey's work from the time of the writing of his dissertation (but only in a
comparative way). In fact, with the publication of *Maker of Heaven and Earth: The Christian
Doctrine of Creation in the Light of Modern Knowledge* (Garden City, N.Y.: Doubleday, 1959),
based upon his doctoral dissertation, this dialogue took a somewhat neoorthodox shape. Gilkey
has characterized himself in that period as an "enthusiastic" and "aggressive" proponent of
neoorthodoxy, although not of its Barthian variety (Gilkey, "Retrospective Glance," 13). In his
exposition of the meaning of the Christian idea of creation, Gilkey pointed out that the Christian

present thought about Christianity's relation to the other religions, Gilkey strongly resists any conception that would reduce the uniqueness of any religious tradition by identifying a so-called common religious core or root within any special tradition and, then, by constructing a theology of religions on that basis. Rather, he argues for the notion of parity between the religions as the place to begin to understand the relations between the religions. Gilkey's concept of the relative-absolute originates from that source: the commitment to the truth and grace of one's own religious tradition while affirming (although not necessarily participating in) the reality of the revelation of truth and grace in other religions. On this basis does Gilkey, as he has poetically confessed, "poke about" upon the seas of the relations between religions "in a small sloop named 'Dialogue.'"[8]

TIME OF TROUBLES

Gilkey's repeated description of our contemporary situation as a "time of troubles" (in the sense meant by Arnold Toynbee) discloses a fourth feature. That this is a time of troubles remains true in spite of the chances for economic success and security in some of the brighter but smaller corners of our tiny world. Gilkey's analysis reveals an exceptional discernment. Not so much in his insistence upon the decline of the Western world—a decline already emitting the odor of putrefaction in our culture, a decline long recognized by many contemporary prophets of doom—rather, in his perception of the positive and life-affirming possibilities in this decline for East and West does Gilkey's analysis of our time of troubles offer its unique contribution. He has been no casual observer; his repeated plea to recognize our critical situation, especially in his essays and addresses from the 1970s and 1980s, points to the key role the shape of events and cultures has had on his theological formulations.[9] But these formulations have been

---

understanding of God and creation conflicts with monistic or pantheistic religious thought, using as an example passages from the Hindu Upanishads (Gilkey, *Maker of Heaven and Earth*, 58). In addition, in the context of a polemic against natural theology, for example, he says the following: "If, then, natural theology is the attempt to reach God the Creator either through man's experience of the immanent coherence of the world or through his general religious experience, it can only uncover an idol, never the true God" (Gilkey, *Maker of Heaven and Earth*, 322). Nevertheless, even within that first book, Gilkey recognized and accentuated the similarities between Christian language about the divine and Hindu and Buddhist language about ultimate reality (Gilkey, *Maker of Heaven and Earth*, 337–39). That neoorthodox orientation, so central to Professor Gilkey in the first one-third of his theological career, has received considerable modification, even transformation. Gilkey understands this as a movement in his thought, in a sense symbolized by the shifts in his choice of theological reference points: from the work of Reinhold Niebuhr through that of Paul Tillich to that of Mircea Eliade presently (Langdon Gilkey, "Theology and Culture: Reflections on the Conference," *Criterion* [Autumn 1989]: 3).

[8] Gilkey, "Theological Voyage with Wilfred Cantwell Smith," 298.

[9] See his short essay "Theology for a Time of Troubles," *Christian Century* 98 (April 29, 1981): 474–80. This was written at the invitation of the *Christian Century* as one of the articles in the series "How My Mind Has Changed." Gilkey preferred to have his own essay entitled

constructive rather than apocalyptic, hopeful rather than anxious. Para-doxically, only by passing through the powerful negations represented by this decline of the West can the West, as well as the rest of the world, hope for new, creative, powerful, and affirmative transformations.

DISCUSSIONS WITH THE SCIENCES

In a fifth although a more subdued feature, this book sustains a critical stance toward the scientific-technological culture of the West. Even though Gilkey appreciates the enormous value of science and technology and recognizes many of their claims, analyses, and methods, he maintains this stance for several reasons. First, he has recognized the presuppositions of the sciences for which they themselves cannot account on the grounds of their own empirical methods. Second, he has discerned a religious dimension in science as well as in politics, the arts, and so forth. Third, he has been sensitive to the presence of the demonic side of this religious dimension in science—in particular, its tendency toward self-absolutization. Although this book documents factors in the world's time of troubles related to the establishment of science, it provides neither the sustained analyses of nor the arguments with the various sciences as in much of Gilkey's other work. One exception is chapter 13 in which, during his treatment of original sin, he analyzes representative viewpoints from the biological sciences. Elsewhere he has developed similar analyses and debates with the physical and social sciences.[10]

TECHNICAL MATTERS

In editing these chapters, steps have been taken both to provide more con-sistency and to draw them together as a book. First, subheads have been introduced into several chapters in order to help the reader follow the analyses and arguments. Second, the chapters have been edited where neces-sary to reflect inclusive language in reference to both God and humans, even though Gilkey has largely been sensitive to this issue. Third, the notes for

---

"How My Mind Is Changing." This response quite appropriately indicates how sensitive Professor Gilkey's thinking has been to the changes within his own time.

[10] Two of Professor Gilkey's books have dealt explicitly with science and religion: Langdon Gilkey, *Religion and the Scientific Future: Reflections on Myth, Science, and Theology* (New York: Harper & Row, 1970); and *Creationism on Trial: Evolution and God at Little Rock* (San Francisco: Harper & Row, 1985). Also, see chapters 6, 7, and 8 in Langdon Gilkey, *Society and the Sacred: Toward a Theology of Culture in Decline* (New York: Crossroad, 1981). Finally, see his earliest approaches to these issues in his *Maker of Heaven and Earth*. He has delivered dozens of lectures and addresses on similar topics. His published articles and reviews on related topics are far too numerous to include in a note such as this. He has also analyzed and directed critiques against the social sciences: See, for example, Langdon Gilkey, "A Response to Ross Reat's Article, 'Insiders and Outsiders in the Study of Religion,'" *Journal of the American Academy of Religion* 51 (September 1983): 484–88. The publications reflecting his sustained interests in and debates with the sciences have intentionally not been included in this collection because Professor Gilkey is currently writing another book on these issues.

the chapters were converted to the same style; several references contained within the text were changed to footnotes in order to establish a uniformity. In addition, some notes and references were added for sources mentioned by the author. Finally, I have provided an index for the benefit of those who may want to pursue particular topics addressed by Gilkey in different chapters.

This collection of essays and addresses represents only a small portion of Gilkey's more recent work. All of these chapters—with the exception of chapter 4 (1974) and chapter 8 (1975)—were written, delivered, or published in the 1980s. Three chapters are here published for the first time. Gilkey originally delivered chapter 1 as an address in Hong Kong in June 1988 at Chinese University. He wrote chapter 8, based on three lectures written sometime after the summer of 1975, during which time he had traveled across Russia on the Trans-Siberian railway from the Pacific Coast of Asia (where he had been teaching for four months at Kyoto University) to Holland. Gilkey originally prepared chapter 13 to be delivered as a lecture for the 1989 Religion and Science Conference in Germany, but cancelled that engagement due to an illness in his family.

ACKNOWLEDGMENTS

First, I want to express my deepest gratitude to Professor Langdon Gilkey. Without his inspiration and help, this book would not have come to be. I thank him first for his gracious reception of my proposal to undertake this project and for his hearty encouragement and confidence. His own generous efforts moved this proposal from the realm of possibilities to the realm of actualities.

Second, I am enormously grateful to Professor Gilkey for entrusting to me the use of his office during the summers of 1988 and 1989, while he was vacationing at his home in Maine. In those two summers, I worked carefully through all of his published and unpublished works to date, a task greatly aided by the access, given to me by Professor Gilkey, to his personal files. I am grateful also for the time he spent with me reviewing and evaluating this material and some of his more recent work in May 1990.

Third, and here my gratitude to Professor Gilkey becomes much more difficult to express, it has been my privilege to be among the last group of his Ph.D. students before his retirement from the University of Chicago Divinity School. I have been taught not only by his writings, both published and unpublished, and his classes in the theology of other great theologians but also by the example of his theological style and insight and by the example of his personal outlook and religious vision. I hope that the labors represented by the publication of this book may express, at least in small measure, my personal gratitude and theological as well as personal indebtedness to him.

Finally, as volume editor, I wish to express profound gratitude for myself and for Langdon Gilkey to the editors of Fortress Press for their encouragement and suggestions from the inception of this book. In particular, two persons at Fortress Press deserve special mention. I wish to remember the late John Hollar for his key role in confidently and enthusiastically beginning this project. Also, because of his efforts to maintain that initial commitment to publication, and because of his creative dialogue and suggestions at each stage, I extend my deepest thanks to Timothy G. Staveteig, Academic Editor, Fortress Press.

Jeff B. Pool
Phillips Graduate Seminary

PART ONE

Contemporary Crises, Religious Symbols, and Christian Theology

CHAPTER 1

THE CRISIS
OF CHRISTIANITY
IN NORTH AMERICA

That there is a crisis of Christianity in the West we all agree. What that crisis is, and what its deeper causes may be, is another matter; diagnoses and suggested cures alike diverge radically. The reason for this is that such analyses of large historical shifts or movements, especially contemporary ones, are, while hopefully informed, woefully speculative in character and certainly not easily verifiable. This is one such precarious diagnosis; it makes sense to me, but its status is only that of a proposal for the reflection of others. I shall confine my attention to North America; its situation appears to be significantly different from Europe's or South America's, and in any case the United States is home ground for me.

My analysis has two stages or tiers: first, an analysis of the encounter of modern scientific, technological, and democratic culture with religion (especially Christianity) and all the effects and surprises that encounter has entailed; then, second, an analysis of the quite recent but deeper travails that have beset modern secular culture itself. In the first our gaze is especially on religion (Christianity) in the West as it has faced (since roughly 1800) the strong, powerful, luring forces of modern scientific rationality, historical consciousness, and democratic idealism. In the second we shift to look at the secular culture of the West to see the perhaps even more fundamental crisis into which it is now passing. Quite deliberately I will seek to evoke echoes of an unexpectedly parallel crisis and reaction to crisis in China's spiritual history in the same period.

THE SPIRITUAL CRISIS
OF RELIGION

The dominant question for Christianity (and perhaps later for Judaism) has been, What shall we do with the modern world? This "world" began to develop powerfully in the seventeenth century with the exploration of the whole earth, the rise of science, the appearance of mechanical technology and so industry, and the slow development of democratic, liberal, and capitalistic ideals. This rapidly expanded and transformed culture became full blown by the eighteenth century; and it has in ever-new forms dominated not only the West ever since but also, until 1945, the rest of the world. At the start this culture was, to be sure, "Christian," and it remained so until roughly 1900 to 1918. It certainly seemed to represent a unified "Christian West" to other invaded cultures. From the eighteenth century on, however, a serious split was occurring. The intellectual and moral heart of the Enlightenment was rationalist and humanist; it believed in the identity of nature and reason and in the autonomy of the rational and moral human being. It was, on the whole, antitraditional, antimetaphysical, and antireligious. Certainly there appeared liberal Christian and liberal Jewish forms of this culture, but as the nineteenth century developed, closed, and then opened into the twentieth century, the intellectual classes slowly moved away from these religious institutions. More and more they became "secular," possibly agnostic, atheist, antireligious, or humanistic. The intelligentsia, on the whole, felt well represented by Feuerbach, Marx, Nietzsche, Darwin, Huxley, Freud, Dewey, and A. J. Ayer.

Strange as it may seem, this encounter was almost as traumatic for Western religion as was the appearance of the scientific, technological, industrial, and democratic West on the horizon of nineteenth-century traditional Chinese spirituality. For both, the question, What do we do with this powerful invader of our spiritual home? became uppermost. The forces of religion in the West, even more clearly than in China, slowly divided themselves (this, admittedly, is simplified) into two increasingly distinct groups: (1) the "orthodox," who resisted many of the general ideals of the modern West (its *Weltanschauung*) in order to retain intact their doctrinal interpretations of God, world, human being, and history; and (2) the "liberals," who accepted (that is, believed in) the results of science, the possibilities of technology and industry, and the ideals of democracy and sought to reinterpret Christian doctrines in the light of modern experience and modern thought. Incidentally, both groups swarmed into China in the late nineteenth and early twentieth centuries, represented respectively, let us say, by the China Inland Mission and the American Board.

It should be noted that the relations of these groups to secular culture, to so-called modernity or modern culture, are by no means simple, not mere matters of the repudiation of the culture by the orthodox and its acceptance by the liberals. The orthodox had no discernible qualms about capitalistic industry and commerce, about private property, even fewer about class, and none at all about nationalism and imperialism; these powerful forces of the modern West they not only accepted but encouraged, usually without criticism. Correspondingly the liberals challenged much of modern culture: its "materialistic" concern for property in capitalism, its virulent nationalism, its slavery (prior to 1864), its disdain for the poor, its racism, and its militarism. They were enthusiastic about modernity's ideas and prophetically horrified at its social realities. It was liberal not orthodox missionaries who railed against Western imperialism in China and frequently pled the cause of the "colonies" against their own country's power when they returned home. Like the most creative of the Chinese reactions to the modern West, the Christian liberals (and the Jewish Reformed) mounted this criticism on the basis of their own deeper spiritual tradition: the value of the person, the love and goodness of God, and the possibilities in history of universal brotherhood, namely the Kingdom. In any case, Fundamentalism appeared out of this split, as the increasingly conservative reaction of the orthodox to the onset of liberalism and modernism. Horrified at the so-called Christians who "adapted pagan ideas"—evolution, historical criticism, and social democracy—many of the orthodox shifted radically to the right and began to defend "fundamentals": verbal inspiration of the Bible, a six-day creation, the virgin birth, the blood atonement, the bodily resurrection, and the approaching end.

In the second half of the nineteenth century and the first half of the twentieth, perhaps after 1918 especially in the United States, the intellectual classes of the West widely assumed that this liberal culture—"modernity" as it is called—would only increase in scope, influence, and dominance. I can recall vividly how this vision was taken for granted by most everyone in academic and liberal Protestant circles in the 1920s and the 1930s. Correspondingly it was certain to everyone that orthodoxy and Fundamentalism would slowly die out as scientific knowledge, technical rationality, and industrial competence increased; and, in time, the world beyond the Western middle classes would be converted to this enlightenment; and, with that conversion, the myths and fears and fanaticisms—the "superstitions"—of past religious history would vanish. Liberals viewed Fundamentalism in America as a traditional, old-fashioned carryover of rural, pre-scientific, pretechnical society and thus soon destined to die out. Ironically this same view of progress led the secular among the elite to see liberal religion itself as on its own way out; in the end, like the archaic religions of Asia, all religion, liberal and orthodox alike, would give way to modern secular forms of society, as history's outmoded absolutist politics and its hierarchical social forms would slowly give way everywhere to democratic and liberal social ideals. As science would become the universal form of inquiry and consciousness, so liberal democracy would become the universal form of social structure and morals alike. Finally, for those who stubbornly remained religious, at home or the mission station, liberal, free-church, Protestant Christianity would provide the model for the universal forms of religious and moral consciousness: tolerant, congregational, autonomous, egalitarian, and above all humanitarian. In sum, as Marx saw the industrial proletariat determined by history to become the universal class of humanity, slowly extinguishing injustice and replacing religion, so, strangely, the Western bourgeoisie — and their intellectuals — saw their own middle classes as forming the center and the model for the universal secular civilization to come. This was progress, the culmination of history's developments from the very beginning; and progress was the symbol dominant in elite religion, education, politics, and social activities.

Gradual Waning of Liberalism

The first level of the crisis, then, and one of the first signs that this vision of progress was in fact an illusion, is the sharp falsification of this prediction of the coming dominance of liberal religion, in fact an almost complete reversal of this entire set of historical predictions. Their future in 1910 is now our present in 1988; and 1988 defies in fact almost all they had foretold — except steady advance in science and in technology. Instead of being the wave of the religious future, liberal Protestantism has, since say 1930, steadily declined in prominence and influence everywhere in the West. Churches remain relatively full, to be sure, in the U.S. and Canada; but neither their belief systems nor their public moral pronouncements — socially daring and even radical as they may be — are noticed, except where (as with race and Vietnam) they partly joined and partly led a wider political protest movement. Catholic episcopal pronouncements (on nuclear arms, capitalistic exploitation, and sexism), equally daring and radical, attract more attention. Catholics agree that it is the lingering shadow of traditional episcopal authority that accounts for this (as well as the intellectual and moral excellence of the statements); but most add that in time that authority too will wane. Catholicism in North America has since 1964 joined "the modern scene"; in that sense it is liberal and at one with the liberal Protestant churches. Altogether, however, their influence, even in ecumenical unity, has dramatically receded even in the last sixty years. This could be documented in any number of ways. So far the secular critics of religion seem to be correct: In a scientific, technological, and democratic culture, liberal religion is as inexorably if gradually eclipsed as orthodox religion is.

Why has this happened? Why have weakness, irrelevance, almost invisibility become the apparent fate of precisely those churches in modern culture that sought to be modern, to make accommodations to science, democracy, autonomy, psychoanalysis, reform politics, and the like?

1. Certainly the rise of the "secular option" is at work here; more and more (since say 1930) the lure, the advantages, the sheer possibility of being secular, unreligious, and unchurched has spread among all classes. This is by no means universal; the core of present churches, especially in the cities, is constituted by persons who have tried that option and found it lacking and are in church through deliberate and eager intellectual and spiritual decision. For many of these a more "biblical faith," "neoorthodoxy" — modern and yet also traditional — represents by and large the appropriate theological center.

Clearly these are a minority now, although the churches represent large sections of the larger population.

2. The union with modern science and historical consciousness has inexorably relativized any particular statements of religious faith; the older certainty and exclusiveness is, fortunately, gone; and an irenic, cooperative, ecumenical, and tolerant spirit reigns. Inescapably, however, there is a bill to pay: Why relate in commitment to a perspective? Why give your soul to a view and a community that is tolerant of other views and inclusive even of its own opposites? Is there anything here that can break open the bondage of sin, conquer the anxiety of fate, dispel the fear and grief of death, or heal the exploited? If not, why be religious?

3. All of these mainline churches, Protestant and now Catholic alike, have precisely by their responsible acceptance of science, social science, psychoanalysis, and liberal politics associated themselves with the classes who are the bearers of those functions in society, that is, the middle classes. Inescapably, despite the predominantly leftish ("liberal") character of their clergy ("social gospelers"), these churches have more and more become bourgeois churches supported, financed, and populated by the professional and managerial elements of society. Like *Time,* a college education, and the station wagon, these represent a part of successful corporate, even suburban, America, despite their liberal, "protesting" leadership. Their clients like and seem to need church, even though they disagree with their minister's "naive liberalism." In the meantime, however, the WASP (white, Anglo-Saxon, Protestant) component of the middle classes has dramatically shrunk, from an unequivocal dominance to perhaps a third or a quarter, as Jews, Catholics, the unchurched, Orthodox, Asians, and blacks have moved into the bourgeoisie. Thus, the membership of the mainline Protestant churches is no longer, as it once was, identical with the dominant portion of the managers, the owners, the professionals, the academics of North America. It represents a minority at best. Finally, this association with mainstream, bourgeois America (its industry and commerce, its science, technology, and academia) means that if anyone becomes spiritually "alienated" from that ambiguous world and protests religiously against it, such a one will find some other religious home — and hence the vast number of "cults," some imported, some homegrown, that have arisen among the children of the bourgeoisie since 1960.

In short, a vast new pluralism has become realized in America. A wide variety of ethnic groups (East Asian, Indian, Hispanic, southern and eastern European, Jewish, and Arab) and religious groups and communities now move in and out of mainstream American life; their numbers are slowly entering the business, commercial, and academic communities. Only the black population, which is also entering the mainstream, retains its concern for and loyalty to its Protestant churches. Although the churches are in this way bourgeois, the day of the Protestant and even of Christian dominance of this class is over. The Christian voice is heard, but it is one among many, and thus it is far more muted than it once was. Liberal Christianity encountered modernity, accepted much of it, and now, instead of inspiring, directing, and renewing it, it has almost disappeared within it.

SUDDEN RISE OF FUNDAMENTALISM

The gradual waning of liberal religion was one surprise. A far greater surprise has been the sudden and even accelerating rise of fundamentalist religion. The juxtaposition of these two represents what I am suggesting to be the first tier or first level of the spiritual crisis of the West, unless of course one assumes that empowered Fundamentalism represents a renewal and not a crisis! For almost three decades it has been clear that very conservative Protestant communities (conservative Baptist, Assemblies of God, Pentecostal, and so on) represent the fastest growing segments of Christianity, as Mormonism (also conservative religion) has been the most expansive single group. About two decades ago the immense popularity of TV evangelists (Oral Roberts, Pat Robertson, the Bakkers, Jimmy Swaggart) became evident to all, as did the vast amounts of money they were collecting, not to mention the estates and commercial enterprises they were purchasing, and the universities, institutes for research, and vacation resorts they were establishing. Associated groups were concurrently seeking changes in local and state laws to foster and to establish in the wider society their beliefs and their morals, particularly the creationists, who sought to ban the teaching of evolution.

Finally, with the Republican convention of 1980, at which the fundamentalist Evangelicals played an important role, it became clear that already they represented a powerful political force. Many spoke now of the aim of dominating the Republican party; many important fundamentalist leaders (Jerry Falwell and Pat Robertson, for instance) began to call the country "back" to its foundations as a "Christian nation governed only by committed Christians." Without exception they all represented the most right-wing political and economic views at home and the most militaristic and imperialistic anti-communism abroad. The alliances they said they could trust would be those with some of the world's remaining dictatorial regimes: Marcos, Pinochet, Noriega, and of course the government of South Africa. In 1988 one of them sought to run—unsuccessfully, to be sure—as the Republican nominee for president. Fundamentalism has become a powerful religious, moral, and now political force; its aim is openly nationalistic and theocratic: to glorify America, to return America to its purported Christian beginnings, and thus to restore its moral and religious authority in the world and its moral values at home. To those who fear it, it has racist potentialities; and certainly, like all theocracies, it can easily move in a repressive, totalitarian direction. Fortunately, the pluralism and the secularism that are eating away at the cultural and economic dominance of the liberal churches from above also prevent this new theocratic mode of dominance from below.

Nevertheless, this crisis represents a threat for liberal religion, for free and open education, for rational and irenic international policy, and for a humane domestic economic and social policy. To everyone's surprise, the "illiberal" religion that seemed adamantly to resist the world now appears to be almost winning the world; and even the atheists are astonished that, far from an innocuous and waning epiphenomenon in a scientific age, religion has shown itself to be a powerful, effective, and dangerous modern force. Similar manifestations of "fundamentalist" religion have appeared in Canada and Australia, in important segments of Judaism, in Sikhism, in Hinduism, in Japan, and of course in Islam. If ours began as a secular century, it is certainly ending as a religious one.

This contemporary relation of resurgent Fundamentalism to the modern world is even more complex than was that of the orthodox or the older Fundamentalism that preceded it in the first decades of this century. There is no question that these groups, such as the creationists, deny crucial general ideas associated with modern science and modern culture: the immense age of the universe, the fundamental changes that have taken place in all its aspects, the changes of forms of life and of species, the relativity of all historical expressions to their time and place (including religious Scriptures), the uniform working of "natural law" in nature and of strictly historical causes in history. The liberal ethical and democratic political ethos of modern culture — tolerance of other ideas, concern for economic and social justice, for peace and for individual liberties — all of this the fundamentalist leaders repudiate; social reform, civil rights, and freedom of ideas and of speech seem to them un-Christian and even communistic. For them the Scriptures are verbally infallible, the creation a recent (ten to twenty thousand years) six-day sequence of events, the biblical history of Eden, of Noah, and of the patriarchs more authentic than the secular history of hunting, gathering, and early urban societies, and so on. To them also the Bible is a repository of scientific and historical facts, of theological doctrines, specific laws, and particular commandments that, properly interpreted, can give utterly authoritative guidance for any sort of theoretical question or moral dilemma raised in the course of ordinary life. All this seems — and for good reasons — to hark back to at least well before the eighteenth century in Europe and the early nineteenth century in North America. Are not these premodern groups, then, antithetical to all of contemporary civilization and not merely to its science? So it seems, and so most members of the academic and the scientific communities view them.

A closer look reveals something else, in fact another set of surprises. Socially and economically the fundamentalists do not represent rural backwaters on the periphery of contemporary commercial, technological, and even educational culture. On the contrary, they own, manage, and participate in large-scale commercial enterprises; they own, manage, and staff nationwide, even worldwide, TV chains and programs; they have easy access to more wealth and property than most of the mainline churches; they operate schools, colleges, and some universities; they are effectively organized politically at every relevant level; and finally they study science, participate in technology, engineering, medicine, and law — and to cap it all, they now claim that their worldview represents "true science." At the Scopes trial in 1925, the fundamentalist movement repudiated completely any relation at all with science, technology, and commerce, with what they called "urban, Wall Street, university and scientific paganism." Quite to the contrary, the present leaders and authors of the works of "creation science" possess Ph.D.'s in natural science from such recognized universities as Berkeley, MIT, Ohio State, University of Pittsburgh; and creationists are visibly present on the scientific faculties of many reputable scientific universities: Purdue, Carnegie Tech, Iowa State, and in the many research laboratories of large industrial concerns. As we have noted, resurgent fundamentalism has moved power-fully into the political and commercial worlds.

Without question, therefore, these groups have accepted the economic, political and social structures of modern civilization (capitalistic, national-istic, technological, and scientific) and the more "worldly" of its goals (monetary rewards, financial success, political and cultural power). What they have not accepted are its worldview, on the one hand, and its deeper personal and social moral ideals (democratic reform, individual rights, co-operation and peace among cultures and religions), on the other. They are, in other words, fully as much modern as they are traditional, and they cannot be understood except in this dual light. It might be interesting to note further that they are one example of the adoption of only the "material" level of Western culture, that is, only its science (in part), its technology, its indus-trial, commercial, and organizational assets; having then repudiated the best of the moral and political traditions of the West, they seek to combine this material and technological side of the West with their own traditional and so virtually unchanged religious and moralistic viewpoint. If this is in fact what they are, then some of the suggestions among nineteenth-century Chinese intellectuals that "only the material capabilities, the science and the technology of the West be adopted" might look more ambiguous now than they did then. Here an uncritical and unrevised form of traditional Chris-tianity reappears powerfully in contemporary life armed now with the science, the technology, and the industrial and commercial potencies of modern culture. Many in the West feel that this union of unrevised religion with the material powers of modern culture is frightening.

This Century's Dominant Question

Once we understand contemporary Fundamentalism as in fact a union, however unexpected, of fundamentalist religion with modern culture, even a "supernatural" religion with science, we see how false and misleading were several of the liberal culture's widely held assumptions about religion. One assumption was that modern scientific culture was antithetical to orthodox faith. Another was the assumption that science always separated itself from, in fact actively repelled, religious and ideological fervor.

Two facts seem certain about contemporary cultures: First, all intend to become scientific, technological, and industrial as quickly as possible;

second, they intend to do this on their own terms—that is, in union with their own religious or ideological stance. When one realizes these facts, a new view of the twentieth century becomes possible; at last we can understand some of the bizarre marriages of science and religious ideology as more than merely inexplicable anomalies. Several examples of this, in fact, dominate the landscape of the twentieth century.

Japan witnessed the union of science, technology, and industrial power with Shinto religion in the 1920s, 1930s, and 1940s. The Nazi ideology undoubtedly co-opted the immense German scientific and technological establishment in the 1930s and 1940s; the effects of this union on the human sciences of anthropology, cultural history, psychology, and sociology were disastrous. Concurrently in Russia Stalinism united with science and technology, affecting biology as well as cultural history, economics, sociology, and political theory. Next in line—but never able to become actual—would have been Maoism's union of powerful ideology with science and industrial technology. And, finally, there is Iran with the prospect of a Shiite science, technology, and industrial establishment. Hundreds of Iranians are being trained at present in science and engineering in the United States; most will return to Iran, and all who return there will perforce adapt the science and the technology they have learned to the self-understanding of the Shiite religion and the stern *Sharia* (law) of that Islamic community. None of these represents the "science" of the American Association for the Advancement of Science, either in method or in the content of their theories. Are they, then, science or not? This question—like What is real Christianity? or What is real Confucianism?—is not easy to answer.

In any case, let us note (1) that the relation of the modern scientific, technological, and industrial culture (developed in the West but now not confined there) to traditional religions and to religious ideologies remains perhaps the dominant question of our century. Further, let us note (2) that many unexpected and bizarre marriages of that modern culture to religion and ideology have occurred, despite the seeming impossibility of such rapprochements. Note also (3) that all this reminds us of the long-debated issue in China: How are we to accept the valid elements of modern culture without losing our own identity, in fact without losing our souls? How are we to unite modern science and technology to traditional Chinese religion, philosophy, and social viewpoints? Finally, (4) let us not forget that this same question, and the crisis it has precipitated, has forced itself on Western Christians—only over a much longer stretch of time—much as it has disturbed Chinese Confucianists.

THE SPIRITUAL CRISIS OF
MODERN CULTURE

We now turn our gaze in another direction, looking not so much at religious institutions and movements as at the career of Western culture itself. For as yet we have left quite unexplicated the causes or sources of the unexpected resurgence of Fundamentalism: Why has supraorthodox religion suddenly reappeared with great power when fifty years ago every sign seemed to promise its steady decline? We must not be fooled by the words *spiritual crisis*. Of course, this phrase can refer to crises of religious belief, to doubts as to whether there is a God, a next life, or an immortal soul—and generally the phrase does mean this. But "spiritual crisis" can, and most importantly does, refer as well to states of deep anxiety, of not-at-homeness or alienation in the world, of lostness or uprootedness, of meaninglessness and emptiness in life, of futility and despair about the future. These represent the crisis referred to when loss of faith in God appears. Loss of belief in God can surely cause such a crisis, but so can other apparently "unspiritual" matters, for example, changes in wider history that affect the quality or security of life. Times of social upheaval, or the threat of it, are themselves also times of deep anxiety. In turn, anxiety signals the most important and often most dangerous of spiritual situations; out of such situations of anxiety—if courage, confidence, and self-control do not appear—can emerge radical sin and its consequence, injustice.[1] Every important social structure has its spiritual symbols that in turn support, invigorate, and direct the common life (such as those of Confucian China and of democracy). A structure in disarray is reflected in the spiritual situation of anxiety, thus possibly in radical fanaticism or radical despair and, in the end, in a kind of blind paranoia: *atē,* madness. Thus, when we speak of the contemporary time of troubles besetting Western culture, we are not looking away from spiritual crisis—away, for example, from the deeper causes of fundamentalist and fanatical religion—but precisely at the sort of situation or condition that engenders crises of the spirit and thus the disarray of religious institutions.

I have mentioned already some of the possible so-called religious causes of the fundamentalist renewal. Certainly the relativization of scriptural authority, treasured doctrines, and moral rules has encouraged a conservative reaction. Certainly, also, some accurately sense the loss of traditional values (sexual continence, the stability of marriage, parental authority and responsibility, hard work and honesty, self-control, to name a few). Again, the reaction is to depend on and to stress an oppressive religious legalism. Many also feel the clear loss, already referred to, of the predominantly Christian character of American life, and so are convinced that the spiritual bases of society are seriously evaporating. (Is this an echo of the earlier sense of the loss in China of the Confucian character of its common life?)

In addition, in school, in public discourse, and through the media much of the population has become conscious, for virtually the first time, of the thoroughly secular character of modern civilization. Many had no idea that

---

[1] For a most perceptive analysis of the relation of anxiety, sin, and social injustice, see Reinhold Niebuhr, *The Nature and Destiny of Man,* vol. 1, *Human Nature* (New York: Charles Scribner's Sons, 1941), chaps. 7–9.

the autos, TVs, consumer goods, and airplanes they had learned to depend on and to rejoice in were themselves directly and inherently dependent on a science and a technology whose naturalistic and, at best, agnostic world-view challenged their own spiritual assumptions. They view such a secular ("atheistic") vision of reality as a recent intruder into American life, a kind of conspiracy of Satan or of communism, a set of "heresies" quite separable from the science and the technology they admire as "American" to the core, a conspiracy generated by such notorious, if as yet unread, heretics as Marx and Darwin. Present Fundamentalism understands itself as a reaction to modern "godless" culture rampant in public schools, secular universities, and mainline churches, not to science, technology, and industrialism; and it sees itself as the one bulwark against the moral decay evident in promiscuity, abortion, divorce, and drugs. Not unlike the consciousness of many of the Islamic and communist countries, its own self-consciousness is that it is counteracting—while the other churches are encouraging—the religious and moral laxity of present American life.

Deeper than all of this, however, lie cultural stresses and strains that equally disturb the spirit; at least that is my thesis. Here is where the most interesting parallel with familiar spiritual problems in China's encounter with the West appear. I have spoken of the time of troubles of Western culture, a phrase Arnold Toynbee used to describe a period in a culture's life when breakdown or decline first become possible, though never necessary, and consequently when awareness of the fragility of both security and mean-ing in life tends to become both sharper and more painful. I shall refer to this time of troubles on two different levels: the social bases, on the one hand, and their spiritual consequences, on the other. In such periods of significant social disarray (for example, the late Hellenistic era and the late medieval period), religion, both fanatical and profound, bizarre and traditional, tends to increase in scope and intensity, as the profusion of new cults in the late Roman Empire illustrates.

SOCIAL BASES

In describing the time of troubles facing Western culture as a whole, the place to start, I believe, is the West's precipitous loss of dominance in the last four decades. Since the mid-sixteenth century the dominance of Western nations over the rest of the world had steadily increased; it was a dominance more and more unchallenged by any non-European power. By the mid-nineteenth century, Western nations enjoyed a sovereign control over nearly the entire globe, ruling in fact whatever they did not own, as the Chinese are well aware. Four hundred years is an incredible length of time; a sense of what we might call a "natural right" to sovereignty, of superiority of intellect, of power, or even of virtue and of religion inevitably appears and becomes habitual, taken for granted (recall the film *Passage to India*). Such ruling communities feel incredibly secure until they begin to cease to rule, until that rule is challenged. In our present that rule has suddenly vanished;

the empires are gone, and with them the monopoly of dominance has fled. America has inherited what is left of the West's power. But the sovereignty over the entire globe that Europe once possessed, that America has not inherited. Other powers outside the West (some of them present allies of the West, some alien and opposed, and some even neutral), all significantly different, have appeared and will only increase in economic, political, and military strength. The Boxer Rebellion at the start of the century was quelled in two short weeks by a small European force; seventy-five years later no amount of American power could even rescue the hostages in Tehran.

This fast change is good for the world, for justice, humanity, and peace. But at the same time this represents an utterly new role in the world for the West: the world's present barely remains "Western," the future almost certainly will be non-Western. As a consequence, the sense of security that an assumed dominance breeds is much more vulnerable, and an anxiety about the shape of the future is manifest all over the West. Not many leaders articulate these realities; most of them are not, I believe, fully aware of them (most Europeans and Americans mistakenly think America has simply replaced Europe as the world's leader). But this slippage of sovereignty, of security, superiority, of the proud sense of the universality — yes, even of the eternity — of their culture is deeply felt. The result is anxiety and the need for roots, for deeper structures of courage, confidence, and meaning.

Toynbee describes a "time of troubles" as appearing in connection with the fundamental institutions of a culture — those institutions on which the security, creativity, power, and so growth of the culture had depended. At some point, because of important historical changes, these institutions get, so to speak, out of sync, start to malfunction; and at this point these essential institutions, instead of resolving fundamental problems, begin to cause ever further and deeper problems. Such was the ultimate fate of the feudal system in Europe; creative of necessary order in the chaos of seventh- to eleventh-century life, the feudal aristocracy became an oppressive burden by the time of the sixteenth and seventeenth centuries, and only radical revolutions could reopen Europe for a new creative phase. Unquestionably those institutions on which the astounding growth and predominant power of the modern West have depended have been science, technology, and industrialism. In our lifetime, however, each of these has undergone an unexpected and disorienting metamorphosis. From an apparently unqualified blessing each has changed into an exceedingly ambiguous social reality, bearing in itself a threat as well as a promise, a curse rather than its opposite. Advances in science now frighten us as much as they excite us;[2] technological developments threaten our existence and our humanity in ever-new ways; industrial expansion seems to have destroyed beauty and quality of life everywhere; and, finally, science, technology, and industrialism together

---

[2] For example, see Spencer R. Weart, *Nuclear Fear: A History of Images* (Cambridge: Howard, 1988).

threaten the natural harmonies and resources on which our common life depends.

Civilization, as developed by the West, has become *zweideutig,* ambiguous, able to destroy us more quickly and surely than it can secure us. The dramatic symbol of this terrible ambiguity is, of course, the bomb, symbol of science and yet also of death. We are aware, moreover, that with that self-induced destruction appears the possibility, also new, of the virtual end of humanity, of nature, and so of history itself. Who could have thought that this was a possibility in 1910 or even in 1930? Again, this unconditional danger consequent on an unconditional power is more felt than articulated, but it surely is widely felt. Ironically and surprisingly such a worldly apocalypse, in the hands of humans, poses an ultimate threat and nurtures an ultimate anxiety. Emotionally and imaginatively, it seems to call for a corresponding divine apocalypse and divine rescue to reintroduce some hope. No wonder supernatural religion flourishes because of the advances of science, technology, and industrialism rather than despite them.

SPIRITUAL CONSEQUENCES

Important military, political, economic, and social changes — and the threats they may well pose for the sense of security and meaning among those long accustomed to both — engender spiritual crises, crises of the soul. In such times religion tends to prosper, especially supernatural religion, which promises to bring in from elsewhere permanent rescue from beyond the obvious, "empirical" confusion and disarray of the present. Empiricism in a time of decay, let us recall, generates not optimism but despair, not a sense of freedom but of fatedness, not confidence but the loss of confidence. Even more, such social catastrophes, or the threats of them, can represent a direct threat to the religious beliefs themselves of those suffering from the catastrophe. When a city or a country is overwhelmed by the superior force of a conqueror, the "gods" of the victims, themselves suffering defeat, tend to lose status and glory, and their devotees may well look elsewhere for help. (The notable exception was of course Yahweh on the occasions of both the exile and then later the demolition of the temple.) Something like this, let me suggest, has been happening to the gods of the West in the twentieth century.

Many people in the West, and perhaps especially in North America, are genuinely Christian or deeply Jewish. Nevertheless, as we have noted, the West in significant part has become spiritually secular or quasi-secular; and the major religious groups of the West have identified themselves at very deep spiritual levels with the modern culture in which they have found themselves. The beliefs, even of religious groups, that have motivated and empowered most persons, secular and religious alike, therefore have been beliefs that characterized the culture as a whole; most forms of religion have been spiritually as well as economically, politically, and socially acculturated. Furthermore it has been almost uniquely characteristic of the modern West that what it believed in was itself; that is, in its own creative achievements, in its science, technology, democratic ideals, freedoms, and predominant modes of being human. Until recently most westerners — and perhaps especially most Americans — were convinced that in the various facets of Western civilization, humankind had reached its apogee, its supreme level, its classic excellence. In Western civilization all other civilizations had reached their fulfillment. During the long processes of historical change, culture had gradually developed and improved: in knowledge, in technical capacities, organized skills, social institutions, and in moral sensibility. Slowly these developments, on all fronts, had reached their modern form: in empirical science, mathematics, democratic politics and ideals, and in Western (Christian) morals and social institutions.

This confidence in development toward the ideal was precisely what they meant by progress, and everyone who regarded themselves as modern took such progress, ending with the achievements of Western civilization, quite for granted. I am sure Chinese were well aware of the presence among Westerners of this assumption of superiority; and strangely, to almost all, Western and non-Western alike, this assumption seemed strongly credible, for the dominance remained unchallenged. As Vice-President Lyndon Johnson said in 1959 (I heard him say it), "Everyone on the globe wants to be an American — and for good reason — it is the natural way of being human!"

Nature and history had combined to produce, over centuries of struggle, modern Western civilization. History here had reached its highest point, and America especially represented that culmination. Having come this far, history would continue to develop this model and so continue in ever-new forms to develop these Western modes of excellence. Time was increasingly sacred, increasingly fulfilled by the development of civilization in the West; and the sacred space where this wonder was placed was in the West, particularly in the Northern Hemisphere. Such was the common faith, the religious substance, of most of modern Western culture.

Those familiar with the sacred connotations in classical Chinese culture of China, as the Central Kingdom at the center of the universe, and of *jen* as the fulfillment of humanity itself in relation to the cosmic *Tao,* will feel a parallel — however surprising — in these notions of Western superiority. Perhaps they will understand, therefore, how such an apparently incredible view of itself was possible for the West and for America. Perhaps the main difference in these visions was the shift from the center of cosmological space to the fulfillment of time as constituting the central axis according to which ultimate meaning became concrete on earth. This belief in progress, and in Western civilization as its embodiment and bearer, represents the spiritual substance or the religious substance of Western culture. That culture proved more powerful in spreading this substance than Christianity, the "official" religion that it proclaimed. This pseudoreligion appeared among intellectuals and authors, usually in secular form, as evolutionary and historical progress; it appeared in religious form, in liberal Christian theology and

Reform Judaism, as a doctrine of divine immanence in history; and it inserted itself as the worldly aspects of the faith of most orthodox Christians and even Jews in the West. Few denied this sense of the progress of civilization and history, and few did not associate the meaning of their own lives, the tasks of their country, and the career of their local community with that faith. As is obvious, Marxism represents another, socialist, form of this belief in historical development as fulfilling itself in the gradual creation of an ideal community. Again, social community, the developmental progress of civilization and of meaning, and the processes of the whole of history combine in what can only be called a religious belief or myth.

Now, the point is that the social time of troubles described above has directly challenged this spiritual or religious set of beliefs about history and its meaning. In fact the process of the falsification, if I may use that strong term, of the hypothesis of progress has been growing in intensity. The former bases of confidence in progress have been eroded; the West's dominance of the globe has gone; the advances of science and technology and the spread of industry have created many more lethal problems than they have resolved; and social suffering, if not on the increase, seems as much the lot of humanity as before. Above all, history itself seems to have lost its one clear thread of meaning. The West finds itself not only in serious internal self-contradiction but suddenly displaced from the center, and the future appears now radically uncertain, even frightening. If all this is so, what then is the human story all about? Is it about nothing? Is it going nowhere at all? Is there no center to space and no direction to time? These questions — again posed on the feeling level if not yet articulated — signal a death of the gods of the West and the consequent need for some new, more deeply grounded faith. The present and future appear in disarray, out of touch with order, with *Tao*. Fundamentalism is, I think, one alternative answer — and a powerful one — to this deeply felt anxiety.

One further point: As the West developed, its sense of confidence in rational autonomy and in its ability to know and to control the world expanded. It became enamored with the external control its knowledge gave it rather than with its inner awareness of its roots in the depth of being and in authentic humanity. With that expansion of self-confidence, seemingly objectively confirmed by the expansion of Western political dominance, by technical dominance over nature, and by industrial control of human wants, came a disdain for mystery of any sort: the mystery of the self, of history, of social community, of reality itself. Questions that can be answered by empirical inquiry became the only legitimate questions. Problems of technical competence became the only real problems and dilemmas of practical action the only questions for common debate. To the empirical and pragmatic mind of the West, symbols and myths no longer spoke to real spiritual needs but reflected only the ignorance and weakness of premodern human being. Even rational reflection on the nature of reality, truth, and the good became "meaningless." In short, the mind of the West moved itself radically and exclusively toward concentration on the surface of life and evacuated life's depths. Thought concerned only means and not ends; it dealt alone with successful practice and not reality; its sole purpose was to fulfill our immediate wishes rather than to criticize, control, or ground them.

Such a mind-set, long at ease in a time of progress and long at home in the sacred space of the West, was ill prepared for the sudden appearance of radical evil, of triumphant evil, and so of the inexorable return of the tragic, of "mysteries" that could neither be solved nor removed. It had cut itself off from its own deepest roots, those symbols and concepts that could disclose to us universal reality, all-encompassing truth, and ultimate good. For it is only through such symbols associated with mystery that what is permanent and what is healing can be glimpsed, approached, and grasped, even within the shadow and the terror of the tragic. The West had been founded on such symbols and concepts, such "myths," one might say. Greek, Judaic, Christian, and Enlightenment symbols had long fed its spirit and made its creative development possible. It had powerful roots, expressible in religious myths, theological symbols, philosophical concepts, and normative judgments, a deep symbolic structure that undergirded the humane elements in its ethics and political theory. In fact, on these bases depended its empirical science, its democracy, and its socialism, its humanitarian legal and social developments. These symbolic foundations, however, were progressively ignored, scorned, even ridiculed in an increasingly positivistic and pragmatic culture. Natural and social science, technical and organizational rationality alone remained as legitimate activities of mind. But this restricted scope of reason or spirit provides poor defenses indeed when the religious substance of the culture falls apart and when the deeper questions concerning reality, truth, and not least of the grounds in cosmos and history of values push themselves brutally forward in consciousness. Again, it is no wonder that naive but unassailable dogmas, identifying ultimate reality and traditional values, and so providing answers to these now-looming questions and above all promising security and meaning to spare, appear powerfully on the scene.

It is not only interesting but surprising to find that this situation, with all its dangers of spiritual superficiality accompanying radical irrationality, parallels the problems in Chinese culture seen so clearly by Hsiung Shih-Li in the first half of this century. Hsiung feared above all that Chinese intellectuals would adopt "surface" skills of the West (science, technology, and industrialism), without establishing them in correlation with China's own deeper moral, ontological, and even religious roots; that is, abstracting its *yung* from the profound *t'i* on which every *yung* is necessarily founded. As Hsiung realized, Western skills themselves rested on a profound symbolic ontological and moral base reaching back into the intellectual and spiritual traditions of the West. This was, however, neither the way the West presented itself (e.g., in Dewey) nor the way most Chinese intellectuals wished to receive it and adapt to it. Only if China reexamined and rethought its own spiritual foundations could it accept these new modes of knowing and doing in correlation with those foundations without disaster.[3]

As my analysis has sought to show, this problem faces not only the Chinese in their relation to the West. It faces Westerners in their relation to the scientific and technical culture the West itself has developed. The loss of the West's own ontological, moral, and religious roots has resulted in an excessive spiritual vulnerability. This cultural travail is the deepest level, I believe, of the West's spiritual crisis, one it surely shares with China, if for different reasons. One has only to look at this crisis to gain insight into the sources of the Fundamentalism that has suddenly appeared all around us.

---

[3] Tu Wei Min, *Humanity and Self-Cultivation* (Berkeley: Asia Humanities Press, 1979), 229–40.

CHAPTER 2

PLURALITY: CHRISTIANITY'S NEW SITUATION

How can the church and its leaders be "servants" in a pluralistic environment? The word *plural* here refers to a religiously pluralistic world, a world of many and varied religions. What effect does such an environment have on the pastor?

The meaning of the present plural world signifies more than the merely plural. Many religions have always existed, and the churches have been more than aware of that fact. I mean something different, something new; I refer to a new problem or an opportunity raised by plurality, that is, a new consciousness with regard to plurality. I suggest that this new consciousness entails a feeling of rough parity, as well as diversity, among religions. By parity I mean at least the presence of both truth and grace in other ways. I shall assume that this is the common consciousness on this issue. This consciousness is new for the churches. From the earliest period through the Patristics down to the liberals of the nineteenth and twentieth centuries, the absoluteness and superiority of the Christian faith were assumed without question. Even to consider parity with other religions is, therefore, a radically new departure. As a consequence, it represents a quite uncharted sea both for theology and for the life and attitudes of the churches.

CAUSES OF THE NEW SITUATION

I begin by looking at some of the more important causes of this new situation. The theological causes stretch back into the liberal period, that is, back

21

into the Enlightenment and its effects on theology. Two changes in theology have helped to usher in this new consciousness. Although these changes occurred under the auspices of liberal theology, they managed to retain their strength during the neoorthodox period and well into our own.

The first change is the renewed emphasis on love rather than on purity of faith. In the *Institutes* Calvin held that the latter requirement took precedence over loving one's neighbor; in effect, it is the defense of God and the name of God and thus is a practical application of the first commandment. On this basis every Christian is required to struggle against and even to eliminate false doctrine and heresy wherever they appear. One need not cite the appalling results of this interpretation of Christian requirements in the baleful history of the churches. It was, therefore, no small matter when liberalism asserted the obligation of loving one's neighbor as taking precedence over defending the purity of doctrine. As a result of this shift, the values of tolerance and ecumenical fellowship — even among those who disagreed theologically — became true marks of the Christian spirit, replacing the dogmatic fervor and the intolerance of "blasphemy" that had once characterized the earlier situation. One basis for the ecumenical movement among the churches was thus established.

The second change in theology leading toward this new attitude complements the first. It is a new sense of the historicity of all doctrinal and confessional statements. With this sense, which also arose under Enlightenment influence, each set of dogmas or doctrines was viewed as a perspective on a truth beyond all of them, a perspective reflecting the cultural and historical viewpoints of that group at that time. Thus, none of them is absolute; and, while each contains important elements of the truth, none of them excludes the others completely. Together, as complementing one another, they contain more of the truth than any one does singly.

Out of these two changes — the primacy of love and the relativity of every doctrinal or dogmatic proposition — the ecumenical movement among Christians was born. An attitude not only of tolerance but also of positive interest and concern appeared within differing positions in Christianity. By the mid-twentieth century the stage was clearly set, therefore, for the new view of plurality among religious faiths and their communities. During all this ecumenical progress, however, the assumption remained that Christianity represented the final and definitive form of religion because its founding revelation was unique, *einmalig,* and so, in its own way, absolute.

If this last remark is valid, then we Christians must move to causes other than theological ones if we are to understand how this new attitude among religions, an attitude of rough parity, has arisen. I suggest that these other causes arise from the cultural and historical spheres in which fundamental changes were taking place during this period. These changes can be summed up as, first, the decline of the sense of Western superiority and, second, a new ambiguity about the major elements of Western culture.

I cannot overemphasize the importance here of the assumption of Western culture's superiority. This long-held assumption, running deep indeed, dominated every level of cultural life. For well over four centuries (from the early 1500s to 1945), the West had no military, political, or economic rivals elsewhere on the globe. As a consequence, Western nations ruled everywhere without challenge — except from one another. History had seemingly disposed of the competitive power of other cultures, and thus it had validated thoroughly the Western claim to superiority.

This mastery, although at first most evident in the areas of science and technology, did not stop there. On the contrary, it spilled over onto every level of life: democracy in politics; personal autonomy in family and marriage; equality of men and women (the West thought itself farther along here than it was!); humanitarianism in ethics; and, of course, to crown it all, Christianity in religion. This combination of military and economic mastery plus a presumed spiritual supremacy was devastatingly powerful, breeding in Westerners easy assumptions of the absoluteness of their own culture and of the irrelevance, if not primitivism, of the cultures of others — assumptions that are to us now both odious and incredible. (The films *Gandhi* and *A Passage to India* illustrate these attitudes well.) It was also assumed without question that the underdeveloped cultures of the rest of the world would quickly transform themselves into latter-day copies of the West. The reality of this domination and the assumption of this superiority lasted until the end of World War II. Then all this changed with lightning rapidity.

In the 1970s and 1980s the effects of this change began to be felt if not yet articulated. Now militarily and politically the vast empires of the West have vanished. The direct rule of the West has thus shrunk into its own borders. As a culture, its rule no longer spreads across the globe. Other centers of power now manifest themselves as possessing genuine parity, if not yet equality. Correspondingly, other cultural alternatives, other ways of life, have appeared as real options: from the older cultures of Asia, from diverse communist experiments, from the societies of the so-called Third World. A pluralism, including a plurality of military and economic powers and of cultural perspectives, dominates our common world scene as never before.

As part of this same process, the institutions and goals of Western life seem neither as permanent nor as beneficent as they once did. For example, the Western autonomous family, once the ideal for most of Asia, now seems ambiguous at best, riven with divorce and threatened with transience. The future of Western society itself appears less the goal of history and more precarious. Those elements that once made it clearly superior — science, technology, and industrialism — now, on the contrary, create its own deepest dilemmas. They even threaten its continued life. Thus, instead of representing a clear progress, Western institutions now appear, at home and abroad, as deeply ambiguous: creative, alluring, but possibly lethal and (not irrelevantly) oppressive. The assumed superiority of the West has dissolved into a new pluralism and a new ambiguity, a new sense of parity among cultures and among alternative ways of life, and a new sense of the precariousness and even the menace of our own. The modern sense of change has itself changed. From one of buoyantly anticipating changes in Western culture, the sense of change has shifted to the more ominous feeling that changes will be from Western culture into something as yet unknown.

The present-day consequences of this process of change are directly relevant to my subject, the appearance of religious plurality. The first is the deeply felt malaise or anxiety about Western life and its prospects that pervades much of our society. This is not articulated widely, but it is there and its effects are everywhere: in the efforts to retrieve former values; in the return to a conservative posture; in the pathological fear of seeming weak ("a paper tiger," as Nixon put it); in the certainty that the beliefs and norms that "made us great" are being lost. In all this we see a spiritual situation of deep uncertainty and anxiety, a situation ripe, as history shows, for the upsurge of religion. Correspondingly, the same situation is evident in the sudden and pervasive appearance of new religious cults and movements: some conservative, even fanatical, forms of traditional religious groups; some importations from Asian religions; some new, homegrown cults. The tide of the missionary enterprise has reversed itself, and the flow is now in exactly the opposite direction. It flows into a spiritually barren and anxious Western culture, not out of it into the rest of the world. Here, then, is a quite direct source for the new sense of the parity of religions—namely, the experience of their effective appearance in power among us on our turf!

It is then in terms of this new global setting that we can understand the appearance of a new attitude toward other religions, the attitude of parity. Western dominance, both political and spiritual, is quite gone. Western culture finds itself unsure of its own foundations and anxious about its future. New religious movements reflecting viewpoints different from traditional Western ones begin to appear with power among us, converting our friends—and frequently our children—and offering to us insights and practices that we both need and yet do not find at home.

It is in this context that dialogue among diverse religious traditions becomes a primary interest, indeed a need, for many to whom relations with other traditions had formerly been purely cursory, a polite but fleeting contact at best. Dialogue presupposes that each partner recognizes the other as equal in some significant measure, the bearer of a distinct truth and grace. Dialogue is, therefore, perhaps the clearest indicator of the new situation that we are analyzing, as it is also the most interesting new factor on the theological scene.

A SPIRITUAL VACUUM REVEALED

The new task of the Christian church is to uncover some of the important consequences for the life of the local church and for its leader, the pastor, in this new situation. What does it mean to be a servant, or the servant church, under these conditions? The Christian community is now the native ground for powerful mission movements representing alien and yet attractive religious alternatives—far more fascinating than rival denominations—and thus threatening us in a quite new way with the loss of members. How can the church react creatively rather than defensively to this new situation?

It is, of course, natural that the reaction of Christians be defensive and negative. The growing impact of non-Christian religions does represent a genuine threat to the stability of many congregations and families—as the numbers of former Protestants, Catholics, and Jews among each of the new religious movements (new to Christian communities) show. It is, however, both more creative and more accurate to react positively to this challenge, to welcome it as an opportunity, and to take full advantage of the possibilities for spiritual growth that it unquestionably offers. This attitude is not just a whistle in the dark. It is undeniable historically that many religious movements in India, China, and Japan, to take only three examples, were effectively revitalized by the challenge of Christian missions. One can clearly trace the changes that the power and influence of the new Christian groups effected in these religions, forcing them to new levels of self-understanding and perhaps especially to new ways of relating themselves to their world. Part, although not all, of the new power of these movements in the present—of Vedanta, Sikh, Yoga, and Zen mission groups—derives from this vigorous reaction to the impingement of Christianity on them during the past century and a half. Correspondingly, from them, and from the necessities of our reaction to them, we may discover new emphases, new vitality, new methods.

One of the ways in which such reassessment and revitalization occur is through the uncovering of the weaknesses and deficiencies of the Christian community. Alternative forms of religion throw a sharp and critical light on older, taken-for-granted forms. Powerful options, offering much that we do not, reveal precisely where we fall short. Their presence thus not only impels us to change but also shows us many of the most important directions of change. My own experience within both Sikh and Zen groups, here and in Japan, leads me to suggest that the weaknesses they help to uncover in our own parish life center around the area of spirituality, the practice of religion and so the direct experiencing of the holy. It is on this assumption that the following remarks are based, and it is in its light that my suggestions for the growth of the servant church and the servant pastorate are made.

It has long been noted that American churches have been suffering from a loss of powerful and meaningful public liturgy. It is not my purpose here to argue this point or trace out its multiple historical roots. It is sufficient to agree, as most would, that a sense of the holy does not pervade most of our present Sunday worship. Long before questions about the absence of God arose theologically, an awareness of that absence was present in many of our church services: hymns were sung, prayers were said, sermons preached. But anything more than that, any sacral presence to which the response of worship was being made, was unfelt and unknown. Strangely—and here the psychology and sociology of religion might help us—this lack seems particularly characteristic of the middle-class, bourgeois congregations of mainline Protestantism and, increasingly, Catholicism. The same problem did not and does not arise in "gospel" churches, in which the Spirit always makes itself known as it did not in traditional Catholicism, in which the presence of the holy in sacramental liturgy was assumed. In both, the reality of the holy was directly apprehended, and worship, whatever its form, was experienced as a response to that felt real presence. Contemporary worship, however, has few traces left of this presence or of the sense of the reality of the divine that is addressed.

It might be disturbing to most modern congregations — to most of us — if indeed the holy were there. It might appear unmannerly, archaic, super-stitious, fanatical (as many Christians tend to regard both "gospel" worship and traditional sacramental realism). One can think of many ways in which Christians would seek to evade it, for it would probably threaten our sense of what is real and what is appropriate. Yet it is undeniable that we seek for it and long for it. In the ways Christians tend to speak theologically about both sacrament and proclamation, we show that we must think of them in the terms of divine activity and presence rather than in terms of human works, human signs. Thus, our theologies of liturgy soar higher than our experience of it, which remains generally earthbound, listening to a passable sermon and sharing in a meaningful rite. In any case, much of our present church life is more barren liturgically and in its communal experiences of the divine than it is void in profundity of theological or ethical reflection.

Far sharper, however, is the crisis within the area of personal religious life. It is, of course, difficult to accumulate data in such regions, but one can talk with friends and colleagues and one can commune with oneself. Hypotheses in this area are, therefore, not so much the result of objective surveys as of reflection on small but still relevant ranges of experiences. My numerous conversations with those who have recently moved out of church life into one of the newer sects validate over and over what these experiences intimate.

Contemporary churches suffer from a spirituality vacuum, a vanishing of the habits and the rewards of personal piety. This vacuum seems to balance and feed the emptiness of common worship. Protestantism is not so much at fault as some are inclined to believe. First in Puritanism, then in Lutheran pietism, and certainly within the personal habits of "sectarian" Protestant groups, there was a rich tradition of personal piety: of regular Bible reading, personal prayer life, family worship, obedience to set rules governing all of life. These firm and all-encompassing habits or practices kept the daily lives of ordinary people in the closest touch with the holy. It was because of this daily communion with the sacred that Protestant individuals could come together in common worship and jointly commune with the holy, even in the most barren of liturgical structures. It is noteworthy that these habits of personal devotions and discipline lasted long after their orthodox theological background began to be criticized and revised — that is, well into the first half of the twentieth century. Even though the pastor's house in which I grew up was theologically and ethically "liberal," I can well recall my father's daily devotions, his regular period by himself of Bible reading, and the family prayers that were taken for granted in our home. Although he had broken radically with traditional Protestant orthodoxy in theology, in his reading of the Scriptures, and in his commitment to the social gospel, his habits of personal piety remained a steady inheritance from that older world.

My point is that much if not all of this vanished, as did the prayer meetings in the Protestant churches, during the middle years of this century. Few of the neoorthodox generation, whatever their devotion to the evangelical gospel or to liberation in the world, were able to continue these habits of life, this life-style of personal piety and discipline. The causes of this are multiple and need not concern us here. Suffice it to say that even deeper than the vacuum in current worship is that in the area of personal piety and devotion. For most Christians, then, faith and obedience are largely inward, within consciousness, on the one hand, and ethical, in actions within the world's life, on the other hand. In that central region of the self's experiencing — of itself, of the Word, of God's address to the self — there is all too little going on. Moreover, it is hard for those who note and regret this situation to return to the evangelical personal piety of the end of the past century. There is little, in other words, that such Christians "do" — except attend church and exercise ethical actions within the world — in the task of embodying and nurturing their faith. Inwardness, sheer inwardness, rules; and as Kierkegaard, the apostle of inwardness, noted, inwardness without significant external embodiment can easily slip away.

What does all this have to do with my topic of religious pluralism? First, this analysis of the shortcomings in both our liturgical life and personal piety has been validated over and over in conversations with those who found themselves leaving the churches (and a few the synagogues) and joining a community from a quite different religious tradition. I have been amused and a bit chagrined to find that none left for theological reasons. It was not the pull of a new interpretation of themselves, their world, or their destiny that lured them! Nor was it a new set of ethical insights or obligations, although issues of life-style and of personal discipline, as shall be seen in a moment, were certainly relevant.

Rather in each case it was in the general area of spirituality that their interests were first quickened and their loyalty maintained. Specifically it was by beginning to participate in yoga exercises and meditation (or, correspondingly in Zen groups, by doing *Zazen* meditation) that they found themselves greatly helped, their lives rather dramatically rearranged, and, above all, that once in, they literally, as one said, could not stay away. When I asked them what it was that they found there in these processes of meditative exercise, all agreed that, first, they felt real inside, real as a personal identity (as one person put it, "Because I experience here the unity of myself with my body"); second, they felt part of a genuine and supportive community; and, third, through these meditative practices they experienced a vastly "higher self," or, in other language, the presence in themselves of the divine energy. (This is Sikh language and would not be used by the Zen, but the principle of the transcendence of the ordinary self is the same.)

After this positive witness most of them add that it was this that they had missed—although they did not then know that they did—in their former religious communities. The patterns of worship, so they felt, were merely traditional and had little personal or creative meaning. There was, as one said, no experiencing of the divine available, "only faith" and the affirmations of faith. Most important, however, was that they were never urged, told, or advised to do anything with regard to their personal life or life-style or taught to develop new habits of personal piety. "There was nothing we could do to aid us on the religious path, to move us forward in spiritual development." Or, as another put it, "All I was told was to believe and to do good, but that left me unchanged inside. Here I was shown how to begin, how to move from stage to stage—and the difference for my inner self, and for my experiencing of the divine, has been immense." Such comments came from mainline Protestants, Catholics, Jews, and conservative Evangelicals, with, of course, the appropriate changes in their descriptions of their former religious communities.

If these reports are accurate, then they do validate, provisionally, my analysis of the crisis in common worship and in personal piety in our churches. If in turn this is so, then it has many implications for the present role of the pastor as servant. For surely it means that if pastors are to be effective servants of their congregations (and of the world), they must start in the area of spirituality, of the cure and nurture of souls, of the development of personal experiencing of the religious and of God. The servant pastor must not only be preacher, counselor, and ethical adviser (as well as organizer and money raiser), but also, above all, "spiritual leader," one who can lead his or her community from the beginning of the spiritual life through its many stages to some form of fruition. This has been one of the classic roles of the pastor; it has tended to vanish since the Enlightenment. We now see that it must return in force, if the religious strength of the churches is to be maintained.

PASTOR AS SPIRITUAL LEADER

The presence in power of alternative forms in religion can uncover our weaknesses and omissions. It can also provide us, if we are open to the assets these religions manifestly possess, with positive suggestions for dealing with these omissions. This seems almost disloyal at first: How can a Christian congregation accept suggestions from the forms and practices of another religion? Two things may be said in reply.

First, many of these faiths—in India and Japan, for example—have experienced renewal by adopting suggestions from competing Christian congregations about emphases in belief, relevant ethical principles, forms of worship, congregational life, and about new and creative relations to the world. It is not demeaning for us to do the same.

Second, the theological assumptions underlying this resistance constitute the exclusivist viewpoint traditional to our faith but currently repudiated by some and certainly by me. If there is truth and grace outside Christianity, if, therefore, these other ways do have something from God to offer us, then there is every reason to accept and use, albeit also to transform, the practices, emphases, and techniques that apparently have such healing and renewing power today.

Thus, the most important suggestions in this essay for the pastoral vocation — for the servant ministry today — is that the pastor view himself or herself as a spiritual leader and that, as a consequence, he or she present to members of the congregation techniques for developing their spiritual existence. Many such techniques long used by other traditions are now available; and many of these have for some time been practiced by Christians. Strangely seminaries and graduate schools, high on theology, ethics, and the techniques of preaching, are generally barren of these aspects of the religious life and religious leadership. The presence of these groups around us is, therefore, genuinely an opportunity to learn from them in areas in which we are poor and they are rich. Possibly through the development of these new ways of practicing the religious life, we may become strong enough to return to our own traditional ways — unavailable to us now — and adapt them to our present spiritual situation.

One final word on this point: The reintroduction in the theology of the twentieth century of the Reformation emphasis on the priority of grace, on the inadequacy of works, and on the futility of all self-help techniques (one can think of the long diatribes against "all works righteousness" written by nearly every one of the greats of the neoorthodox period) has made many of us wary of techniques for the spirit. How, if we believe in grace, can we hope to bring its presence about by doing something, by repeated practices, by techniques? This question represents an interesting theological problem we cannot explore here. Still, there are a couple of things that can be said in reply.

First, a study of the biographies of the Reformation "saints," the Puritans, and, as I have noted, typical Evangelicals shows that despite the immense emphasis on grace within each of these movements, the lives of these recipients of grace were filled with important religious practices: the reading of Scripture, personal devotions, a religiously determined life-style, and so on. Outwardly their lives were not religiously incognito at all. In contrast, there remain few religious practices, except attendance at worship service, that in the same manner feed the inner spirituality of most contemporary clerical persons and laypersons. If the new religious groups show us how vital such practices are, so also does the history of our own traditions.

Second, there can be little question that modern interpretations of grace, however much they may emphasize inner spirituality, find much more place for human response and activity than the founders of the Reformation did.

There is hardly a modern theologian who does not make central the responding acknowledgment and decision of faith, the self-direction within
the new life, and the responsibility of the new self for itself and its actions.
From innumerable modern sources (especially the Enlightenment), a new
emphasis on freedom and self-constitution, the autonomy of the self, has
appeared in theology. This new emphasis on human response, on the personal, has reshaped recent theologies of grace into new forms, forms in
which personal decision and action combine with grace rather than being
ruled by it. Thus, in contemporary theology the apparent contradiction of
practice, works, and self-help with a theology of grace is more seeming than
real. Responsive action on our part and the nurture of the soul through practice are both warranted if our existence, as well as our thoughts, is to be
suffused with grace and with the experience and consciousness of grace. An
emphasis on spirituality and the practices that lead toward it is not antithetical to the workings of grace; it may be that which makes those workings
within us more effective.

THEOLOGICAL IMPLICATIONS
OF PLURALITY

I want to conclude this essay on plurality and the pastoral vocation with
some brief comments on the theological implications of plurality, since the
pastor also wonders about theological questions and is dependent, implicitly
or explicitly, on answers to those questions. I cannot overemphasize how
new these issues are, and thus how few guidelines from tradition, even from
the tradition of early twentieth-century theology, there are. This is literally
an uncharted sea; few have yet ventured out on it, and the early maps of
those hardy souls who have are still far from satisfactory. Let us then look
at some of these problems, at the rocks and the monsters out there, and see
what we can begin to make of them.

As I have noted, one can discern three stages, so to speak, in the church's
relation to other religions. First is the stage of clear exclusivism: other ways
are simply false, if not blasphemous; Christianity represents, therefore, the
only way to salvation. There is neither truth nor grace without it. Second,
God works universally, and thus there is some measure of truth and grace,
even a saving measure, in other faiths. The definitive faith, however, the final
revelation among all, is in Christ. Christianity is thus the criterion for all the
others, even if it is not the exclusive locus of divine grace, for the love known
in Christ is present outside the influence of Christ. This is the view of the
liberal tradition and, interestingly, of most of the neoorthodox. Both traditions were implicitly, if not explicitly, universalist, and yet both insisted on
the finality of Jesus Christ. If one makes the appropriate theological changes,
this general position also represents the views of Hinduism and Buddhism
on other faiths; to both of them other religions are ways or paths on the
journey to truth and Nirvana or *Moksha*. But it is, of course, Hindu or

Buddhist enlightenment that defines that journey and its goal. In this sense there is still no parity among ways. At this second stage, therefore, all serious paths or ways are true and in their own way effective; but one among them is taken to be absolute, the defining criterion for the others.

I contend that even this second stage is unsatisfactory. It does not represent parity; it sets one faith clearly above the others; and it defines every other viewpoint in the categories of that one. The theological question is, therefore, How does one move to the third stage to affirm the religious pluralism of which the Christian church is one facet, that is, to affirm parity? The dilemma, of course, is that every faith proceeds theologically on the basis of some central starting point, some absolute ground or locus of interpretation, some standpoint from which all else is viewed and understood. For Christians, this is the event of Jesus Christ; for Jews, the Torah and the interpretive existence of the community; for Hindus and Buddhists, the higher consciousness in relation to the Scriptures and traditions of their community. If one relativizes each of these starting points, how can one proceed to reflect on the world from the point of view of one's religious faith, which is the task of theology? How can one relativize an absolute starting point? Can there be such a combination of relativity and absoluteness, of standing here and yet recognizing other places to stand?

This question goes deeper than the issue of the relativity of theology and so of doctrines and dogmas. It has long been recognized that there are no absolute and timeless propositions, even the ones the church officially makes. All are relative to their cultural setting and to their epoch, not to mention to the class, race, and sex from which they emanated. Thus, there is a history of theology; and thus, theology must be brought up to date and set within the categories relevant to our epoch and place. All this is now recognized. It has relativized every form of theology within the Christian community. It also made possible and fruitful the ecumenical movement. Are we not dealing here with the same problem, only now extended to other faiths as well as to other denominations?

The answer is, no; the issue here is far deeper. For, in the case of the former "relativizing," the human responses to final revelation (in Jesus the Christ) were relativized, not the revelation itself. Those who freely admitted the historicity of their own theologies, the liberals and the neoorthodox, nevertheless insisted on the absoluteness of Christianity or the finality and *Einmaligkeit* of the event of Jesus Christ. They had no sense of the relativity of that revelation or event of revelation among other revelations. If, however, one grants parity to each faith, then this is precisely what one is doing. It is not just our response to revelation that is relative; it is the revelation to which we are responding that is now roughly equal to the others. This is the new situation, a new and deeper interweaving of the relative and the absolute.

As is evident, this new situation represents a genuine puzzle. Let me suggest, however, that difficult as it is to think one's way out of it, still there are times when we act our way out of it, when what cannot be resolved in theory is nevertheless resolved in practice. For example, in dialogue between diverse religious faiths, a new combination of relativity and absoluteness, of standing firmly in one's own place and yet seeing its relativity, is enacted. I recall vividly many conversations with my Buddhist philosopher friend Takeuchi Yoshinori in Kyoto. Once he said to me: "I do not wish you to cease being a Christian, just as you do not wish me to cease representing Buddhism. This is the condition of our dialogue, that we each continue to stand where we stand. If we cease to be Christian and Buddhist, and each becomes secular, then there will result a different, and much more boring, conversation between us. Yet we each recognize the presence of truth and grace in the other and that recognition of equality is also the condition of our dialogue." Here was a puzzling but fruitful union of a relativizing of one's position, on the one hand, and yet a firm affirmation of that particular religious viewpoint, on the other. If either the firmness of affirmation or the sense of its relativity in relation to the other were to be lost, the dialogue would cease. Perhaps, therefore, we should start here, in our experience of constructive dialogue, and, from that puzzling point of unity of what is relative with what is absolute, try to think out a new Christian theology of the encounter of faiths.

The new reality of pluralism, however, does not merely present us with theological problems and puzzles, although it surely does that. As in church life, it also presents us with creative possibilities. When we begin to explore existence from within another faith, we see how deeply it can help us wherever we are ourselves weak. Let me give just one example among many.

It has become increasingly evident in the past few decades that the Western view of nature is in sore need of repair. Or, to put this point more specifically, it has been this view of nature that has incited and allowed, even encouraged, the industrial exploitation of nature, which is such a danger to our world and to us. This Western view of nature is not solely the fault of the biblical and the Christian tradition, as some maintain. But clearly that tradition is in part responsible. In its view humankind is distinguished from and set between God and the natural world. A three-level universe is thus imaged with God above, humans just below, and nature as the mere backdrop or stage on which the drama of the relation between the other two is played out. That this image has been creative there can be little doubt. It has been the source of the sense of the significance of history; even more, it has been the deepest root of the emphasis on the uniqueness of the human, on the value and power of the human, and so it has been the source of the creative humanitarianism of the modern Western tradition in our social, political, and ethical life.

Nevertheless, this view of nature as below ourselves, as subject to our domination, and thus as the mere stage for the really significant action of history, has teamed up with the objectifying of nature introduced by the new science. Nature in this view is not only distinguished from the human, and so from the realm of grace, it is also transformed into merely a system of objects, a passive, vacuous, and in itself valueless realm to be used by us for our creative purposes. As Dewey said, "We bring purposes and ends to nature; we give her values which she does not in herself have." Such is the theory. The practice has been exploitation.

No one is so optimistic as to think that, on the one hand, a new view of nature will prevent by itself the continuing exploitation of nature or that a new view can simply be constructed, so to speak, by fiat. On the other hand, different attitudes do have a significant effect, as changing attitudes toward other races and religions show. We also realize that the sense of the human relation to nature in other religious traditions is very different from our own. As an example, Buddhists feel themselves to be participants in the whole cycle of nature, each of us having been during other incarnations a participant in several parts of nature, of the animal and even of the plant kingdoms. While the uniqueness of the human level is perhaps less evident in other religions than in the Christian traditions, still there is the clear advantage that the line between the human and the rest of nature is much less sharply drawn. In Buddhism, for example, nature is by no means merely subservient to human purposes; rather nature has its own integrity and destiny, one in which we humans can participate in order to fulfill our own destinies. It is, therefore, a destiny with which we should cooperate. This sense of nature as a wider realm of mutual participation, as a vast cycle of existence through which we all pass, is close to the sense of nature the ecologists give us when they speak of the total natural system on which we are all dependent. And this sense of the wholeness and value of nature is as much a part of the truth as is the uniqueness of the human over against the rest of nature. Our Christian as well as our cultural traditions can well learn, therefore, from these religious movements that now make up our new plurality. As with the issue of spirituality, many of these movements have forms of wisdom that Christians sorely need. They present us not only with uncomfortable and taxing challenges but also with great opportunities for growth.

One final word: The confrontation with plurality in the sharp sense of parity is at present a very real fact in the life of contemporary churches. They would be well advised to face up to this reality and learn from it rather than to avoid it or struggle against it. As everything I have here stated indicates, however, this problem is not only for the churches and for religious traditions; it will soon be a problem on an even deeper scale for our Western cultural life. For if what I have said is true, Western culture will soon have to face its own context of plurality, the parity of competing cultural forms. Western scientific and naturalistic culture, which once thought itself to be the one chosen form of future cultural life, now finds itself only one of the many forms of modern cultural life functioning in our world; and almost certainly the strength and lure of new alternative forms will grow in the next decades. Soon we shall not be able to think of "Westernizing" other cultures — for that is not what happens in fact. Soon the reality of cultural pluralism will be as evident to Western academia as it is now to the leadership of the world's religions. It is no small part of the servant task of the churches, therefore, to help prepare their people and our common secular society for this even stronger wave of pluralism.[1]

---

[1] The following are suggested readings on religious plurality: John B. Cobb, Jr., *Beyond Dialogue* (Philadelphia: Fortress Press, 1982); Charles Davis, *The Christian and Other Religions* (New York: Herder & Herder, 1971); John Hick and B. Hebblethwaite, eds., *Christianity and Other Religions* (Philadelphia: Fortress Press, 1980); John Hick, *God and the Universe of Faiths* (New York: St. Martin's Press, 1973); John Hick, ed., *Truth and Dialogue in World Religions* (Philadelphia: Westminster Press, 1974); John Hick, *God Has Many Names* (London: Macmillan, 1980); John Hick and Paul Knitter, eds., *The Myth of Christian Uniqueness* (New York: Orbis, 1987). Paul Knitter, *No Other Name?* (Maryknoll, N.Y.: Orbis Books, 1985); R. Panikkar, *The Unknown Christ of Hinduism* (New York: Paulist Press, 1979); R. Panikkar, *Myth, Faith, and Hermeneutics* (New York: Paulist Press, 1979); W. C. Smith, *The Meaning and End of Religion* (New York: New American Library, 1964); W. C. Smith, *Towards a World Theology* (Philadelphia: Westminster Press, 1981); and F. Schuon, *The Transcendent Unity of Religions* (New York: Harper & Row, 1975).

CHAPTER 3

THEOLOGY: INTERPRETATION OF FAITH FOR CHURCH AND WORLD

Let me begin our thoughts on the vocation of the theologian with the realistic distinction between the glorious possibilities of that task and its actuality. When I was in graduate school at Union Theological Seminary in New York, we rightly took it for granted that the vocation of any theologian worth his or her salt was to address the whole church about the faith and to speak the Christian word to the world, and we assumed therefore that theologians in fact did this. After all, had not Reinhold Niebuhr not only dominated the last World Council of Churches meeting but also addressed regularly the CIO, and had not Paul Tillich spoken to a hushed American psychoanalytic society, not to mention the assembled greats who had graced the covers of *Time* magazine? Needless to say, it did not take long for some of us more ordinary mortals to realize that the full embodiment of our common task is rare indeed and far beyond our reach. I am lucky to speak once in a while to, say, Nebraska's Methodist ministers or to a group of concerned laity in a local church. Full embodiment of our task comes only with the providential gift of near genius; but still the task is constant and stands as a challenging, if unrealized, possibility, even for each of us. It is of the full structure of this task, not of the limitations that our own meager talents set on our enactment of it, that I wish here to speak.

ASSUMPTIONS ABOUT DIVINE PRESENCE

Not surprisingly, the only grounds for envisioning, shaping, defining, and limiting the task of the theologian are themselves theological. Thus, we must start with two theological assumptions that set, for me, the contours of the theologian's vocation. Both concern God and the manifestation or presence of God; it is from the modes of that presence that the theological task of declaring, interpreting, and elaborating that presence and its implications takes its shape. The first assumption that creates the community of the church and so theologians as well is that God is present decisively and for us men and women fully through the life and work, past and present, of Jesus who is the Christ.[1] It is here that the community of the church finds its empowering center. It is here too that individual Christian life and Christian theology find their source and center, their most significant authority, standard, and commission, that on which and by which the first—Christian existence—lives and that of which the second—Christian theology—primarily speaks. The second assumption is that God is also manifested, as an unconditional and ultimate creative presence, in the world and thus in culture, as the source or ground of creativity, of judgment, and of new possibility in ongoing historical life. It is, I think, simply biblical to affirm that social and cultural life also stand *coram Deo*—in the presence of God—in history, and thus, in however dim or distorted a fashion, does that cultural life represent a response to the continued divine presence creating, preserving, and directing finite being. As there is a cultural side to the presence of God in Christ in the church, so there is a religious substance, a dimension of ultimacy, in every communal and cultural whole.

While they are very different and should be carefully distinguished, these two modes of the divine presence, in church and in culture, are inseparable, deeply intertwined, and interdependent—as both the Old Testament account of Yahweh's presence to Israel through history and the eschatological goal of the Kingdom uniting covenant community with the redeemed world make clear. The task of the church—that is, of the grace and truth promised to it—is in large part the support, criticism, and healing of the world as well as of itself in the world. No theological or sermonic expression of the church's message is possible except it embody as well as reshape the forms of thought and value of its culture. The inner religious life of each of us, the forms of our anxieties, our sins, our deepest loyalties and hopes, is shaped by our outer world: by the structures of our social world and by the events that transpire there. Inner and outer, personal and social existence create and re-create each other, inner creativity and courage resulting continuously in new outer structures and new solutions to outer problems, but also the present sins of our hearts warping the historical institutions we do shape into a hard, semipermanent objective fate for our children and our children's children. No church can exhibit the presence of God if it ignores the sins and injustices of its community; it loses its own inner soul, its religious substance, when it loses touch with its task of criticism and healing in its own world. Then it becomes merely its world blessing its community's injustices and

---

[1] This essay preceded by five years the publication (in 1989) of the previous chapter.

encouraging its community's aggression, as the German churches did and as the American churches may again. The message of the church has thus, through no accident, a dual focus: Christ and his kingdom. We are called to deal both with sin and with the outer social results of sin, with self-interest, pride, and greed and their consequences on the historical fatedness of rapacious and oppressive institutions, unjust and exploitative social structures, and aggressive communities. As estrangement from God results in inner distortion and despair and in outer injustice and destruction, so God's creative and redemptive grace and meaning are present in both church and world, in the means of grace and in the creative structures of culture. From these basic presuppositions about the divine presence and about human need, theology derives its task and the theologian her or his vocation.

DUAL ROLE OF THE THEOLOGIAN

The theologian therefore has a dual role, churchly and public, on the boundary between church and world, as Tillich put it, at home and yet not quite at home in either one. In both, the theologian has a vocation and a message, but in neither church nor world can that message be uncritical, undialectical. The theologian's churchly role — when seeking the ear of the church — is not fulfilled by an uncritical proclamation of the American world around the church, nor is it fulfilled by an unchallenged championing of the church to itself as the light of its world. Hence the theologian is, as the minister is, uneasy in the church. Correspondingly, the public role of the theologian — when seeking the world's ear — must also be paradoxical, dialectical, and thus uncomfortable. A continued defense of ourselves as the church to the world, of the church as a significant institution, or of God as a rational idea among other rational ideas, and of theology as "a respectable discipline," a defense conducted on the world's terms and according to its criteria, is far too insignificant a theme, is not only defensive but a bit narcissistic. Moreover, by submitting the Christian message to the barren standards of the world without a struggle, it tells the world little it does not already know. What our role may be in the church and in the world is the subject of the rest of my remarks. For the moment, one implication of my argument is that, in contrast to Van A. Harvey, it is for me no accident that from the beginning theology has resided — albeit only with a temporary lease — in both church and academy, in the world's universities as well as in the church's seminaries. Theology is, as Tillich showed, a compound both of message and of cultural situation, and so it needs both, and, as we have noted, it speaks to both. But it is also true that this theological compound, when true to itself, represents a bitter as well as a healing prescription for both of the institutions (church and university) that bear the necessary elements of that compound and that alternatively house its practitioners.

The major role of the theologian is clear enough: It is to produce relevant, contemporary, and appropriate constructive theology and to present this to the Christian community. Its job is, therefore, to reflect on the Christian message in relation to the human situation, personal and social, and in the light of the present cultural situation. This task of theology can be defined in two ways: It presents an understanding of contemporary human existence as that existence is interpreted through the symbols of the Christian tradition, or, alternatively, it presents a contemporary interpretation of Christian faith in its relation to human existence. It sets into contemporary conceptual form the Christian gospel as that gospel addresses, challenges, and heals the personal and social history of men and women. Clearly first of all, then, theology is a function of the church, of the Christian community. It represents that community's effort to understand itself and its message, to define what it is in the area of belief, of fundamental conviction, that is to say, what basic symbols or sets of symbols constitute that community, that distinguish it from other communities, and that therefore guide and empower its life, its decisions, its actions and policies, and its rites and customs.

We should note, however, that even in realizing this churchly task of understanding and thus of defining itself—and continually reunderstanding and redefining itself—theology relates itself also to the world. The gospel addresses universal human existence, yours and mine, that of churched and unchurched, of *ecclesia* and world alike. For the destructive problems that wrack the world, on the one hand, and the creative meanings that would heal it, on the other, represent the same problems and the same answers that the gospel pictures. If sin and death are what the gospel as a message addresses, these two do not confine their destructive power to the people who hear the Word, nor are faith and love relevant only for the existence of the churched. A relevant, intelligible, appropriate constructive theology is thus not only a necessity for the church's life, it also represents an important message for the world, an interpretation of our common existence that the world might well heed to its benefit, that must be presented to the world with the same seriousness it is presented to the church.

DISTINCTION BETWEEN FAITH
AND THEOLOGY

Theology is a reflective task. Its goal is understanding, understanding through a valid theory, shaped by Christian symbols, of the nature and problems of human existence, personal and social, of the nature, activity, and promises of God, and thus of the hopes for personal and historical life. To be a Christian is to live Christianly, with faith and love, to have one's existence characterized by a Christian relationship to God and to others. This is personal and existential, and here all of us are radically equal, for none has more talent for this than others. Theology and doing theology are significantly different from this. Theology represents a Christian theory about existence and the God to whom it is essentially related. It is Christian understanding, and it characterizes our thinking, whereas Christian life or faith characterizes our existence, the way we are and act. One implication of this distinction is that "wrong" theology does not signal a lower level of Christian existence; nor does a "correct" theology (or one's Ph.D. in theology) signal a higher level of Christian existence. Any one of us can grade a systematic paper or review a theological book; none of us, only the Lord, can grade a neighbor's faith or give a final review to another's religious existence.

Another implication of the distinction between faith and existence, on the one hand, and theology, on the other, is that theology relates itself first of all to other theories and only indirectly to concrete situations in actual life. It seeks, for example, to clarify the relationship of the Christian understanding of human being with the psychological theories of Freud or Piaget; its understanding of history with the views of Toynbee or Marx; its views of knowledge and/or of reality with those of Whitehead, Heidegger, and Wittgenstein. It gives understanding, and through that gift it may provide inspiration (and possibly may even become a vehicle of new faith and action). But its primary goal is to help us to understand what we believe: who we are, what our deepest problems are, who God is, what we believe God has done to reconcile us with one another and with God, and what we are to do in obedience and out of love. Preaching proclaims the gospel to particular persons in particular situations, persons faced with particular problems and obligations—that is, with regard to their religious existence, their faith, and their love. Theology (even liberation theology) presents an understanding, an interpretation, of the gospel in relation to the human situation generally and thus in relation to our culture's understanding of that situation: its relevant sciences, social science, psychology, historical knowledge, and philosophy. While it is surely true that a theologian must understand the ups and downs, the absurdities and pathos of life and be in touch with his or her own existence and that of others—else he or she can hardly be creative in theology—still most immediately a theologian must be intellectually conversant with the theoretical interpretation of the human situation (for example, with Marxism) that characterizes contemporary culture. In any case, it is only in the latter area—in the area of theories relative to theological understanding—that we can hope formally to educate and to assess or "grade" one another.

THE STATUS OF THEOLOGY

The distinction between religious existence and theological reflection on that existence helps us to be clear about the status of theology. It used to be held that the center of valid dogmatic theology was itself revealed, that a sound theologian could therefore unambiguously "state the faith of the church," and as a consequence that true theology was absolute, changeless, and universal. Now, however, we realize that theology is not directly God given but represents a human response to the divine presence. To be sure, our commitment, loyalty, and obedience — our religious existence — must be, or should be, unconditional; but we should always recall that our theology is not. Theological propositions are our reflection on our faith and the revelation that is its object, not propositions revealed in themselves. Thus, any given theology is relative and partial, as all our thinking is, one perspective on the Christian message, in the present case the perspective of a male, middle-class, white, Protestant, and married American (possibly even Chicagoan) of advanced middle age. If I don't recognize this partial and thus relative character to my theology, you may be sure others will: blacks, women, Europeans, South Americans — even misguided colleagues — and if by accident any expert should come across this in a hundred years, she or he would be able to say, even after only one paragraph, "an understanding of theology typical of late twentieth-century American Protestantism during the decline of the Anglo-Saxon Western world." To believe that theological truths are absolute, changeless, and universal is to forget that theology represents human thinking, and that all our thinking, even that creative of theology, has a historical character.

Any particular theology is, therefore, a proposal to the church community, not an authoritarian or dogmatic edict, a proposal for understanding our common faith, a proposal for our consideration about our Christian existence, and thus a proposal to be assessed, criticized, amended, or rejected by each of us and by the community as a whole. Even if there is one Lord, there are many theological points of view pointing toward that one Lord. One does not therefore believe in a given theology, even one emanating from Emory or Chicago; one believes in God and God's Word, and holds, or may hold, that a given theology is the best expression for the moment of that which is believed. Let me add that the inevitably parochial, even local, character of our theology does not mean that we should try to write a "male" theology, an "American" theology, a "southern" theology. We should attempt to point our propositions toward the universal, as proposals about human existence generally for the whole church's understanding; soon enough their relativity will become evident. But we should not try to present only part of the truth.

THE NECESSITY OF THEOLOGY

Granted, then, the theoretical and the relative perspectival character of theology, why is theology important or even necessary for the Christian community, for the church? If constructive theology is not a vocation for everybody in the church — as are faith and works of love — why is it a vocation for anybody? The necessity, it seems to me, is based on the historical, the communal, and the personal character of our faith, and on the transcendent character of God.

Christianity is a communal, an interpersonal form of religion. As a message about a historical event rather than a universally available experience, Christian faith is generated not in individual experience but is communicated from one person to another by proclamation, preaching, teaching, and witness or example. As it comes to each of us and is passed on, it is a Word that must first of all be said or declared. In order for this to be possible, the message must be thought out, reflected, set into intelligible, coherent, and relevant concepts for it to be spoken, on the one hand, and heard and acknowledged, on the other. Preaching and teaching presuppose a theology, a coherent, unified interpretation of the faith. By the same token, this faith, if it is to have any reality at all, must be personal, assented to by the mind of each one who affirms it. For it to be ours at the deepest level of our existence, we must understand its meaning and be assured of its truth, we must be able to think what we believe and so assent to it, if we are to believe it. If we are to guide our lives by it, again we must be able to think it. As do proclaiming and speaking a message, so believing and affirming one presuppose a theology, again a coherent, intelligible, and credible interpretation of the faith. Both reasons call, moreover, for a continually renewed or revised theology, so that the message can be said relevantly and credibly to us and affirmed personally by us with understanding and conviction.

Finally, the transcendence represented by the object of our faith calls for theology in those who receive and acknowledge this transcendence. The message comes to us from beyond ourselves, from beyond our experience and everything that is immediately around us. To be sure, grace is communicated to our experience, in our liturgies, through our sacraments, through our preaching, and through persons transparent to the divine. But grace is not merely our experience, nor identical with the liturgical rite, a sacramental reality, even a powerful sermon, or the most loving person. The divine Word and power communicates itself through each; still each is only a medium, and our reception must be pointed through the medium to what lies in and also beyond it. In us it is in large part reflection that lifts us up beyond the immediate, the visible, the present medium of grace, that, in other words, makes the divine presence in and through these means into means of grace, the divine immanence into what is also the divine transcendence. Correspondingly, though grace is in the church, it also judges the church and so transcends it. Again, reflection, and thus theology, is the condition for that dialectical yes and no, for that acceptance of and yet transcendence over the immediate in order that the medium be a true symbol of grace. Thus, because of the historical, the communal, and the personal character of Christian faith, and because of the transcendent character of the God of faith, theological reflection is a necessary component in the life of the community. That community must understand that which it believes and that by which it guides its life, and that striving toward understanding culminates in and is represented by the vocation of the theologian.

THE POLAR CHARACTER
OF THEOLOGY

It is evident that for theology to perform this necessary function in the Christian community, it must be polar in character. On the one hand, it must express the original and central message of the faith and thus point us beyond our immediacy in our cultural present to God's presence in the event of Jesus Christ and subsequently in the means of grace related to that event. On the other hand, it must bring that message to us, to our understanding and our modes of thinking and thus express that message in a form intelligible, credible, and relevant to us — that is, in the form of modern concepts, categories, standards, and aims. If it is too orthodox, too time honored and thus timeless, theology will enshrine a message addressed to a day other than our own, a message that may evoke nostalgia but will not penetrate into our personal being as relevant to our existence here and now. If it is too timely, it will merely repeat the world's wisdom, and failing to communicate anything new and healing to our world, it will leave us again untouched. Constructive theology is, therefore, an infinite risk: The tradition must be revised and set into modern categories lest it not be heard at all. But it must also transform those categories into Christian form — into a Christian interpretation of contemporary experience — lest no message be there. If we merely re-present tradition, we lose our touch with the world and with ourselves; if we merely re-present our world, we lose the message. Here lies the double risk. We see, then, how important it is that there be a variety of constructive theologies and that each recognize itself as a proposal to the church community. Each new theological construction represents a creative reinterpretation and thus an infinite risk, a risk to be assessed in openness, in critical judgment, and in infinite interest by the community.

THE FUNDAMENTAL TASK
OF THEOLOGY

The fundamental task of theology is, therefore, that of revision, of re-presentation. With the obfuscation characteristic of any profession, we now term this the "hermeneutical" problem, the problem of interpreting what was said or written in one age into the categories and concepts of our own age, or, as Tillich called it, the union of the eternal message with the cultural situation characteristic of our time and place. There is no question that this hermeneutical enterprise defines the constructive task and, thus, that the hours recently spent pondering its problems and the pages used explicating its method have been necessary and well used. If we seek to do constructive theology, each of us has to formulate as carefully as possible a procedure for this translation or revision and to test that procedure against the often polite but more frequently horrified rejection of our colleagues.

At this point, however, we encounter the present temptation lying in wait for the contemporary theologian, especially one in a major university graduate school. This is the temptation to linger so long in the preparatory enterprise of hermeneutical method, of answering the question of how to go about doing theology, that the theologian never in fact realizes, re-presents, or reexpresses a single aspect of the original message. Let us remember that a modern and contemporary method of constructive theology, however brilliant it may be, is not itself the gospel or even a modern, contemporary reinterpretation of the gospel, and that the problems that a method of theological inquiry faces in the academic community are not the same as the problems that wrack and threaten to destroy the world's existence. Thus, doing theological method is not yet doing theology, however much it may seem in academia that the two are one and the same. As with getting in shape, the concentration on method is important and necessary, but it is not the same as running the race that must be run. To repeat, the central churchly task of the theologian is to re-present the Christian gospel—that is, the full set of Christian symbols—as an interpretation of our common, human existence; and to re-present this in a form appropriate to its original sources and intelligible and credible to contemporary minds. Thus can theology aid the community of the church in reshaping its own life—its own "religious substance"—closer to a genuine Christian substance. For only in this way can that community become (like its Lord) a symbol, a medium, a sacrament of grace to its world.

The primary task of the theologian is the revision of the Christian message in contemporary terms, a message addressed, of course, first of all to the community of the church, which seeks to live by that message. The corresponding temptation of the theologian (now that we have lost all power in the world; there were many other temptations before that power slipped away from us!) is so to concentrate on that hermeneutical task, and especially the interesting, alluring intellectual problems connected with it, that the message itself and especially the relevant, biting, healing relation of that message to ourselves and to the world cease to be central objects of reflection. The gospel, we have said, contains a Christian message to and about human existence; it presents an interpretation of our common existence that is both true about it and healing to it. It is, therefore, addressed to the world and not alone to the saints, judging, challenging, shaking, healing, and transforming the world. Correspondingly, while the primary requirement for any theology is that it be a re-presentation of the message to the church, it is no less also necessary that it be a re-presentation to our world, to the cultural and social life of men and women in our time.

I have cited a number of reasons why this last point is important. Let me summarize them in a slightly new fashion and thus with a somewhat new emphasis. First, the church and therefore the message to the church cannot be separated from the world around it. If it seeks to do that, the church fools itself about itself and thus loses itself in a morass of self-deception. The anxieties and fears that bother and threaten the listeners in our pews are the world's problems: unemployment and inflation; disease, age, and death; loneliness and conformity; public violence and racial conflict; nuclear war and national weakness; our way of life in relation to the world's future, and so on and on. Thus, in addressing our own anxieties as Christians in church, we are in fact discoursing on our wider culture's problems. If we would understand our personal crises, therefore, we must as theologians understand also that wider structure; if we would speak a healing word to personal problems, we must envision new possibilities for our cultural history. To separate personal problems relevant to religion from social problems relevant only to political and economic policy is to divide us up artificially; it is we who suffer from both sorts of problems and we who seek to deal with them. Thus, correspondingly, if we seek to solve our personal economic and social problems either by drink or by an inordinate ambition, we are enacting and embodying a wider social problem. If we attempt to resolve our economic and social anxieties by anti-Semitic or white racist attitudes and actions, even more are we embodying and spreading a social disease. And, finally, if we think to ease our fears for America's security by amassing unlimited nuclear arms, by electing to support friendly dictators, or by commandeering all the natural resources we can, we have ourselves incarnated, joined, or become the forces of destruction rampant in our world—in effect, voluntary instruments of a scourge in modern history.

Personal crises tempt us to individual sins. In much the same way—though perhaps obscured by their size—social crises represent not just political and economic problems or puzzles. They also bring with them moral crises and they demand moral decisions. They make us deeply anxious and tempt us, only now all of us together, as a community, to attitudes of self-concern and to acts of selfishness: of expropriation, aggression, violence. The German church was silent in the face of deep social, economic, and political crises, and it remained craven before the demonic reactions of its community to those crises; likewise, much of the American church has been silent in the face of racial division and nationalistic expansionism. Both made evident that a church that ignores the injustices and the upheavals in its immediate world ends by becoming part of them, an instrument of them, and so corrupts itself endlessly; and it makes of its message, however sublime, an "ideology" justifying that sordid historical reality. Let us recall that it is only the sinners in a given historical situation that ignore social sins, that try to be indifferent to the injustices of the world they rule and profit from: to the masters, the oppressors, and the aggressors, social sins of inequality, injustice, and imperialism seldom have relevance to their private religion! Those who suffer from these acts, however, those who are sinned against, the oppressed, slaves, and servants, the dominated and the persecuted, the hungry, do not regard that worldly situation as religiously indifferent or even as unrelated to the divine judgment.

The gospel can hardly be the gospel if it does not address the ills that beset us and the sins with which we seek to escape those ills. Those ills and sins are for any church community the sins of its own social world, nothing else.

Thus, for the gospel to challenge, judge, heal, and transform, it must relate itself not just to the contemporary church, not just even to cultural theories and to cultural self-understanding; it must relate itself also to the social structures of destruction and of possibility in that historical world, to its economic, political, class, racial, and national developments. It is no accident that the gospel is a gospel for persons in community, for inner individuals in their social roles, for personal commitment and decision in the wider kingdom. As a consequence, a theological interpretation of that gospel must include both the theoretical and the practical relationship of the gospel to the world's life, to its crises and its political meanings, to the total life of contemporary history.

There is another point in this regard significant for the wholeness of theology as a contemporary expression of the Christian message. The primary task of theology, the hermeneutical task, represents the effort to unite our message from the past to the intellectual, social, moral, and political characteristics of our culture. For theologians acutely conscious of the anachronistic character of their tradition, its pseudoscience, its literalism, its frozen immobility and dogmatism, even its pallid humanitarianism and its male bourgeois prejudices, the task of hermeneutics unwittingly encourages the assumption of the stability, credibility, and viability of the modern culture to which it seeks to adapt the gospel. The gospel that we bring often seems to us precious but precarious, barely acceptable by the world's hardheaded wisdom. Whether this attitude is more true for theologians in academia somewhat nervously present in the self-assured atmosphere of an academic council, made up of prestigious scientists, sociologists, and psychologists, or of preachers trying to communicate to a committee of important and self-confident bankers, brokers, manufacturers, and labor leaders, I will not say. In either case the first task of theology, the revisionary task, is apt to encourage a serious misunderstanding of the gospel and a vast illusion about the stability and viability of the world to which it is now addressed.

For the simple fact of our present is that the contemporary world to which we rightly seek to adapt the gospel is, if anything, in worse shape than either the gospel or the church that proclaims it is. It is probably more anachronistic and illusionistic; it is a good deal more threatened from the outside; and it seems bent on a path of self-destruction even more than the forces of traditional religion do. This is not to state that modern Western culture, and with it the American way of life as its latest edition, is necessarily on the decline; no one knows that much about even the immediate future. It is to state that culture faces serious internal and self-generated difficulties, even contradictions, and that the precariousness of its present dominance and, through that, the precariousness of its continued life have revealed themselves with increasing clarity in our generation. A sophisticated industrial society has begun to develop economic problems of inflation and of supplies and social problems of urban decay that it never dreamed possible; a technological industrial society, fated to an uncontrollable expansion, seems to be doomed shortly (by, say, the year 2000) to consume the resources on which it must live and to destroy the nature system through and in which it must exist. Meanwhile, let us recall that dominant power was long resident among the Western nations alone — the last time a non-Western power threatened or could threaten the West was in 1456, five hundred years ago, when the Turks stormed Vienna! Such dominant power in our lifetime has fled the West and is now beginning to manifest itself elsewhere. Only one of the four major world powers is now Western. And if you don't think America exhibits this precipitous loss in anxiety, puzzlement, frustration, and panic, then just listen. Correspondingly, like many an aging leader, anxious over the loss of former power, we are beginning to shed the courage of our creative ideals and to retreat to the cynical and eroding interest of mere self-protection. The strident call to forget human rights and prudently to bolster those sorry tyrants who depend on us around the world is a sure sign of anxious weakness rather than of mature strength, of a community that, in fearfully whiffing the dank odor of its own mortality, empties its ideals of all real content in order to save — in order, that is, to endanger more dramatically — its life.

This is our real world. It is grim, it is precarious, and it will not go away. It needs desperately, as the church does, clear understanding and interpretation and, above all, judgment, grace, and hope. Merely to adapt the gospel to that world is to misunderstand the meaning and the purpose of the divine judgment and of grace and to harbor vast delusions about that world. Perhaps the most vivid example of theological insight in Christian history, of a vision of what theology might and ought to be, was when Augustine realized, just before the demise of the Roman Empire, that the effort, long honored in the established church, merely enthusiastically to adapt Christianity to that Roman culture — creative, powerful, glorious, and eternal as Rome had long seemed — was mistaken, that the Christian vision must transcend as well as engage that culture, and that this too was a part of the calling of theology. In that act of transcendence of the Hellenistic world, as well as of adaptation to it, he sowed the seed of endless new ecclesiastical and cultural possibilities, possibilities by no means yet visible to him as he watched the Vandal hordes circling the walls of besieged Hippo waiting for the kill.

It appears that I am saying that the theologian must know everything about present culture, even its probable future, as well as everything about the gospel and its tradition — a large order indeed. Certainly the theologian's interest and curiosity about our social as well as our personal situations must be wide, for the fire from heaven bursts into light and heat only when it strikes the earth, not before. But we can restrict that demand somewhat . The constructive theologian is not and cannot be a specialist in each of the important contemporary disciplines: in the sciences, economics, politics, sociology, and psychology. The construction of theories and policies in these areas is not the theologian's responsibility. No area of culture, however, is separate from the "religious substance" of the culture, from the effects, theoretical and practical, of that culture's most fundamental beliefs. There is a central spiritual ethos of a culture's life that unifies each element and each vocation into a cultural whole, that gives to each of a culture's sciences and arts its particular stamp, and that provides standards for its actions and content to its aims. The economic, political, social, and individual life of our culture is, for example, permeated by a matrix of crucial symbols drawn from the hopes and aims of science, technology, democracy, and capitalism, which together make up what we call the "American way of life" in all of its facets. This religious substance is a legitimate and crucial object of the theologian's concern, of, that is, the theologian's "theology of culture." To this "secular mythology," if I may so term it, theological self-understanding must continually relate itself: in analysis, in retrieval and support of what is creative in that cultural tradition (for much is), in criticism and judgment of what is false and dangerous, even demonic, there, and in the promise of grace and of hope for its future. The task of the church, and thus of theology, in the world is to shape that cultural religious substance positively closer to a Christian form (more just, more equal, more compassionate and humane, more peaceful) and, negatively, to guard it from the self-destruction of anxiety, insecurity, panic, radical self-love, sin. Put in terms of disciplines, systematic or constructive theology, then, is fulfilled only when it is supplemented, on the one hand, by theology of culture and, on the other, by liberation theology. Without them, constructive theology is apt to collapse into method and remain formal, academic, unrelated, ineffective, narcissistic, ideological. Without the theological center of the gospel in relation to our existence, however, theology of culture and liberation theology remain void of significant criteria or standards and, therefore, empty of deeper purpose and hope.

An old summation of the gospel, and thus of the task of theological interpretation, says, first, that it deals with sin, with fate, and with death, and, second, that it is respectively God's mercy and grace in Christ that addresses sin, God's providential power in history that overcomes fate, and God's eternal being that triumphs over death. All of this is included in the gospel and thus in the task of theology. In the church, where word and sacrament are present and where the gospel is re-presented, the depths of sin are uncovered and faith and love may be borne. But the world is in the church and the church is in the world. Both the church and world together participate in the estrangement of sin. Both suffer under the fatedness of history: its unjust institutions, its terrifying trends, its destructive and irrational events, its menacing future. And both together face the inevitability of death. To re-present in constructive form the whole gospel means, therefore, to encompass all three: God, ourselves before God, and the contemporary historical situation in which God's power, judgment, and new possibilities are manifest. What is it we need and must know in theology? It is God, the soul, and the world we souls share together—that is all, but it is enough!

CHAPTER 4

SYMBOLS, MEANING, AND THE DIVINE PRESENCE

Symbol making in America is my theme, but inevitably this means theological and liturgical symbols in America. More precisely this means liturgical symbols in the secular American world, a world not yet lost for God and yet in vast difficulty with its liturgical symbols. How are theological and liturgical symbols possible in secular America? My central thesis is perhaps better expressed by Raimundo Panikkar: Liturgy must express the sacred quality of the secular if it is to be meaningful. I shall here try to follow out the implications of this thesis with regard not only to theology and ethics — as many Catholics have already sought to do — but with regard to liturgy.

HOW SYMBOLS MEAN FOR US

How do symbols mean for us? Further, how is it that, in meaning for us, symbols seem to put us in touch with what is real and to communicate to us a cohering and transforming power? These are the basic questions of both contemporary theology and liturgy — the two disciplines, separate as they seem, that live in and through the same mystery of divine communication, of reality and power transmitted through symbols. In both cases, although we can reflect on this mystery of divine communication, we cannot ourselves create or evoke it or increase it by rearranging the furniture. The direction of the movement comes the other way: the divine communicates itself to us through symbols; its presence is there already in the symbols; and our worship, like our theological affirmation, is a response to this objective presence, as the classical doctrines of revelation, *ex opere operato,* justification by grace through faith alone, and Barth's theory of religious language each in its own queer way affirm. With this caveat in mind, that neither the most intelligent theological reflection nor the most sensitive liturgical rearrangement can itself evoke the divine presence, we can nonetheless reflect on the mystery of this presence and of its communication to us and thus possibly see in which direction we might turn in order to sense it anew.

How do symbols mean and, in meaning, communicate reality to us? Not all symbols are alike, and the rules appropriate to one kind do not necessarily apply to symbols at another level. The closest sort of symbols to the kind we are here concerned with, liturgical and theological symbols, are our more basic social symbols; that is, those symbols shared by a society that structures its life-world by shaping its ultimate horizon, defining its constituent parts, placing each part in its relation to the others, assigning tasks, goals, privileges, and obligations to people, and thus giving unique shape or form to that social world. Clearly such symbols are political, economic, social, and individual in content, since they help define both ourselves in our various roles and our interlocking social relations. Together this set of interrelated symbols defines symbolically — as our customary social behavior may define "incarnately" — a community's total way of life, the kind of community and people that group is among the world's peoples: in our own case, as a democratic, bourgeois, affluent, materialistic, moralistic, semi-Christian society, one involved in incarnating something called the American way of life.

There are some symbols here to which we probably really respond: individual rights, free speech, equality before the law, consent of the governed, emphasis on personal integrity. There are others at which academics and religious tend to shudder: individual accomplishment and self-reliance, the self-made person, the sanctity of property, the overriding rights of hard work, the centrality of private or individual happiness, the wonders of affluence, the beatitude of success. These more reflective or notional symbols, if elaborated into institutions, form the basis for such theoretical disciplines as political, economic, and social theory and ethics. They can, however, also be incarnated into more concrete earthy, material symbols: a conglomeration of geographical references (wide plains, high mountains, green valleys), ethnic peculiarities, historical events, culminating in such familiar and potent symbols as the Cadillac, the milk shake, the busy executive, the accomplished, sunny young mother, and so on. One thing is immediately clear from this brief sociology of Americanism: Even the most secular society lives by its fundamental symbols. Its institutions as systems of shared meanings and expectancies are structured by these symbols, and thus the roles of each of us, and so the meaning, purpose, and aims of our lives, are symbolically determined — even if, as in our case, the symbolical determination is toward a mode of existence that is oriented away from inward and symbolic spirituality and toward things and outward security and success. As in religious societies of old, we in a consumer culture still live in and through the unseen, an unseen that comes to us in symbolical forms.

As is evident, a whole way of being in the world is expressed in the symbols common to American life. But, even more to my present point, a way of life is created, re-created, and generated here. We Americans do not make these symbols so much as they make us: our expectancies, goals, hopes, fears are determined here; and, correspondingly, our most fundamental moves in life, voluntary and involuntary, are shaped by these symbols. They make us who we are. We should therefore note the normative, even prescriptive, character and role of these social symbols: they tell us what authentic humanity is to be for us, what its role, possible vocations, goals, and joys should be, and above all what an authentic community is. They structure a world in which we find a place and a task, and they point out to us the task that is to be ours — whether making money, being a distinguished scientist or a Hollywood star. According to these norms, we are told what humans really are and so what fulfills our humanity, and how to gain that beatitude. Americans are not pushed by some sardonic fate into reduplicating endlessly the national type; we are, rather, each one of us for herself or himself and one by one (as Schleiermacher said about sin) lured into embodying these types or models communicated to us through this whole range of common symbols. They are for us then "ultimate" in twin senses: (1) they guide and shape our cognitive and moral judgments; and (2) they determine the one life we have, its shape, its destiny, its weal, and its woe.

Intrinsic to such potent social symbols, moreover, is an inevitable reference to reality. They communicate to a people what humans really are, what community really is (not just what we or they think it is), and so what the grain of history itself involves. No society can function, no social roles can lure our activity and devotion, no government can inspire our obedience, no politics can incite us to action unless the symbolic world each offers communicates to us reality as well as value and thus promises to usher us into the real world latent in history's obscure developments. In other times fundamental social structures were divinely ordained, and the symbols expressive of them became part of the structure of the society's religion, if not identical with it. Of late, the divine source has for our common life fled, but neither communist nor American society fails to believe and assert that its symbols represent the grain of history itself. The meaning, legitimacy, and power of social symbols thus unite descriptive, normative, and ontological elements into what can only be called a religious symbolic structure. Culture and culture's symbols do mediate an ultimate concern, as Tillich said, and possess a religious substance; and the problem of the relation of cultural symbols to Christian symbols has been and is a crucial issue for theology and liturgy alike.

If, then, we pose my initial question (How do cultural symbols mean and how do they communicate transformative power?) to these symbols, the answer is obvious. They mean so powerfully to us, in fact they almost are us, because they shape and thematize our real world, our life-world, the ordinary social world in which we really are and know that we are. The sense of reality and so of authority and power in these symbols comes from their intrinsic relation to our common and shared life experience. After all, we are born into the world shaped by them, almost everyone we know is determined by them, and all our shared possibilities are expressed by them. Their reality and power are self-evident; they are the structure of our most real world. Such symbols communicate reality to us because they are ingredients as reality's essential structure in our daily experience, not because they are "proved"; and they mean because they shape us and so have a vital use and role in our being and becoming ourselves. They shape our real world and ourselves; and to what else could the words *meaning* and *validity, use* and *verification* be pointing? By the same token, functioning social symbols are not "disproved"; rather, when they do die, it is because our life-world has receded from them, as when we move from home to another culture, from ethnic ghetto to the wide world, and find our once-real social world now only a quaint, queer, arbitrary, and slightly absurd corner of a much vaster reality.

Thus, it is clear that without touch with ordinary, shared experience, with the real life-world of day to day and so of today, symbols weaken in intrinsic power and validity and lose their function and role. At first they become merely traditional, rote, even magical devices, extrinsic, heteronomous forms that crush rather than shape our true existence now rooted elsewhere. At last, however, all reality having fled to the new life-world, they are left inert and flat ghosts, emissaries of a lost world that is no longer real and embodiments of meanings that no longer mean. This slow bleeding to death of once-omnipotent symbols is not totally strange to present Catholic experience.

It might seem from this that in a secular world, religious symbols, now separate from the secular life-world and so inert and dying, must revitalize themselves by "getting with" our dominant and robust social symbols, our civic religion, and thus find a real role by putting into Christian form the democratic, egalitarian, possibly the revolutionary symbolic structures of a secular society—as a good number of anxious Catholics seem to suggest. Such a temptation is by no means new, and debate about it has a long and honored tradition. There has in fact been a kind of love-hate, attraction-repulsion relation between cultural and religious symbols throughout history, and possibly our analysis helps to reveal its anatomy. Religious symbols lose their reality if they are separated entirely from the life-world; yet they lose their integrity if they are simply identified with the social symbols that structure that world.

On the one hand, religious symbols are drawn inexorably to participate in the life-world if they are to survive at all; for here alone is where reality, meaning, and transformative power are. Thus, if during their vigorous days they find they cannot so relate to culture and retain their integrity, then they do not abandon the life-world of their votaries but they remove that life-world itself from the wider culture and set it within their own religious orbit, as in the early church, in monasticism, and in all the forms of sectarian withdrawal where religion itself structured the daily life-world in order for religion to survive. On the other hand, religious symbols cannot become merely identical with the social symbols that structure and lure our common life, lest again they lose their integrity and die. In such an identification there arises an Americanized Christianity whose real criteria of reality, truth, and value are shaped by the symbols creative of the social world of a suburban, corporate, consumer, and nationalistic culture and so whose real sacramental elements are an enlarging church role, a new church plant, a full school, expanding committees, the executive desk, two telephones, and a plaque as the best "corporate representative" of Vatican and Pentagon alike. What can liturgy be then if the only reality its symbols really mean, and so which they can communicate, is the profane reality out the church door in the town? No wonder such a church is finally emptied when its people more and more enter the town itself and find they can live there without the church's help. Religious symbols that lose a special judgment and a special promise over against culture also lose their life and reality.

The classical answer, in both Catholicism and Protestantism, is to recognize two zones of influence: that of the life-world where social symbols predominate and that of the religious world—above, beyond, and after in Catholicism, within and later in Protestantism—to which religious symbols, theological, moral, and liturgical, refer. One problem of this solution, just now vividly seen by most Catholics, is that our most fundamental Christian symbols refer to precisely that life-world and not to some other zone; they are here to shape, thematize, empower, and direct ordinary life to its natural goal, not to shape some other level of existence somewhere else. Thus, the two-zones solution misses the basic point. And the end of that road in a developing secular period is the fatal separation between secular nature and supernatural grace, a profane life-world and special religious places, leading to inert and extrinsic theological symbols, unreal and meaningless because out of touch with ordinary experience, and empty sacramental elements. Thus occurs the same result as above; namely, a church whose religious elements are frozen and empty and whose real life is its life as determined and empowered by the social life-world, the life of culture, and so a church using the remnants of its sacrality to bless instead of transform, as Ralph Keifer put it, "all the most oppressive elements of our culture." Religion can neither safely incorporate itself into culture nor completely separate itself from culture; in either case, paradoxically, ordinary life is shaped by other symbols, and religion is left empty in itself and so with only a demonic role in the world. Put theologically, as Augustine might have phrased it, our existence is in this world of time, and only if the divine is incarnate here in our life-world can we listen, be moved, and be redeemed; and yet this world where we are is fallen, and so only if religion challenges, judges, and transforms that life-world from beyond itself is there also any hope for redemption.

How then can Christian symbols mean for us if they can neither be separated from nor identified with our life-world as it is shaped by social symbols? If symbols mean and communicate in so far as they shape and transform our common, ordinary experience, to what ordinary experiences or level of common experience in a secular world do Christian symbols refer? If we do not mean ordinary experience as is — as it is formed and lived in culture — nor a special religious level or type of experience, what experiences do Christian symbols shape? Or, to return to our first theme, if Christian worship is a response to the objective presence of God in experience and not just a presence in special experiences in church or monastery, how is this possible in a secular world? Where and how in our ordinary life does the presence of God manifest itself?

In reply let me begin by stating boldly another thesis that is, I believe, consonant with the most creative and important trends in present Catholic thought and life; I shall try to interpret worship in the light of this thesis. As the best present Catholic ethics views Christian obligation as directing us not toward a level of grace beyond nature but toward the reshaping of human natural and social life to its own creative end, so Christian worship should celebrate not the God of special religious places but the God of all places and times, the God of the world and the world's process. Christian worship can no longer be tied to a two-zone Christianity that celebrates alone a special divine presence appearing exclusively in sacred events and that points to a level beyond and above the secular level. Rather Christian worship in our world should seek to celebrate in the Christian community the presence of God's creative and healing grace in natural, secular experience. Worship, then, responds not merely to God's special presence through liturgical action, although there must be that special presence lest all become blurred in one fallen world. Rather its goal is, first, to reawaken through concentrated expression our awareness of the ultimacy that grounds, permeates, and guides our entire life in and out of church and, second, to relate us all in shared celebration, contrition, praise, and commitment — in short, in faith — to that ever-present ultimacy through Christian symbols and thus in Christian form.

Such awareness and such faith are, I believe, dependent on the special works of divine grace; but what we are aware of when we have faith, what we have faith in, and thus to what in the end our worship, trust, and commitment respond is the divine presence throughout the scope of natural and social life. If, as modern Catholic theological ethics assures us, the purpose of the gospel is the liberation of human natural and social existence into its essential human form, rather than the translation of our nature to a new level, and if, as the same writers say, in that sense the eschatological promise embodies the fulfillment of God's creative and providential work in concrete social history and not just its transcendence beyond history, then it must follow that the divine presence that a contemporary Catholic worship celebrates, to which it responds, and that heals and transforms is a presence within the secular and the historical orders, the order of natural and social existence, not exclusively a presence specially lowered down into an alien world of nature by miraculous acts of grace. As Catholic theology and ethics have moved radically away from the two-zone world of their past, so liturgical and sacramental theology must seek to reinterpret themselves so as to relate our ordinary social life-world to Christian liturgy in ways other than a theoretical separation and so frequently an actual capitulation.

THREE LEVELS OF SYMBOLIC MEDIATION

This conception of worship as the celebration of a divine presence through-out our ordinary existence and yet a presence obscured in our secular world is paradoxical in the extreme. How do Christians celebrate a presence in office, bedroom, supermarket, or country club that they do not and seem-ingly cannot feel, dominated as they are by the social symbols of a secular worldly culture? The two-zone theory seems to make obvious sense — until we recall it has been tried for generations and with fatal results for the present situation. To help us understand this conception I suggest a further thesis concerning the three fundamental meanings of symbol in Christian theology, three levels of symbolic mediation. Let us note, as I develop these three levels, that each implies what can legitimately be called a sacramental theory of religious symbolism; namely, one in which the divine is mediated to us through its presence within the finite.

UNIVERSAL CREATURELY EXISTENCE

A religious symbol can be defined as a finite medium, or creature, in which the divine power is active and transformative and so that manifests or reveals through its own intrinsic being or activity the creative presence of that divine power. Thus, the sea, a mountain, a people, a person — in fact, any creature — can and have thus become "symbols" of the divine being and activity: each in its own way, and each through its own character and integrity as a creature, becoming a medium or symbol of the ultimate. If in our faith God is never experienced directly in this life, the divine is expe-rienced only in this way through symbols, through the creaturely world God creates, sustains, permeates, and guides to its fulfillment. The notions of creation and providence, then, applied to our question mean that poten-tially every creature is a symbol, and even more that it is itself only as a symbol. As a creature of God upheld by the divine power alone and good through God's presence alone, each creature is, as Augustine insisted, itself only when its autonomy, its essential character, reflects that creative divine power. Humans achieve humanity when they are images or reflections of God, when their autonomous freedom unites with grace. Providence, God's ordaining work in the general life of history, means in turn that human community achieves itself, becomes truly human, when community too exists as a symbol of the divine providential purposes, when its being as just and human shows forth the divine rule and manifests the divine being; and such is the eschatological conception of the Kingdom. But this sacramental or theonomous principle of the nature and perfection of the creature in God reaches its clearest expression in the incarnation; for our faith, the presence of God is paradigmatically seen in and precisely through the fully human person of Jesus, and thus is Jesus the true *humanum* precisely in reflecting throughout his existence the divine presence.

In each case the sacred or the divine is present and manifest in and through the finite; in turn the finite becomes its true self only as it becomes a vehicle or medium for that inward grace, reflecting and so revealing its presence. To understand itself and its destiny truly as finite, and so to achieve its true or natural integrity as a creature, is, as Augustine said, to understand and constitute itself precisely as a creature, a finite being upheld, directed, called, and healed by the divine power. Nature, thus, can never be, either in reality or in conception, separated from grace; each creature in its essential or natural being, as itself, is a "symbol" of the presence of the holy, and it becomes its authentic self when the pattern of its life in faith inwardly and outwardly in action reflects that creaturely status and role as an image of God.

If this is so — and it seems the clear implication of the most fundamental Christian symbols — then the primary (logically and ontologically, if not in honor) meaning of the word *symbol* has reference to the creature as creature, lest we conceive of the creatures about us and of ourselves as merely natural, as essentially secular and profane, alien from God and strangers to grace, and lest we be driven, as all classical doctrine seems to have been, to a separation or division of the divine and the human natures of Christ, a separation of heaven from earth and liturgy from life-world. Thus is the divine present throughout the life of the creature: in its being, its meanings, its relations, truths, judgments, norms, temporality, and death. This presence in all of life gives "secular" and so real meaning to our theological symbols of creation, providence, judgment, and promise; and our continual experience of this dimension of ultimacy in our entire existence alone makes it possible for us to be human, and so to question, wonder, talk, doubt, and believe religiously and so to think theologically. These are the experiences of the ordinary life-world for which we were searching, obscured as much as revealed by our common social structuring of that world.

Worship, therefore, is primarily related to this presence of the divine throughout the human creature's existence. Its central purpose is to bring to awareness and celebrate that universal presence, to shape that awareness into Christian form and, through that shaping of our natural existence by sacrament and word, to elicit gratitude, contrition, recommitment, and transformation of that natural existence. It is the holy as it permeates our entire life as creatures, and at every level of that life, to which worship primarily responds: the holy that founds our being, that undergirds our creative meanings, that enlightens our truths, that inspires our creativity, that cements and deepens our relationships, elicits and demands our moral judgments, and directs our common efforts to re-create and liberate the world — and forgives and completes the waywardness in those efforts and grounds our hopes that they will be so completed. This ultimate dimension to our personal, social, and historical being, which constitutes that divine presence in ordinary experience, provides the real basis of Christian worship.

Here we, too, are in principle the symbols or media receptive of the divine and so potentially reflective and even revelatory of grace. If this presence of the holy in our own existence is completely unknown, the other levels of religious symbols will communicate little or nothing to us. This, therefore, gives to them their feel of reality, their meaning for us, and their transformative power. The inward "spirit" side of revelation, the work of God in us that makes possible God's communication to us through Christian symbols, is constituted by our awareness of ourselves as symbols of God's presence and power; through the Spirit as this self-awareness of God's work in us, we see God's truth. This also gives another view of the problem of the two-zone view in a secular world. If we conceive of worship as for people who live in a totally secular or natural world, grace being on another level found only in church, then there is in ordinary experiences no base for the special acts and experiences of liturgical life. Creatures in a two-zone world where nature and grace are radically separated cannot become symbols, participating, in becoming their natural selves, in the divine power and grace; and thus do their symbols in worship become empty of natural common content.

ORIGINATIVE HISTORICAL EVENTS

As is evident, however, the finite creature—at least the human creature—is estranged from his and her own essential nature. An alienation from the natural self and from its natural relations has occurred because a prior alienation from the ground of that self, from God, has occurred. Thus are God, the true self, and the true other all obscured, veiled, lost, and forgotten; and the relations between the three are radically distorted. Men and women remain rooted in deity but forgetful and unconscious of this rootage; they remain centered in love for others, yet forgetful of this in love for self, and so on. The divine presence in all creatures, hidden originally within the integrity and autonomy of the creature, is now doubly veiled by sin, by our alienation from the sacred source and ground of our life. In all of us, therefore, it must be reawakened and reappropriated by special manifestations of the sacred. As a race and as individuals, we must be "twice born," because we are separated by our common sin from our essential natures, from our true role and status as symbols, and so precisely from an awareness of and life within that continued divine presence. Here arises, then, a second sense of the word *symbol;* namely, those special and unique finite media through which a particular revelation of the ultimate and the sacred, universally present but universally obscured as well, is now manifested in a particular form to a historical community, and so through which a group becomes newly aware of its own status as symbol (in the first sense), as existing in and through the power of the divine. Through the Son made flesh, the

Spirit descends again upon the community. In our tradition the originating symbols in this second sense, symbols of special revelation or of redemptive grace, are the history of the community of Israel and the person of Jesus.

The estrangement of natural existence from its natural personal and communal life—surely as predominant an aspect of our secular experience as it is of our dogmatic theology—explains the dual, ambiguous relation of religious symbols to the cultural symbols with which we began. For this estrangement means that our social symbols themselves—those notions that, for example, structure and maintain the American way of life and that, heaven help us, relate us in most of our life to ultimacy—are, though real and pervasive enough, by no means "natural" in the real sense of that word. That is, they themselves reflect our estrangement from our authentic selves and from authentic community as deeply as our concrete behavior does, and they reflect this because they imply no real self, no real relations, no real community, and above all no real relation to the ultimacy on which we all depend. Thus, while social symbols exemplify and communicate reality, meaning, and power, they exemplify and create distorted forms of human life and must, therefore, be judged and transformed from beyond themselves.

In the divine economy one of the strange purposes of human social history is the creation, embodiment, testing, judging, and transformation of such systems of social symbols; and one of the crucial roles of the Christian liturgical community is not only to draw to *itself* the power and vitality resident in the structures of ordinary life but also, in creative and prophetic outward response, to criticize and refine the social symbols within which ordinary life is lived. The liturgical community can do this through the criteria of its own symbolic understanding of authentic humanity and authentic community as manifested in Jesus and the Kingdom; for they represent the promised fulfillment of our human history of social creativity and social estrangement. In any case, returning to our theme, the universal fact of alienation requires a second level of symbol; namely, a particular, finite medium as incarnating at once the essential nature of the *humanum*, of human community, and of their eschatological fulfillment.

REPRESENTATIVE ACTS AND LANGUAGE

In each tradition this presence of the divine in and through special revelatory events and persons is over time communicated to the continuing community founded upon that special presence. This communication over time is in turn achieved through symbols in a third sense. Again, finite entities have become media that point to, recall, and reintroduce by representation the originating presence of the holy in the revelatory symbols creative of that tradition. Such tertiary symbols are infinitely various in religion; in our tradition they are most importantly composed of communal acts and elements (sacraments), on the one hand, and spoken and reflected words, on the other (*kerygma, didache,* and the theological symbols that further reflection draws from such, including creation, providence, incarnation). Both sacrament and word are essential if our theological understanding of the divine presence is correct. Ultimacy is present in our living and being human, in the totality of our existence, not just in our minds and consciences. This ontological presence of the holy can be brought to awareness and recommunicated to us only through media that are as we are and that analogically also communicate our being to us: water, bread, and wine. On the other hand, the presence of the holy is hidden in the finite, or incognito, in ourselves and in these special media. Its presence must be evoked for us by a word that penetrates through the creaturely vehicle to the transcendent that appears within it, and so a word that brings that transcendent dimension to our personal awareness—whether it is the transcendent at work in a historical event, in a sacramental element, or in our own existence. Sacrament and word, ontological presence and *kerygma,* are essentially and yet dialectically interrelated in communicating the divine presence.

In turn, our awareness of and response to the presence of the sacred, which is the heart of the problem of worship as response to the holy, combine these three senses of the word *symbol.* All Christian worship points to and finds its center in the revelatory events or symbols originative of that tradition, to the word in prophecy and Word made flesh. Correspondingly, the role of the tertiary symbols is to accomplish that pointing and centering, the sacraments of baptism and Eucharist with all of their manifold symbolic power re-presenting to us and in us these originating events, and the *kerygma* or proclamation opening up to us the transcendent meaning of these events and so calling us to decision and commitment in relation to them. The classical forms of Christian worship, Catholic and Protestant, have emphasized, and often overemphasized to the exclusion of the other, one or the other of these two forms of tertiary symbol.

I suspect, however, that the present weakness of both classical forms of Christian worship lies not so much in this traditional overemphasis as in their common indifference to the third meaning of symbol as I have delineated it and in the crucial relation in worship of the other two meanings to this primary one; namely, that the divine works in and on us as creatures, too, and that awareness of our role as symbols—in our being, our meanings, decisions, and hopes—lies at the heart of any experience of the holy that is to be relevant and effective in us. My argument is that unless the symbols of our tradition in word and sacrament are brought into relation to the ultimacy that permeates our ordinary life, unless traditional symbols reawaken in us our role as symbols of the divine activity, there is no experience of the holy. The Spirit must speak in and through us and must reawaken us to our role as symbols, if the Father is to be known through the Son. In a secular age, when ordinary life is separated in its self-understanding from its own transcendent ground, sacramental symbols unrelated to the transcendent dimension of our own existence in life become magical or merely traditional, and kerygmatic symbols change into empty theologisms or anachronistic signs of our moral and intellectual autonomy.

To be alive, religious symbols must provide shape and thematization to the patterns of ordinary life; correspondingly, natural, secular life must receive its fundamental forms from these symbols, not from our "normal" but distorted ones, if it is to achieve its own essential goodness. God is already there in our existence as its ultimate ground and its ultimate goal. The role of sacrament and word alike is not so much to insert the divine activity into nature, into the ordinary course of our lives, as to bring that prior relation forth in awareness and to give it the shape, power, and form of Jesus Christ. (The clue to renewed worship, as of a renewed Christian existence and theology, insofar as by reflection we can take hold of these matters, is to reappropriate through the forms of Christian symbolism the presence of the holy in the totality of ordinary existence.) The goal of worship is to reawaken through concentrated expression (an expression formed by Jesus Christ) our awareness of the ultimacy that grounds and permeates our entire existence, an awareness in all of our existence of our role as symbols of the divine being, logos, and love—a veritable participation in the life of the Trinity, but a participation that is the fulfillment of our nature as human beings rather than a translation of that nature to a higher sphere.

As is obvious, essential to this view is the affirmation of a parallelism or correlation, as well as a crucial distinction, between the workings of the holy in and on us in our daily secular life and the deeper meanings of the Christian symbols or doctrines, and so between life in the world and worship, between general and special revelation, nature and grace, God as creative providence and God as redeemer. Thus do the symbols (in senses two and three) of our faith manifest to us our own status and role as by nature symbols (in sense one) or creatures. And thus, in turn, does our ordinary experience, apprehended in its ultimate dimension, give to our Christian worship its life, relevance, and power.

Also essential to this view is the affirmation that while grace in and through Jesus Christ (what I called the secondary level of symbol) brings something radically new and utterly unmerited into our ordinary existence, it does so only because of our fallen state, our separation from God and from our own natures in the exclusively autonomous rather than theonomous character of our lives. It is not to make up for a lack in our created nature that the unmerited and surprising grace communicated to us by the special revelation in Jesus Christ comes to us. It comes rather to overcome the distortion we have made in our natures and so in our history. Redemption fulfills creation; it does not transform it into something else or even something "higher," as if to fulfill our created human natures and to liberate men and women in their historic existence were not high enough goals for human lives, and as if that human goal did not have its own genuine glory in being at one and the same time a creative creature and also a symbol of the divine activity in history. But we must add that, in refashioning our human being into its own created structure and purpose as such a symbol, grace also thereby projects us into a new future — of ourselves and of history — which itself has a goal far beyond that of a mere repetition or even a restoration of the temporal past. Directedness toward an eschatological goal is the essential nature of both divine and human being, and so again grace in no way transcends nature but rather makes its realization and fulfillment possible.

WORD AND SACRAMENT

Let me close this discussion with a few remarks about word and sacrament in the new setting of a worship oriented not just toward a special religious sphere, the two-zone view, but as the ground, critic, and inspirer of the secular sphere, the ordinary human life-world. Since the Enlightenment it has been frequently assumed that with the growth of autonomy, self-consciousness, and subjectivity in modern culture, the Protestant principle of the word addressed to intellect and conscience would slowly displace the anachronistic, materialistic, and "magical" Catholic sacramental principle. Not a little in recent modern Catholic liturgical reforms — most of which I heartily approve — seems to agree: the emphasis on the vernacular, personal participation by the laity, biblical sermons, and the like. I would like to dispute this general view of the decline of the Catholic principle, however, and, unless such a caveat is too paradoxical from a free churchperson, to assert in our day the priority of the sacramental in Christian liturgy, after saying some of the reasons the Protestant principle of the word is also important for us all.

I have already supplied the most fundamental reasons for the word: the transcendence of deity and the integrity of the finite. Thus, when the divine is either active in the life-world or present in specifically liturgical action, its presence is "hidden" within the finite media. There are few visible theophanies in our traditions; thus, unless that presence had been proclaimed and interpreted, as is clear in both the prophetic and the apostolic traditions, it would have remained incognito to those who witnessed the events and to us who ponder them. Further, this presence is neither the visible creaturely medium itself to which faith is directed nor even the transcendent in and of itself. Rather faith addresses itself to the two in dialectical conjunction, as covenant, law, and Christology made plain. Thus, it is the word of witness alone that directs us beyond the medium to the holy present within it. Without the principle of the word, the sacramental principle of presence is always in danger of confounding the sacred and its medium, of relinquishing therefore both the transcendence and sacrality of deity and the autonomy and integrity of the creature. This identification of the finite medium with the sacred transcendent to it has been fatal at every point that it has appeared in church history — when ecclesiastical media and sacred grace or doctrinal media and divine truth, canon law and the divine will, were confounded — but it would be especially so in the secular context we envisage if the sacred were identified with the creaturely symbol as such, with ourselves, our community, and our social world.

The word, thus, is also necessary as the principle of judgment on the estranged character of all human life, even life lived in the presence of deity; for the servants of God are by their very closeness to deity the most prone to identify themselves with it. The word is that in revelation which manifests the infinite qualitative difference between holy and profane and between the sacred and its medium; in judging, therefore, the word brings the only grounds for hope for a reduction of that difference.

Finally, the word addresses uniquely the inward and the temporal human spirit; sacramental presence is fundamental to our faith, as I shall argue, but that presence is both inward and personal—and so must be spoken—and it is proleptic, a promise for the future. And neither the grace of judgment, forgiveness, acceptance, and justification nor the eschatological promises can be communicated except by speaking the personal word.

Lest this seem, however, to end in a Protestant peroration, let me say that to me the Catholic principle of sacramental presence, taken in its epistemological and ontological as well as its liturgical scope, is basic to our faith. All I have said should make this obvious. After all, the theory of revelation enunciated here is a sacramental and not a verbal theory of divine manifestation, in which the divine presence in a multitude of forms and modes, rather than the "divine speech," is regarded as the ontologically and epistemologically prior level of revelation. Incidentally, the essential and prior character of the principle of sacramental presence must be asserted not only against Protestant theologians of divine speech but presently also against the siren calls to the best Catholic theologians to abandon the divine presence in past and present and to "speak" only of an eschatological presence to come in the future—a theology of the word alone with a vengeance even when connected to Catholic ontologists!

All I have said about the divine presence throughout experience, at every corner of our life-world, and about our role as symbols—in our being, our meanings and work, our relations, our goals, our movement into the future—indicates that the possibility of meaningful theological speech, and so of the word itself, depends upon our awareness of that sacramental presence. No God of the future can be promised meaningfully to us, and no future kingdom can be relevant to what we do politically today, unless there is that presence already at work in our common life. Sacramental presence, the divine activity in and through all of creative process, precedes and grounds word and promise alike, as Catholicism preceded and grounded the personal and autonomous forms of Protestantism.

This sacramental presence, however, is not merely a matter of grounding; no great tradition likes to feel like a basement, however essential to the upper floors. My further point is that the character of modern culture calls more for a Catholic and so sacramental principle of mediation than it does for the Protestant verbal principle; this is why I emphasize it everywhere. Ours is an age in which all that is historical is relative; thus, all speech, words, concepts, propositions, dogmas, laws, and forms of liturgy are to us historically relative, pinioned in their medieval epoch, subject to qualification, infinitely human and so contestable. Ours is also an age fortunately reawakened to the intimacy of the relations of body to spirit, of the spirituality of the bodily and the sensual. The sensory and the aesthetic are thus for us again, after centuries, possible media of spiritual insight.

Again, the word alone, addressed to intellect and conscience, is inadequate. With sacramental media, by contrast, we can recognize the finite and relative character of the media and not lose the mediation; *symbol* is a better word than either *dogma* or *doctrine* on this point. Sacramental mediation more naturally than verbal can relate us to the absolute and unconditioned by means of relative symbols, for the symbol both participates in the relativity of the creaturely world from which it arises and communicates an infinity in which it participates. Such mediation, moreover, can relate us to ultimacy through a wide variety of symbolic forms: verbal, conceptual, active, aesthetic, bodily. A Catholicism that has learned to relinquish its Catholic absolutism and has the courage to recognize the new world of relativity — the relativity of its institutional structures, ecclesiastical hierarchy, dogmatic formulations, canon law, liturgical forms — and yet that as Catholic and sacramental can relate grace and the wondrous width of divine activity through a multitude of media to the total life-world of men and women — this Catholicism may well find itself more relevant to modern needs, more creative in the modern situation, and less anachronistic to modern sensibilities than any form of Protestantism is. Strangely, in denying or abjuring — or being forced by twentieth-century historical consciousness to do so — the great temptation of a sacramental form of religion to absolutize the relative and so to sanctify the ambiguous, Catholicism may discover the vast strength of a sacramental form of religion; namely, the divinely granted capacity to allow finite and relative instruments to be media of the divine and so to endow all of secular and ordinary life with the possibility and the sanctity of divine creativity, and thus more than Protestantism to bring Christianity alive, well, and active through the turmoil of the modern world.

If Catholicism, or Protestantism, is to achieve this task of mediating the divine grounding, the divine judgment, and the divine possibility to our entire secular existence, it must widen the scope of both word and sacrament far beyond their present religious, ecclesiastical, dogmatic, and merely "redemptive" limits. If, for example, the word is to provide, through the proclamation and teaching of verbal and notional symbols, the basis for all of our existence, personal, social, and historical, our understanding of those symbols must include their relation to the social, public life of humans, as well as to their individual virtues and vices, weals and woes. The proclaimed word must intersect, in judgment and approbation, in critical analysis and deep support, the whole realm of social symbolism and of social behavior we analyzed, a relation of deep and dangerously potential idolatry, on the one hand, but, on the other, the necessary condition for creative human life. We humans cannot *be* at all, especially in a divine kingdom, without a symbolic social structure. As Augustine said, every state strives for ultimate peace and justice and then fails, establishing at best only a perverted peace, a perverted justice, and an incomplete humanity. To refashion our social world into an approximation of the promised Kingdom and thus to help in the liberation of women and men is one of the major themes of the gospel and so one of the major tasks of the church catholic. Only thus can it be creative in a secular world. A world moving deeper and deeper into a dehumanizing technology, into fundamental shifts of world power, into the new nightmare of scanty resources will need all the humanizing of its social structures it can get.

Even more needs to be done to widen the scope or range of the sacraments. Ideally the sacramental system of an unfallen church (is such a notion conceivable?) would mediate the divine grace to every facet of natural life, to all the major stages, crises, and points of intense meaning of our ongoing life-world. Thus, in a sacramental universe the sacraments would bring to explicit expression at appropriate points the divine presence in all of life, as the divine word would mediate the divine judgment and mercy to all the issues of common human life.

Yet look at the sacraments, all seven of them. This is not what they do, or even seek to do, at all. Rather, in their classical form, they relate the divine presence not to human life generally and in its natural course but only to human beings as they enter *ecclesia,* the covenant community, the special and separate realm of redemption, the churchly realm of grace. Baptism is not at all a sacrament of birth, of the divine gift of being, of life, of human existence, though our faith and our creed emphasize the centrality of the divine creation. On the contrary, baptism is solely a sacrament of the forgiveness of sins and of entrance not into the human but into the religious community! What a strange Marcionic vision within a Catholic system that names God "being" and then acts sacramentally as if the divine gift of being were secular and not worthy of sacramental notice! Confirmation, the Christian rite of initiation, is not with us a rite of entrance into adulthood and the adult community, a sacrament celebrating, blessing, and molding the divine gift of human autonomy and responsibility and so of adult and responsible community, as if these were purely secular at their heart. Rather confirmation represents solely the entrance into Mother Church, as if there for the first time we met the divine presence. How strange, again, that a Catholic system should contest the Enlightenment secularization of human autonomy and responsibility and then reduplicate that very secularization in its sacramental system. The sacrament of ordination or of orders is the blessed sacrament of vocation, the divine gift of meaningful activity in the world and for the neighbor, and thus for God and God's kingdom. Do we clerics alone do this work in and through our religious tasks? Does the creative activity of our lay or secular sisters and brothers, an activity instrumental in increasing the Kingdom as we now define it, namely, as a social

order of liberation, justice, and humanity, then derive not at all from the
divine power and purpose? Are divine orders only clerical?

Theologically and ethically, we proclaim that the meaning of the gospel
and the task of the church is that of liberating and humanizing God's world,
and we define the eschatological promises in that light. Yet, as we see, our
sacraments fail to point us in this direction, toward the world and its life.
A similar analysis could be made, obviously, of marriage, penance, and
unction: again, each in principle directed at central issues of human existence
but traditionally concerned only with the way those issues appear or reappear in the special covenant community of grace. The Eucharist needs no
redirection, for in mediating the presence of the risen Lord in the communion, it is the center; but it needs, I believe, freeing; its scope needs an infinite
widening and extension over the whole earth. This widening could, I suggest, be the special role of the other sacraments; namely, to relate not only
(as traditionally) to rebirth but also to birth, not only to life in the *ecclesia* but
to life in God's world, and thus to help mediate the divine presence to all of
life as it moves into God's future.

This widening of the scope and range of liturgy and sacramental action
is not at all a matter of relinquishing the sacramental relation to rebirth in
Christ and so also to life in the covenant community. This essential tie with
special revelation, with Christology, redemptive grace, and ecclesiology,
represents that continuity with tradition which we lose at our peril. Rather
this widening of scope is a matter of realizing anew and afresh — and possibly
for the first time in church history — that rebirth in the covenant community
is in no way ultimately separate or divorced from being human, from achiev-
ing and fulfilling the *humanum,* and thus is also intrinsically related to birth,
to human autonomy and responsibility, to our human relationships, our
human vocations, and our human death as expressions of the mode of their
perfection.

The eschatological fulfillment of Christ's existence, given in promise in the
classical sacraments, is also and primarily the fulfillment of our life in the
world as simply men and women; to become one with Christ in the loving
community is to become one with God and so one with one's neighbor in
the world: and so to become at last human. Thus, each sacrament has, so to
speak, a multiple reference: first to its eschatological perfections; then to its
partial fulfillment in the life of the church; and finally its possibility — and
more than mere possibility — in the life of all of us in the world as humans,
to our role and status as symbols, in all the stages and modes of our life, of
the divine being, the divine truth, and the divine love. This wider reference
to our life as human in the world might represent in our liturgy the radical dis-
continuity with tradition necessary in our situation; for it is this reference to
the sacred quality of the secular that our liturgy desperately needs for its
realization and validity, and in order that it may fulfill its task of sanctifying
and liberating the world's life. Entrance into the center of the secular life-world
is a necessity for a reinvigoration, as it is the criterion for a reassessment and
reshaping, of the Catholic tradition and the Catholic liturgy in secular America.

PART TWO

Christian Symbols
of Divine Being
and Activity

CHAPTER 5

THE CHRISTIAN
UNDERSTANDING OF GOD

The idea of God is at once the most important and yet the most questionable of all religious doctrines or symbols in the West. This idea or symbol points to the central object of both Christian and Jewish faith, the sole subject of their revelation, and the final principle of both reality and meaning throughout human existence. Nevertheless, of all concepts in modern cultural life — and in varying degrees for believers and doubters alike — the idea of God remains the most elusive, the most frequently challenged, the most persistently criticized and negated of all important convictions. Is there a God? Can such a One be experienced, known, or discussed? Is such experience testable, such knowledge verifiable, and such speech meaningful? Or is all such experience illusory, such seeming knowledge in fact a projection, such speech empty? These issues represent the primordial issues for philosophy of religion, for philosophical theology, and for confessional theology alike.

Almost every dominant motif and movement in modernity — its expanding scientific inquiry, its emphasis on what is natural, experienced, and verifiable, its persistent search for the greater well-being of humans in this world, its increasing emphasis on autonomy and on present satisfactions — has progressively challenged the concept of God and unsettled both its significance and its certainty. This challenge has been on two fronts: (1) The traditional concepts of God, inherited from the premodern cultures of medieval, Renaissance, and Reformation Europe, revealed themselves in almost every aspect to have anachronistic elements and to be unintelligible in the light of modern knowledge and modern attitudes toward reality, with

the consequence that these concepts have had to be reformulated on a fundamental level. (2) More importantly, these same aspects of modernity have
challenged the very possibility of an idea of God, its knowability, its
coherence, and its meaning; to much of modernity such an idea is on a
number of grounds an impossible idea, and, as a consequence, the whole
enterprise of a theistic religion appears as a futile, expensive, and even
harmful activity.

Because of this second point, the prime problematic connected with the
symbol of God has in modern times differed noticeably from earlier prob-
lematics. Our fundamental questions in religious reflection are not about the
nature of the divine and the character of God's activity or will toward us,
which represented the main questions of an earlier time. The question now
is the possibility of God's existence in a seemingly naturalistic world, the
possibility of valid knowledge of God and meaningful discourse about God,
and the possibility of any sort of "religious" existence, style of life, or hope
at all. As a result, the efforts of religious thinkers in our century have by and
large been directed at these two interrelated problems: (1) a justification of
the meaning and the validity of the concept of God in relation to other,
apparently less questionable, forms of experience—scientific, philosophical,
social, political, artistic, psychological, or existentialist; and (2) a reformulation of that concept so that it can be meaningful and relevant to the
modern world.

CLASSIC FORMULATION OF
THE DOCTRINE

Despite the new and sharper edge to the question of God in modern times,
certain continuing issues characteristic of the traditional discussion of this
concept have also been present, albeit in specifically modern form. In the
concept of God, as in the reality experienced in religious existence, dialectical tensions have appeared and reappeared as the center of theological
discussion. It is a strange notion, filled, as we shall see, with paradoxes and
polarities. These perennial problems internal to the concept of God (whether
orthodox or reformulated) also characterize modern discussions and manifest themselves with each option characteristic of modern theology and
philosophy of religion. In the following I shall seek to explicate the career
of these problems in modern theologies as well as to show the way modern
views of God have handled the question of the reality of God and of the
possibility of such a concept.

The General Idea of God

In Western culture, dominated as it has been by the Jewish and the Christian
traditions, the word or symbol *God* has generally referred to one supreme

or holy being, the unity of ultimate reality and ultimate goodness. So conceived, God is believed to have created the entire universe, to rule over it, and to intend to bring it to its fulfillment or realization, to "save" it. Thus, as a functioning word in our own cultural world, *God* in the first instance refers to the central and sole object of religious existence, commitment, devotion, dependence, fear, trust, love, and belief—and to the center of worship, prayer, and religious meditation. "God" has also been the object of religious and philosophical reflection, the supreme object of theology and of most (though not all) forms of speculative metaphysics.

So understood, God represents a puzzling and elusive notion by no means easy to define, as the traditions of Jewish, Christian, and Islamic religious thought have clearly recognized. As the supreme being or ground of being, the Creator and ruler of all, God transcends (exceeds or goes beyond) all creaturely limits and distinctions, all creaturely characteristics; the reason is that the divine, so conceived, is the source and therefore not simply one more example of those limits, distinctions, and characteristics. As Creator of time and space, God is not in either time or space as all else is; as the source of all finite realities and their interrelations, God is transcendent to all experienced substances, causes, and all ordinary relations; as that on which all depends, God is neither essentially dependent on nor a mere effect of other things. Thus, deity can hardly be spoken of as simply a being among other beings, changeable as all else is, dependent and vulnerable as every creature is, in time and passing as we are, or mortal as all life is—lest the divine be a mere contingent creature and thus not "God." For these reasons, the concept of God inevitably tends toward that of the transcendent absolute of much speculative philosophy: necessary, impersonal, unrelated, independent *(a se)*, changeless, eternal. In addition, for these reasons as well as others, the customary reference to God as "he" is now seen to be extremely problematical!

Yet, as we shall see, God in Jewish and Christian witness, piety, and experience is also in some way personal, righteous, or moral, the ground or base in actuality of value, concerned with all creatures, with people and their lives, impelled and guided by important purposes for them individually and collectively, and deeply related to and active within the natural world and the course of history. The reflective problems in this concept of God, illustrated by debates throughout Western history, therefore have a dual source: in the fact that God, however described, is unlike ordinary things of which we can easily and clearly speak, and in the fact that inherent in the religious reality itself and in its reflected concepts are certain dialectical tensions or paradoxes—absolute-related, impersonal-personal, eternal-temporal, changeless-changing, actual yet potential, self-sufficient or necessary and yet in some manner dependent. Such dialectical tensions stretch, if they do not defy, our ordinary powers of speech, definition, and precise comprehension. However one may approach the divine, religiously or philosophically, therefore, one first encounters "mystery," and with that encounter appear, among other things, special procedures and special forms or rules of speech, characteristics as old as religion itself.

BIBLICAL AND EARLY CHRISTIAN CONCEPTS

Before I trace the development of these polarities in Christian history, I would like to examine the diverse origins of the paradoxes or dialectical tensions in this notion I have noted earlier. The origins of this understanding of God lie in the Hebrew and Christian religious traditions, especially in their sacred Scriptures. In what we call the Old Testament, God or Yahweh is undeniably one and transcendent to all the limited and special forces and powers of our experience of nature, society, or self. Yet Yahweh's central characteristic or, better, mode of experienced being or self-manifestation is a concern for and relation to history and especially to a particular people in history — Israel. Although God manifests power and glory throughout the vast scope of nature, the main arena for the divine works is the particular sequence of historical events related to the calling, establishment, nurture, and protection of the chosen people. In this activity in history, moreover, God is revealed as a moral or righteous God, the source of the law, and quick to punish those, even chosen ones, who defy this law. Yahweh is also, however, a God of mercy, patience, faithfulness, and grace, since according to the prophets, despite Israel's obvious unworthiness and continued betrayal of her covenant with God, God promises to redeem Israel in the future. This God of history, covenant, judgment, and promised redemption is throughout assumed to be, and often clearly affirmed to be, the ruler of all events. All agree that the divine purposes shape, reshape, and in the end will complete history. Finally, by inevitable implication, this sovereign Lord of history is seen to be also the Creator and ruler of the entire cosmos.

These themes in the notion of God are continued, albeit with modifications, in the New Testament: God is one God, a God concerned with history, judgment, and redemption, the God who is Creator and Redeemer, alpha and omega. Only now the central manifestation of the living God of Abraham, Isaac, and Jacob is in the "Son," Jesus of Nazareth, through whom the divine righteous and loving will for human beings is revealed, the divine judgments made known, the divine power to save even from death effected, and in whose speedy return God's sovereignty over all creation will be fully and visibly established. The presence of God, moreover, is now less in the temple and in the law than in the Spirit, dwelling in the minds and hearts of the Christian community and in their witness and hopeful expectation. Thus appears a new set of Christian symbols helping to define God and the divine activity: not only creation and redemption, covenant, law, and messianic promise, but now also Son and Logos, incarnation, atonement, Holy Spirit, parousia, and, as a summation of these "new" concepts, Trinity.

In briefly tracing the development of this complex notion from the beginning of the Christian era to our own times, we should recall that once Western culture became Christian (A.D. 325), the concept of God became the symbolic center for every aspect of life and for the understanding of nature, society, and human existence generally. Consequently, it became not only the object of endless philosophical and theological speculation but also the foundation for every special discipline of thought, every representative mode of action, and all important social institutions. Thus, inevitably, this notion, and the modes of thinking that expressed it, established union with the sciences, with ethical, legal, and political theories, and, above all, with the philosophy of each epoch.

During the crucial formative centuries of Christendom, the dominant intellectual inheritance through which Western life understood itself and its world was that of Greco-Roman philosophy. Thus, during this long period the biblical notion of God outlined above was naturally given its main conceptual shape with the help first of Platonism and Stoicism and then, during the High Middle Ages, of Aristotelianism. In this classical philosophical tradition, especially in its later Hellenistic stages (200 B.C.–400 A.D.), the sense of the reality, value, or meaning of the changing, temporal, material world and of earthly human and historical life in time noticeably weakened. Correspondingly, for this tradition the divine was precisely that which infinitely transcends change, time, matter, flesh, and history. As a quite natural consequence, those transcendent and absolute aspects or implications of the biblical Creator and ruler were, in the developing conceptualization of God from A.D. 150 to 400, enlarged and extended: God became eternal in the sense of utterly nontemporal, necessary in the sense of absolute non-contingency, self-sufficient in the sense of absolute independence, changeless in the sense of participating in and relating to no change, purely spiritual instead of in any fashion material, unaffected by and thus seemingly unrelated and even unrelatable to the world. It would be false, however, to conclude that the absoluteness of the patristic conception of God stemmed entirely from Hellenistic philosophy, though it was expressed in the latter's categories. It also stemmed from the character of patristic piety. Since that piety emphasized, as did most Hellenistic spirituality, the victory of the incorruptible, immortal, and changeless principle of deity over the corruptible, mortal, and passing character of creaturely life, the divine is and must be that which transcends and conquers the transience of mortal flesh.

THE SYMBOL OF THE TRINITY

In the early patristic period, for example, with Justin Martyr, Clement of Alexandria, and Origen, this absolute aspect of God was unequivocally affirmed and regarded as designated by the traditional biblical symbol of the "Father," the utterly primordial, unoriginate, changeless, eternal, and un-related source of all else. The related aspect of God, equally central to the life and piety of Christian faith, was consequently expressed through the symbol of the Son or the Logos, the principle of divine outreach and self-manifestation (almost a second God, as Justin and Origen put it) through which the transcendent Father, changeless and inactive, created the world, was revealed in it, and acted to redeem it. The Holy Spirit completed the relationship by assuring the presence of the divine in the community and in persons. Thus, at the outset of the philosophical career of the Christian God, the symbol of the Trinity served to provide conceptual expression for the dialectical polarity of the Christian God as at once the self-sufficient Creator of all, transcendent to all finitude (Father), and as the active, revealing, loving Redeemer (Son), present in grace and power to God's people (Holy Spirit).

By the inexorable and possibly ironic logic of events and ideas, however, this important mediatorial role of the symbol of the Trinity soon disintegrated. As the doctrines of the Arians quickly made evident, a Son or Logos that genuinely mediates between the absolute and the relative and that is related to the creaturely, the temporal, and the changing in time can be itself neither ungenerate, eternal, changeless, nor fully "God" if God is defined solely by the traits of a transcendent absolute. An originate, related, mediating principle is by that token hardly God; but in monotheism such a subordinate, semiabsolute, and partly divine being, however "good," is inadmissible as representing incipient polytheism. Besides, if Jesus Christ is not fully God, how can he save? These unanswerable arguments of Athanasius pushed the conception of the entire divine Trinity in an absolutist direction; Father, Son, and Holy Spirit were all defined at Nicaea, and again later at Constantinople, as fully divine—that is, as essentially negating every creaturely attribute: temporality, potentiality, changeableness, relatedness, and dependence. As a consequence the Trinity ceased to be the central symbolic expression of the polarity of the divine relatedness. To put this point more precisely, a distinction now appears in post-Nicaean theology between the *essential* Trinity (the "three-in-oneness" characteristic of the eternal God's inner life) and the *economic* Trinity (the "three-in-oneness" manifested and expressed externally in God's creative, revealing, and redemptive activity in relation to the world). Clearly this distinction, in contrast to the pre-Nicaean concept of the Trinity, where a "halfway absolute" Son mediated between the absolute Father and the world, covered over rather than resolved the fundamental problem or dialectic of the Christian concept of God, namely, how the absolute God can be related to the relative world. Now in the new form the same old question arises: How can the essentially trinitarian God in whom Father, Son, and Holy Spirit are alike eternal, changeless, *a se,* and impassive participate in all the actions and reactions in relation to changing temporality entailed in the economic Trinity?

As the appearance of this distinction makes plain, at no point did Christian theology allow itself to deny God's continual relatedness to and activity in the world of change. How could it? The entire corpus of Christian belief from creation to redemption, every aspect of its ritual of word and sacrament, its entire sacred law and its sanctions, and every facet of its piety of prayer, miracles, and special angelic and saintly powers depended on the reality in past, present, and future of that divine presence and divine activity. Nevertheless, that a deep theological problem remained for the classical theological conception of God is also evident. Once God was defined in theology as "pure actuality," "eternal being," "changeless," and thus quite void of potentiality, alterability, passivity, or temporality, it became virtually impossible, if not contradictory, to express intelligibly the obvious related-ness and mutuality of God to the changing world necessitated by the scrip-tural witness and by the structures of the Christian religion itself.

Although with the Reformation the philosophical or metaphysical defini-tion of God as absolute, changeless, eternal being or actuality radically receded in prominence in theology, the same problem remained. In the "biblical" theology of the major reformers, God is conceived centrally through personal rather than metaphysical categories: as almighty or sover-eign power, as righteous or holy will, as gracious and reconciling love. The "ontological" concepts of self-sufficiency (aseity) and eternity remain, but what now determines the shape of the doctrine of God in each reformer is the center of Reformation piety or religion; namely, the new emphasis on the priority and sole sovereignty of divine grace in redemption, on the utter unworthiness and inactivity of the recipient of grace, and finally on the absolute priority and decisiveness of divine election.

What is here eternal and changeless is the divine decree destining, yes predestining, each creature to grace or to its opposite. The first cause of being that led Thomas Aquinas to the concept of pure actuality has become, if I may so put it, the first "cause" of grace, leading to the concept of the eternal and changeless divine decrees. Thus, for primarily religious rather than metaphysical reasons, the same paradox tending toward contradiction appears: an eternal, hidden, and yet all-sovereign divine electing will, on the one hand, and the affirmation of the presence and activity of God in relation to a real and not sham sequence of historical events and of human decisions, on the other hand. Although Calvin especially drew out most clearly the implications of this new paradox based on Reformation piety rather than on traditional philosophy, still the same paradox in this new form is evident and fundamental for the theologies of Luther and Zwingli as well.

CONTRIBUTIONS OF MODERN CONSCIOUSNESS

At the start of the post-Reformation period there were two dominant con-ceptions of God, one Catholic and the other Protestant. They differed markedly in the categories with which God was described, yet to our twentieth-century eyes they exhibited the same paradoxical (not to say contradictory) character: the Catholic conception of an absolute, purely actual, changeless being "illegitimately" (so to speak) related to the world, and the Protestant conception of an eternal, sovereign, divine will ordaining and effecting all temporal events from eternity, thus again "illegitimately" related and even responsive to historical crises and human needs. Under-standably, subsequent modern reflection on the issue of God has, at least since the seventeenth century, been largely constituted by sustained philo-sophical and theological criticism of these two inherited conceptions, and thence characterized either by humanist and naturalist rejection of the concept entirely or by a more or less radical theological reformulation of it. Perhaps the best way to cover this extensive process is to remind ourselves first of the grounds in modern (Enlightenment and post-Enlightenment) sensibility for this criticism and, second, to describe some of the character-istic forms of these reformulations as those forms appear in the present theological discussion.

The Enlightenment Critique

The grounds for the modern critique of the idea of God have been essentially three: (1) the new emphasis on experience as the sole relevant and dependable source for valued and meaningful concepts and the sole ground for the testing of those concepts; (2) the corresponding shift to the subject as the sole seat of legitimate authority in all matters pertaining to truth and as the sole originating source of significant moral and/or personal action; and (3), since the principle of authority in matters of truth and morals has moved radically inward to the subject, all external forms of authority are radically questioned, especially those coming from church traditions or Scripture.

Thus, as we have already noted, the question of the reality of God, even of the possibility of the concept in any of its forms, has been sharply raised in modern culture. On the one hand, a powerful "naturalistic" viewpoint, which finds belief in God anachronistic and incredible and thus a religious relation to God either offensive or irrelevant, has arisen and spread per-vasively throughout the Western and communist worlds into almost every class. From this viewpoint, "nature," as understood by science, is the seat and source of all that is real; men and women are the source of values, and their needs and wishes constitute the sole criteria of values. Thus, this world and its history represent the sole locus of hope. Whether in socialistic or capital-istic form, or as theorized by Karl Marx, Sigmund Freud, Jean-Paul Sartre, or Albert Camus—or by most if not all the leaders of the scientific and philosophical communities—this naturalistic humanism has dominated the cultural scene. As a consequence, its powerful presence has posed the central intellectual issues for theologians concerned with the defense and reformu-lation of the concept of God.

Whether or not naturalistic humanism, a nonreligious understanding of reality generally and of human history and existence, is a lasting possibility has also become problematic in the modern period. This possibility of a totally "secular" worldview was assumed in the French Enlightenment and taken for granted by most of the nineteenth-century critics of religion (such as Auguste Comte, Ludwig Feuerbach, and Karl Marx). However, recent history has seemed to show that as traditional religion wanes as the symbolic center of a community's life, "ideology" tends to take its place, an ideology with important religious aspects or dimensions. Thus, even if God has receded from the center of Western consciousness, "the religious" has apparently not, for the political and social worlds of Western culture are structured ideologically, and thus its major conflicts are still inspired by competing forms of religiosity.

MODERN REFORMULATIONS

Insofar as thinkers have sought to defend and retrieve a concept of God, these new emphases on the authority of experience and the human subjects of experience have slowly but effectively reshaped that concept. First, the traditional concept of the divine self existing alone, a notion essentially and necessarily quite out of relation to any human experiences of the divine, became understandably a most questionable concept: How could there be experience and knowledge of any such unrelated object? Thus, most modern "doctrines" of God remain within the boundaries of possible experience and speak of the divine (as of anything else) only on the basis of our experience, in terms of either God's metaphysical relations to the world, our immediate experience of God, or God's special activities of revelation in history. Second, if all that is real for us must be within the area of our experiencing, then inevitably the sense of the reality and value of the changing, temporal world of process will increase, for this is the world we experience and know. Thus, however much or little the transcendence of God may be emphasized in modern doctrines, we find now that the relatedness of God to the world, to the events of history, and to temporality itself has become the starting point for discourse about God rather than an embarrassment to it. Most concepts of God in modern times are therefore dynamic, related, even sharing in some aspects of temporality and dependence, whatever sorts of categories (personal and biblical, or ontological and metaphysical) they may choose to use. I shall set forth in more detail the various options available in our day for a concept of God and the issues around which present discussion of this subject centers. It will be evident, however, that whatever the option or issue, it is a God related to us and to our experience, and so a dynamic, active God, who is known, affirmed, and described and not a wholly transcendent, independent, changeless God.

Knowledge of God

The question about how God is to be known—by rational inquiry of some sort, through religious experience, or through a revelation responded to by faith—has been a traditional and recurrent question throughout Christian history. In that history there have been those who, while denying neither the efficacy nor the significance of mystical experience or of revelation, have insisted that the existence of God can be established by philosophical argument, and so the nature of God known and defined, at least in part, by reason alone, that is, by "natural theology." On the other side have been those who distrusted philosophical reason as "pagan" or at least as misguided; correspondingly, they have argued that the true and living God, the God of Abraham, Christ, and the church, can be known only in revelation. As a consequence, for them a valid understanding of the nature and intentions of God must proceed alone from revelation and not also from philosophical reasoning. While the developments in modern culture I have just traced have not effaced this traditional issue and its contesting parties, still these developments have to some extent effected changes in the way each side argues its case. I shall mention briefly three points of difference.

1. The question of the possibility of a concept of God, the most radical question about God's reality, has come to the fore. Thus, each side, the natural theologians and the revelationists, find themselves more concerned than their predecessors were with the source or point of origin (in a "godless" natural and historical world) of this idea in philosophy or in the experience of revelation respectively, that is, with the question, How do we come to know God? as well as with the question, What do we know about God in the way we do know it?

2. Although the sharpness and difficulty of the question of the reality of God and of the intelligibility of that concept has made a natural theology eminently desirable if not necessary for modern believers, still the drift—not to say flood tide—of modern rationality away from metaphysical speculation has raised increasing difficulties for that enterprise in modern culture. Whereas in many epochs only orthodox members of the church might be scornful of or ungrateful for the use of philosophy in theology and especially the idea of a natural theology, now the philosophical community more than the theological community raises questions about the possibility of metaphysics and natural theology of any sort. In modernity (as possibly at the end of the Hellenic era), natural theologians have had to contend with philosophical resistance to their speculative, metaphysical labors as well as with religious-theological resistance, and they face the bizarre and arduous task, not forced upon their predecessors, of presenting a reasoned defense of metaphysical reason even before they begin their quest via such reason for God.

3. The modern critique of authority, the emphatic denial of absolute authority to any document or institution, has transformed the interpretation of revelation and its cognitive meaning. Prior to this the "revealed faith" could refer to sets of propositions in the scriptural corpus or the dogmatic tradition, and how one "knew God" via either one could be plainly and intelligibly stated. With the modern critique of scriptural and dogmatic authority and of a "propositional view of revelation," at best revelation comes through the words of Scripture and tradition and is received not in terms of objective propositions but on the "religious" level as an experiencing or feeling (Friedrich Schleiermacher), as an "encounter" resulting in a personal acknowledgment or a decision of faith (dialectical theology)—that is, as an existential reality and activity, so to speak, below the conceptual and ordinary cognitive level. The obvious problem of a cognitive event (not only

of certainty that its object is but also of knowledge of what it might be) taking place via such a prelinguistic, preconceptual, and preexperiential "experience" thus plagues contemporary revelationists as it did not their predecessors. We should note that neither one of the traditional avenues to the knowledge of God, metaphysics or revelation, is in the least straight and smooth in our own day.

Despite these added difficulties, each answer has in our own time had its powerful and persuasive adherents. Those who emphasize the knowability of God by reason have offered one version or another of the classical "proofs" of God: the cosmological, from the existence of the finite world (mainly the neo-Thomists); the teleological, from the order of the finite world (note especially the brilliant use of this argument by Alfred North Whitehead as well as by a variety of evolutionists such as F. R. Tennant and Teilhard de Chardin); the ontological, from the implications of the concept of God itself as a concept of a perfect and so necessary being (the quite original work of Charles Hartshorne is unique at this point); and the moral argument, from the implications of moral experience. These widely variant forms of philosophical approach have been united in arguing that any theology intellectually respectable enough to speak to modern, intelligent people must re-present its religious heritage in the intellectual form of such a rationally grounded philosophical theology. Without such a philosophical base for our knowledge of God, our certainty of the divine reality and our comprehension of the relation of this concept to our other concepts will be seriously lacking. As a consequence, the idea of God will increasingly be regarded as merely subjective and idiosyncratic, a private matter of feeling and therefore unreal, a private image unrelated to the width of all experience, vacant of content and in the end meaningless. Powerful recent examples of these arguments for a philosophical basis for our knowledge of God have been the Hegelian idealists, the neo-scholastic and now the transcendental Thomists, and perhaps most notably the growing and flourishing school of process or neoclassical theologians.

On the other side have been those who have shared a more jaundiced view of culture's reasoning and of its philosophical "proofs"; on religious grounds they have emphasized the transcendence and mystery of God and the actuality and sufficiency of revelation as the source and norm for the concept of God. They are not at all unaware that most contemporary philosophy has come to regard metaphysical speculation and all proofs of a divine reality as representing a dubious and uncritical use of reason, and therefore itself devoid of certainty, objectivity, or meaning. They also have sensed the ideological and invalid character of much "modern" thinking. For them, modern thought, far from providing an objective and valid ground for our ultimate faith, itself represents a significant aspect of the modern problem, needing itself new principles of illumination if it is to help our religious existence.

Most importantly, the main problem of the knowledge of God, they insist, is not that we cannot know God with our finite minds but that in fact secretly we do not at all wish to know God. Thus, as Barth argued, natural theology represents the persistent and systematic attempt of self-sufficient people to create a "God" of their own and so to avoid relationship with or knowledge of the real God. A philosophical God, the product of our own metaphysical thinking and the construct of our own wayward modern wisdom, may be infinitely more comfortable for us to live with; nevertheless, such a God is a far cry indeed from the real God who confronts us in judgment and may confront us therefore also in grace. Furthermore, the very center of Christian promise resides in the re-creation of what we are and of how and what we think, not in their mere extension and solidification. Thus, God—not "our own words to ourselves"—must speak to us in revelation. Such an event of revelation provides the sole basis and the sole norm for the religious existence of the Christian community from which and for which valid and legitimate theology speaks. To be sure, theology does speak to the world as well as to the church; but in its speech it must seek to re-present not the wisdom of the world but the message of the gospel, not the word of humanity but the word of God. Theology may use philosophy—it cannot avoid that—in explicating this message in coherent and adequate form. Its primal obligation, however, is to be faithful to revelation and not to the pressures of public rationality as the world defines rationality. Faith, therefore, precedes and controls the use of reason in theology; *credo ut intelligam* rather than *intelligo ut credere.*

Language about God

A second issue, characteristic of the whole tradition yet vital to recent theology, is concerned with the question of the nature of the categories or concepts fundamental to or appropriate for Christian speech about God. Should these be "personal," "historical," and "ontic" in character, as they surely are in Scripture, or should they be "ontological," "metaphysical," and therefore "impersonal" in character, as in almost every speculative philosophical system, even an idealistic or a panpsychistic one?

As in the first debate, there are compelling reasons on both sides, reasons apparently intrinsic to the character and claims of the Christian religion. In its fundamental symbolic content, exemplified in its belief in God as Creator and providential ruler, in its view of human beings as finite, temporal, and yet "real," and in its idea of history as the arena of God's activity, Christian faith cannot avoid making assertions about the character of ultimate reality and about the essential structures of natural, human, and historical existence. Thus, inescapably it must employ ontological or metaphysical as well as ontic or existential words to express its own deepest meanings. As intrinsically related to reality as, so to speak, the anchor of value within reality, God therefore must be expressed in categories appropriate to the discussion of the structures of reality as a whole, that is, in ontological or metaphysical categories.

Yet the center of Christian piety, its religious center, has classically been expressible only by means of personal, that is, anthropomorphic, language. Just as a description of a human being devoid of any personal inwardness, decision, action, and so responsibility would subvert all that Christianity has to say about human nature, so a description of God void of all personal categories (intentions, purposes, mercy, love, and so on) can hardly express what Christians intend to say about God. While, therefore, the ontological or philosophical theologians seem (initially at least) better able to explicate conceptually the symbols of creation and providence, the biblical theologians, using personal categories, seem only to gain in strength when they speak of sin, the law, and the gospel, and especially when they speak of God's "judgment" and God's "love."

Divine Agency, Temporality, and History

While the following three issues are not completely new to Christian discussion of God, the characteristic emphases of modern culture have nevertheless intensified each of them, shifted their focus and balance, and thus reshaped these issues dramatically. As a consequence, so it seems to me, the contemporary doctrine of God in Christian theology appears in undeniably new forms, whatever particular symbol (such as creation, providence, eschatology) in systematic theology we are discussing.

Let me first mention what we might call the limitations in God's agency characteristic of recent theology. For a variety of reasons (especially in this case the centering on the subject), the sense of human autonomy and of the depth, reality, and "awfulness" of evil have grown with the rise of modern culture. On both counts, theologians are less and less able or willing to say blandly that God wills, intends, or even effects whatever happens, including those actions and events that we assess to be evil. Apparently, to deny human freedom and to saddle God with evil (the rise to power of Adolf Hitler for instance) runs counter to all we believe about ourselves, history, and God. This has in turn led to two typical theological moves in the present far less prominent in the classical tradition. The first is the denial of the absoluteness and aseity of God in every respect: God's perfection and even God's necessity do not involve God's absoluteness, says Hartshorne; and in order that God be good and we be free, says Whitehead, God must be radically distinguished from the principle of ultimate reality, from the force and power of reality, that is, from what he calls creativity. Thus, the finitude of God, in the sense that God is not the source of finite reality in all its aspects but rather that God is only one of a number of correlated and primal ultimate "factors" constitutive of finite actuality, is now asserted by a most important school of contemporary Christian theology. Needless to say, this is new in the tradition.

Another kind of move, occasioned by the same issues but implying a quite different theological viewpoint, emphasizes the "self-limitation" of God in the creation of a contingent, relative, and dependent creature, but a creature that within limits is genuinely autonomous. Thus is this creature capable of and called to self-constitution, to becoming itself through its own commitments, decisions, and actions; as a consequence this creature is capable of original, novel action and so is "free" to sin and/or to accept grace—that is, free to act in ways neither determined nor predetermined by God. This "Arminian" position (which, whatever its denials, it seems to be) has been, I think, shared by most nonprocess theologians in the present century, with the possible exception of Barth. Some of the most dramatic changes in the concept of God in modern times have, therefore, occurred in new interpretations of God's relation to natural evil and mortality, on the one hand, and of the symbols of providence, election, predestination, grace, and eternal damnation, on the other. In all these loci, creaturely freedom or autonomy now plays a much larger role than before, qualifying the absolute sovereignty of the divine will and the divine power. Correspondingly, the goodness of God and so God's separation from evil have been much more jealously guarded, whether this is achieved metaphysically through the concept of the finitude of God or theologically through the concept of the divine self-limitation.

Again, for the variety of reasons I have mentioned, the sense, on the one hand, of the reality and value of temporal passage, of change, and of the new and, on the other hand, of the reality and value of relatedness has vastly increased. To the Hellenic and Hellenistic epochs, the divine was both more real and more good to the extent that it was not involved in change and relatedness. In our epoch we tend to reverse this apprehension. A changeless and unrelated God probably would seem to most of us not only a compensatory chimera of the imagination, unexperienced and so unknown, but even more a notion void of all real content and value since such a deity would lack relatedness to the changing world where initially all reality and value reside. Thus, the most prominent characteristic of contemporary theologies of all sorts is what may be termed their war with the Greeks. There is hardly a conception of God from Hegel onward that is not dynamic, changing, and in some manner intrinsically related to the world of change, and almost the worst thing any school can say of its opponents is that they are in this or that regard Greek. The instance of this dynamic view of God currently most influential is of course the Whiteheadian, where God is an example of process rather than its negation. God thus shares in the metaphysical categories of process: temporality, potentiality, change, relatedness, development, and dependence or passivity.

With quite different tactics the biblical or neoorthodox theologians have carried on their war with the Greeks. Although they have retained the symbols of the absoluteness and aseity of God, the transcendent Creator of an essentially dependent creature—so that their views are deeply differentiated from a process God—nevertheless, in using the personal and historical categories of biblical speech, they too have produced a conception of a dynamic and related God. Like their rivals in the process school, their main conscious opposition has been to "the Greek concept of God" as changeless, unrelated, aloof. Theirs then is a "God who acts in history," who "comes" or "is coming," who effects "mighty deeds" of revelation and redemption, and so on. All these clearly are temporal as well as personal words expressing actions over time and within time, relatedness, a relative dependence ("encounter," "judge"), words implying temporality, change, passivity, and potentiality as well as "personality" in God. The neoorthodox have not drawn out explicitly the ontological implications of this their central language about God. Often they have left the obvious puzzles in the "dialectical" or "paradoxical" forms they think appropriate to the divine mystery. Or, as Barth was wont to do, they have simply stated that this apparent contradictoriness is precisely what is implied by the divine freedom. Nevertheless, it is clear that their view too entails radical changes from any recognizably "orthodox" conception of God. These changes have been even more evident in the post-neoorthodox eschatological theologies in which, for some, God is so temporal that, far from representing an eternity beyond time, the divine being is now said to be only "future."

As is well known, a major theme in modern culture, practically its defining feature or essence, has been the theme of historical development or progress, a theme asserting the supreme meaningfulness of history as a whole as a steady advance toward higher and higher forms of social life. Insofar as the liberal theologies of the nineteenth and early twentieth centuries accommodated themselves to this pervasive modern theme (myth?), God was interpreted as the immanent spiritual and moral force underlying the historical development of society; the Kingdom was interpreted as that social order that is history's goal; and the Christian community was viewed as having its raison d'être in the political implementation of this historical progress toward the divine Kingdom of justice and love.

Amid the turmoil of twentieth-century history, this vision of a developing historical progress rapidly dissipated. The dominant theologies of the continent — Barthian, Bultmannian, Scandinavian — therefore tended to separate the Christian message of salvation and the redemptive activity of God from questions of political and historical development. In the most extreme form of this theology (as in Bultmann), the gospel breaks into an individual's basic "world," freeing him or her from the past and giving him or her the new prospect of an open future. Appropriate for any time or place, this message has nothing directly to do with the ups and downs of social history; coming vertically into life, it touches and heals only that which can receive it, namely, the individual spirit that can welcome it with decision, commitment, and faith. Although he remained an active socialist throughout his life, Karl Barth was interpreted theologically (rightly, I think) all during his lifetime as in this sense also propounding a nonsocial and nonpolitical interpretation of the gospel. Social history and "God's history" are two different, if interrelated, histories, and Christian salvation in Christ remains at best only indirectly connected with or relevant to improvements in the social order.

In the last two decades a very strong reaction in the other direction has occurred. A number of liberationist or political theologies have appeared, calling upon Christian action and Christian theology to turn again toward the wide spectrum of social history's crises and oppressions as their main if not exclusive area of concern. The new theologies stress their identity with a given oppressed community, call for revolutionary action or praxis, and recognize only theological reflection that arises out of both. Thus, we have black theologies, feminist theologies, and Third World theologies. As a consequence of this identification with groups oppressed by Western social reality, they tend to make alliance with Marxist thought rather than with Western philosophy and social theory in general. They see the divine action as itself adversarial to all that is the case in the sorry present; while they are also utopian, they are markedly antidevelopmental in the essential themes of their thought.

Such adversarial theologies understandably wish to deny the relation of God to all that characterized the dominant and oppressive past or present of Western history. Yet, as socially centered theologies, they wish also to identify God in some important sense with history. Thus, for them God is neither the God of the past nor the God of the present; nor is God a God beyond time, a God vertically above or below each moment, the ground and determiner of all being. Rather, God is eschatological, the one who is coming, the God of the future, the one who from the future will master the present and establish the divine sovereign rule in future history. This conception of God, as one might expect, tends to puzzle theologians still mired in capitalistic and/or male society; but professorial proponents of such praxis-oriented theologies who are also still mired in high-ranking academic positions in that society (and drive a Mercedes) puzzle us even more. Nevertheless, the power with which this movement has redirected the concentration of theology back to history and forward into the future—hopefully not Heilbroner's future[1]—has been impressive and marks this as a most creative form of contemporary theology.

The sharpest theological debates in the last decade and a half (at least outside the United States) have centered on the issues summarized here: whether theology can be carried on apart from revolutionary action; whether God has been active and sovereign in the past and the present and will be in the future; whether the gospel is a promise of redemption for the individual soul or only for historical society; whether that promise is to be fulfilled here and in eternity or solely in a kingdom characterizing the historical, social future; and whether in Christ God's redemptive action was once and for all accomplished and manifest (even if its effects remain

---

[1] See Robert Heilbroner, *An Inquiry into the Human Prospect* (New York: W. W. Norton, 1974). This study is a sober, even gloomy, reflection by a social scientist on the effects of the crisis of the environment—increasing decade by decade—on the comforts, privileges, and especially the liberties of modern society.

fragmentary), or whether in Jesus are to be found solely promises for a future social parousia of the kingdom.

ISSUES AND PROPOSALS

Basic to a monotheistic conception of God in my view is the conviction that God is the source of the totality of being. This affirmation is fundamental both to the main thrust of Scripture and to our experience of the reality, goodness, and possibility of finite life in time. It is also the inescapable precondition for any Christian understanding of our experience of estrangement or sin, for any valid Christian interpretation of history, and for any understanding of reconciliation and redemption that is in accord with Scripture and experience, although these are issues far too complex to resolve here. Thus, my own constructive view differentiates itself as sharply as it can from any of the process views of God that deny that God is the source or ground of finite reality and give to creativity that status of ultimacy traditionally accorded to God. Yet I also disagree with those forms of orthodoxy that have insisted on the active omnipotence or total sovereignty of God in the coming to be of finite events, whether events of natural process or the thoughts, decisions, and actions that constitute the events of history. As always, the central problem for the doctrine of God is how to unite intelligibly the absoluteness of God as the unconditioned source of our total being with the dynamic relatedness and the reciprocal activity of God as the ground, guide, dialogical partner, and redeemer of our freedom.

To the modern consciousness, reality—personal and historical as well as natural—is in passage, deeply and inescapably temporal. Therefore, the world and God must be reconceived in terms of temporality or process if the relatedness of God to the world as Creator, Preserver, Judge, and Redeemer is to be explicated. Radical temporality implies the becomingness of all things, the movement of whatever is from its former givenness to its present state—where briefly it is and constitutes itself in freedom—thence into new, as yet unrealized possibilities. Correspondingly, it implies the vanishing of all possibilities that are to come and all actualities that presently are into the "has been-ness" of the past. Past, present, and future unite in each creative present, but every creative present itself recedes into the relative and ineffective nonbeing of the past, making room for not-yet possibilities from the future to become actual in each subsequent present.

In such a situation of radical passage, where the not-yet future becomes real in the freedom of the present, and each present in turn vanishes into the nonbeing of the past, some deeper reality is required that is itself not in passage, that does not vanish into the nonbeing of the past, and yet is intrinsically related to that passage. This deeper reality, experienced in the continuities present in changing time, in the freedom also present in time, and in the novel possibilities impinging on time, is the initial referent for the word *God.* God so conceived is active in the coming-to-be of our temporal being, in its preservation over time, and in its movement through time into the future.

God is first experienced as the unconditioned ground of the movement from a vanishing past (the recent past) into the new present that constitutes our reality. Such a movement, essential both to present reality of any sort and also to its continuity with the past (and so to substance, causality, sensing, and knowing), can be provided neither by the past itself, which is gone, nor by the new present, which is just coming to be. There must, therefore, be an unconditioned ground of each that does not pass away and yet that is in creative relation to the movement of temporal being.

God is also experienced as the source of our freedom in the present, as the ground of that act of self-constitution that unites the given from the past with the new actuality of the present in the light of the possibilities open to it in the future. Freedom does not ground itself; it experiences itself as given—something to be actualized by us but not created by us. It cannot be given to us merely from the past or merely from the future, for in relation to both we experience freedom. It too is therefore of God and can realize itself only in a dependent relation to God. God in turn is unconditioned in relation to finite past, present, and future, not arising out of the past or dependent and vulnerable in the present or in danger of ceasing to be in the future. Nevertheless, in relation to each mode of time, God is self-limiting, making room for the finite freedom that God grounds and establishes in each present. Needless to say, the ontological distinction between God and the finite world thus established and preserved, as well as God's continual relatedness to it, is vast and, as in all traditional discourse about God, calls for an analogical rather than a univocal mode of speech. This also means that God is in some important sense hidden within temporal passage and that the divine presence is to be recognized and acknowledged more through a religious discernment than by means of objective inquiry.

Moreover, God is experienced as the source or ground of new possibility and of the impingement of the future on the present. These novel possibilities are not produced out of the past, out of preceding actuality, else they could not embody the genuinely new. Nor are they produced by any creatures or set of creatures in the present, else there would be no subsequent order among the near infinity of present creatures. Rather they are "held" in the envisionment of some unconditioned reality that spans past, present, and future and that views these possibilities as possible, as not yet, and still as relevant to and in harmony with past and present actualities. Thus, God, as the ground of future possibility, is at the same time the ground of order and intelligibility, the divine principle of logos—a traditional symbol now reconceived in a dynamic, temporal mode. God is both being and logos, the abyss of reality as the dynamic ground of the actuality of each present and the principle of possibility and order as the ever-moving source of novelty and harmony. Although God so conceived is unconditioned, infinite, and absolute, clearly God so conceived is also self-limited, temporal (the future is also for God possibility and not actuality), changing (in relation to a self-constituting world), and reciprocal (in relation to the freedom of the creature).

God, however, is more than being and logos; God is also love. In order for there to be genuine historical possibility, more than possibility is needed. We historical creatures corrupt our possibilities in enacting them, and so we warp if we do not destroy them—and also we die. The reconciling, reuniting, and redemptive love of God is essential for the fulfillment of possibility in human life and history, and the reality of that love is the essence of the Christian gospel. The re-creative and reuniting power of the divine love is, like the divine being and the divine logos, manifest universally, appearing everywhere in history, especially in history's religions where redemptive forces are at work. For Christians, however, it has its central locus, its deepest reality and power, and its final criterion in the Christ and the community that lives in his Spirit.

This brings us to what may be the most important new issue confronting Christian theology at the present time: the encounter with other religious traditions. In our present situation religious faiths, like political and economic systems, encounter one another regularly and intimately. Since this encounter of the religions has become an omnipresent reality, especially in the past two or three decades, the relation of Christian theology to other, non-Christian modes of "theology" has emerged as a burning issue. In this encounter Christianity and Christians have witnessed these religions as bearing power and embodying vital, healing, redemptive forces providing unique illumination and grace to our ailing cultural life and our somewhat impoverished existence. No longer, therefore, is it possible for Christians to declare other faiths either devoid of truth (as orthodoxy did) or primitive or less developed steppingstones to the absoluteness of Christianity (as the early liberals did). Many admit and affirm the suggestion that within other religions the promise of grace and salvation is present and truth is experienced. What does this mean then for the uniqueness of Christian revelation, for the finality of Christ's incarnation and atonement, for the salvation of non-Christians, and a thousand other important theological questions?

Understandably most of the new debate on these matters has centered on the crucial questions of special revelation and Christology. Many have assumed that were these christological doctrines to be liberalized or toned down, the issues vis-à-vis other religions would dissipate. This is not so. Important divergences (say, with Hinduism and Buddhism) appear in connection with every significant theological or philosophical question, from that of the nature of reality and our knowledge of it through the nature of human being and its "problem" to the understanding of history and final salvation. Not least of all, significant divergences appear in connection with the symbol of God. Some important religions witness to no reality equivalent to the referent of the symbol God. Furthermore, whatever it is that differentiates philosophical and theological systems from one another permeates the entire system, not just some of its doctrines. A Christian theism with a minimal Christology—whether Deist, Unitarian, low liberal, process, or whatever—is as Western and Christian in its philosophical conceptuality, its thematic style and emphases, and its religious implications as a typically neoorthodox theology centered on biblical symbols and Christology; it remains then just as divergent (although perhaps at different points) from a Hindu or Buddhist "theology."

In conclusion it is safe to say that the encounter of religions with one another and their subsequent dialogues with one another will effect radical changes in the discussion of God carried on by every present form of Christian theology. To predict what new directions these changes will represent is really only to state my own preferences, where I think the understanding of God ought to go, granted this encounter. As for the direction it will in fact go, I have no insight except to suggest that, even more than in connection with the new rapport between Catholicism and Protestantism, a close encounter with the nothingness of Buddhism will effect noteworthy changes in every recognizable form of contemporary discourse about God.[2]

---

[2] The following are suggested readings on the problem of God in Christian theology: Samuel Alexander, *Space, Time, and Deity,* 2 vols. (London: Macmillan, 1927); Thomas Altizer, *Total Presence: The Language of Jesus and the Language of Today* (New York: Seabury Press, 1980); Anselm, *Monologion* and *Proslogion;* Thomas Aquinas, *Summa contra Gentiles,* book 1, and *Summa Theologica,* part 1, questions 1–43; Augustine, *The City of God* and *On the Trinity;* Karl Barth, *Church Dogmatics,* vol. 2/1, and *The Humanity of God* (Richmond: John Knox Press, 1960), chap. 2; Emil Brunner, *The Christian Doctrine of God: Dogmatics,* vol. 1; John Calvin, *Institutes of the Christian Religion,* book 1; John B. Cobb, *God and the World* (Philadelphia: Westminster Press, 1969); Gerhard Ebeling, *God and Word* (Philadelphia: Fortress Press, 1967); Edward Farley, *The Transcendence of God* (Philadelphia: Westminster Press, 1960); Langdon Gilkey, *Naming the Whirlwind: The Renewal of God-Language* (Indianapolis: Bobbs-Merrill, 1969) and *Reaping the Whirlwind: A Christian Interpretation of History* (New York: Seabury Press, 1976); Charles Hartshorne, *The Divine Relativity* (New Haven, Conn.: Yale University Press, 1964); G. W. F. Hegel, *Lectures on the Philosophy of Religion,* vol. 1, *Introduction and the Concept of Religion,* ed. Peter C. Hodgson, trans. R. F. Brown, Peter C. Hodgson, and J. M. Stewart (Berkeley: University of California Press, 1984); Hegel; *The Christian Religion,* ed. and trans. Peter C. Hodgson (Missoula, Mont.: Scholars Press, 1979), chap. 2; William Ernest Hocking, *The Meaning of God in Human Experience* (New Haven, Conn.: Yale University Press, 1912); Gordon Kaufman, *God the Problem* (Cambridge: Harvard University Press, 1971); Martin Luther, *The Bondage of the Will,* trans. J. I. Packer and O. R. Johnston (London: James Clarke, 1957); W. R. Matthews, *God in Christian Experience* (New York: Harper, 1930); Jürgen Moltmann, *The Crucified God: The Cross of Christ as the Foundation and Criticism of Christian Theology,* trans. R. A. Wilson and John Bowden (New York: Harper & Row, 1974), esp. chap. 6; H. Richard Niebuhr, *Radical Monotheism and Western Culture* (New York: Harper & Row, 1956); Schubert Ogden, *The Reality of God and Other Essays* (New York: Harper & Row, 1966); Origen, *On First Principles,* esp. book 1; Wolfhart Pannenberg, *Basic Questions in Theology,* vol. 2 (Philadelphia: Fortress Press, 1971); and vol. 3 of this series, published in translation as *The Idea of God and Human Freedom,* trans. R. A. Wilson (Philadelphia: Westminster Press, 1969); and *Theology and the Kingdom of God,* ed. Richard John Neuhaus (Philadelphia: Westminster Press, 1969); Karl Rahner, *Foundations of Christian Faith,* trans. William V. Dych (New York: Crossroad, 1978), esp. chaps. 2, 4, 5, and *The Trinity* (New York: Herder & Herder, 1970); Friedrich Schleiermacher, *The Christian Faith,* trans. and ed. H. R. Mackintosh and J. S. Stewart (Philadelphia: Fortress Press, 1976), 194–232, 325–54, 723–51; Ernst Troeltsch, *The Christian Faith* (Minneapolis: Fortress Press, 1991); Tertullian, *Against Hermogenes;* Paul Tillich, *Biblical Religion and the Search for Ultimate Reality* (Chicago: University of Chicago Press, 1955), and *Systematic Theology,* vol. 1 (Chicago: University of Chicago Press, 1951); Claude Welch, *In This Name: The Doctrine of the Trinity in Contemporary Theology* (New York: Charles Scribner's Sons, 1952); Alfred North Whitehead, *Process and Reality: An Essay in Cosmology,* corrected ed., ed. David Ray Griffin and Donald W. Sherburne (New York: The Free Press, 1978), and *Religion in the Making* (New York: Macmillan, 1926).

CHAPTER 6

CREATION: BEING
AND NONBEING

There is little question that the symbol of *creatio ex nihilo* and its direct
correlate, the naming of God as being, pure being, or pure actuality, have
been both crucial and predominant in Christian theology. Not since the
Gnostics and not until process theology have significant groups within the
general range of Christian reflection questioned this identification of God
with being itself. God as being, the source and ground of finite being, seems
as established and durable a part of our symbolic repertoire as incarnation
and resurrection, and more durable even than sin! Nor is its other direct
consequence, the positive affirmation of time, space, nature, human being
(both individual and social), and history, that is, finite being in all its scope,
any less persistent. In fact, one finds this affirmation of "the world," if not
of the flesh and the devil, a major assumption not only of theologies (such
as process) that relinquish *ex nihilo* and so deny that God is the source of
being; it is also enthusiastically seconded by a variety of secular viewpoints
that scarcely know what either *ex nihilo* or God as absolute being might mean.
   This chapter will not seek to repudiate the legitimacy of any one of these
three symbolic assertions: *creatio ex nihilo,* the naming of God as being or
being itself, and the affirmation of "the world."[1] It will, however, question
the way we have (and I include my own previous reflections) thought of
these symbols, and it will begin to articulate the paradoxical suggestion that
nonbeing be included, in ways it has previously not been, in the consideration

---

   [1] I had better not! My first book, written over thirty years ago, gave unqualified affirmation
of all of these three and sought to articulate their "meaning in modern terms": Langdon Gilkey,
Maker of Heaven and Earth: The Christian Doctrine of Creation in the Light of Modern Knowledge
(Garden City, N.Y.: Doubleday, 1959).

of both creation and God. I begin, then, with a brief summary of the traditional approach, starting with the clear assets of this tradition and then moving to some of its now-apparent liabilities.

GOD AS BEING AND
THE AFFIRMATION OF THE WORLD

Since the important interrelation of the symbol of creation, that is, *creatio ex nihilo,* with God as absolute or pure being and the affirmation of the world, is familiar doctrinal territory to us all, I shall only summarize here. If, as Christian convictions made plain, God is the sole source of all that is and, being God, is the spiritual source of all that is, then the other two follow at once.[2] On the one hand, as the sole principle of the being of things (the first cause of being, as Thomas Aquinas said), God must represent absolute or unconditional being, nondependent being, or being itself. On the other hand, all that is, being the purposed creation of God, must have intrinsic value, or as Bible and tradition have put it, it must "be very good." With regard to the first, God as unconditional being, the primary meaning of ex nihilo was the denial of dualism, *non ex materia sed ex nihilo;* God did not create out of matter but on the contrary posited all of finite being, matter as well as form, into being from nothing. Thus is God the source and ground of finite being in its entirety. As a consequence, God is neither an example among others of the ontological structure of finitude (as in Whitehead) nor the former or fashioner of finitude out of a given material (as in Plato's *Timaeus*). As their source, God transcends all the factors within finite being that depend upon and limit each other: matter and form, creativity and eternal objects, nonliving and living. As transcendent to every sort of dependence and limitation, therefore, God is first cause and without cause, unconditional or absolute being (absolute causality, as Schleiermacher said), or being itself. Thus, as the patristic theologians stated and the tradition has reiterated, God is eternal (not temporal), incorruptible (not mortal), independent (*a se*), necessary (noncontingent), and omnipotent (without external limit). One notes that these attributes are more negative than positive in their meaning. Like the formula ex nihilo itself (*non de Deo et non ex materia sed ex nihilo*), they represent more an explicit denial of the experienced and known limitations of creatureliness than a positive, cognitive grasp of the meaning

---

[2] When I say "follow," I mean to explicate the order of being of these concepts or symbols, not the order of knowing. With regard to the latter, it is almost universally recognized that the affirmation of God's creation of the world followed, as a consequence, the Hebrew experience of the divine rescue and the divine covenant relationship, at Exodus and at Sinai; God was first known as redemptive actor in history and then known as Creator of people, history, and nature. The logical order of concepts, however, the order of being, goes the other way: Because God created the world, including nature, history, and men and women, therefore, (1) God is able to act in revelation and in redemption within nature and history, and (2) time and creation alike were known to be good.

of these transcendent terms. In any case, the transcendence of God over the limitations of finitude follows directly from the affirmation of the divine creation of all things.

In the same direct way the positive affirmation of the world (as good) is correlated with the belief in the divine creation of the world. In an epoch when the goodness of finitude, its potentiality of meaning and fulfillment, was by no means assumed, and frequently repudiated, this was a novel rather than a conventional assertion. It is not that God the Creator was believed to be good because God's creation was known as good, but the reverse: the creation, despite its evident and deep ambiguity, was affirmed to be good because the God who made it was known in the covenant and later in Christ to be good. This implication of creation, therefore, which in periods of optimism seems unnecessary and redundant, became spiritually significant in difficult times, when life otherwise might have been regarded as futile, meaningless, and even evil. The basis for this affirmation of goodness — repeated over and over again in the Genesis account — is, as we noted, the spiritual character of God and, further, what Calvin called "the divine benevolence" known in the covenant and in Christ. Thus, the patristic theologians emphasized that creation was an intended and purposive act of God, not a "mere" metaphysical necessity of the divine nature, either an automatic emanation or an act of divine self-fulfillment. For in neither of these cases would finite being have value in and for itself, but possibly only for its ambiguous divine source. Thus, the spirituality of God, and the non-constrained and so purposive ("free") character of the act of creation, are symbolic grounds of the goodness affirmed of the world and its life.[3] Needless to say, the spirituality of God was also very important in the conception of the human entailed in the creation: A spiritual God created men and women in the divine image, as analogously spirit (and so as both intelligible and responsible, and we would add creative) as well as analogously living, although the latter tended to recede in importance. As, therefore, God is unconditional being, life, and spirit or freedom, so nature represents finite existence and life and so humans represent conditioned or finite being, life, and freedom; all of finite being is in its own way therefore good.

In the symbol of creation, however, both the ontological transcendence of God and the goodness or value of creation were qualified by their apparent opposites: the divine immanence in the world and the ambiguity

---

[3] This point is overlooked in modern attempts to render this account "more rational" by showing the necessity of creation to the nature or completion of God: cf. Hegel and Whitehead especially. To both of them, the goodness of creation was inherent in creation itself, and so obvious to reason. Thus, God's goodness was made more rational, secure, and meaningful, if it could be shown that God's nature entails divine creative activity in producing or fashioning this good world. If, however, the value of the world is (as it is to me) ambiguous, and if that value is dependent on the divine purpose for the world and love of it — both being notions that involve freedom — then the nonnecessity of the act of creation and so even its metaphysical contingency seem to follow.

of creation. Hence results the richness (to some) and/or the confusion (to others) of this cluster of religious symbols. If all the creation is essentially and so permanently dependent on its source (that is, non-self-sufficient or non-ontologically autonomous), God is necessarily continually present in and to finitude, preserving it from moment to moment, on the one hand, and, on the other (again as spirit), giving to it a renewed — and so refashioned or revised — order and purpose. The immanence of God in creation follows as a polar concept to the divine transcendence, as the symbol of providence is entailed in that of creation. God is both transcendent to creation and therefore absolute and at the same time immanent and participating in or relative to creation. To put this in another way, God is absolute, but God is not all that there is, since there is also the real and relatively autonomous creation. Christian understanding does not, therefore, represent a monism in which plurality is unreal, shadowy, or abrogated. Yet God is the source of finite reality and not another finite factor over against and balancing finitude; this is not a dualism or a pluralism of finite principles. Theologians of creation have all teetered on a thin line between monism and dualism, each leaning toward one or the other of these poles. Some have emphasized more the presence of God in creation, and so the continuing and pervasive dependence of finitude on God, tending toward monism (Augustine, Luther, Schleiermacher, Tillich). Others have emphasized the distinction between the transcendent God and creation and thus tended toward dualism (Thomas, Calvin, Barth). All alike, however, have in the end illustrated the dialectical, paradoxical notion implicit in creation: The world is totally and essentially dependent on God (*non ex materia*), and yet the world is not identical with God (*non de Deo*). Correspondingly, God transcends the world as distinct from it, and yet God is immanent within the world as the source of its being, as the principle of its life and order, and as the ground of its hope for fulfillment. As Creator, God transcends and is "independent" of the world; but as Creator, God also participates in and so is in relation to the world. Both consequences are essential for my topic, although they have hardly received equal emphasis at all times![4]

The goodness and value of the world has also been vigorously qualified in the tradition, although it has never been denied. Vast ranges of common experience deeply challenge that goodness, and these, too, represent important aspects of the Hebrew and Christian worlds, not least since both, as noted, begin with unexpected experiences of rescue from apparently overwhelming evil. For neither tradition does belief in creation originate as the result of a rationally responsible survey of the order and goodness observable

---

[4] As an illustration, when I reread, as I have perforce done, my own *Maker of Heaven and Earth,* I am mildly horrified at the way that essentially Niebuhrean viewpoint minimized, nay overlooked, the immanence of God in creation. From my later, more Tillichean perspective, this seems bizarre indeed.

in ordinary, common existence. The depth of this experience of estrangement — as Tillich put it — emphasizes, therefore, the distinction between God and our world. It is the deepest and continuing ground of the *non de Deo*. The world is not God because the world is suffused with an evil in which we all share; and yet it is of God, and thus its undeniable evil is neither essential, necessary, nor unredeemable. As a consequence, the evil is made possible by the ontological distinction between Creator and creature; but evil is effected by the historical enactment of creaturely freedom or spirit. Its cause, as Augustine said, is not nature but freedom — namely, the capacity of freedom to estrange itself from the God on whom it is nevertheless totally dependent; ontologically, therefore, evil has no cause. The paradoxical symbol of creation, that we are dependent on God yet distinct from and even free over against God, grounds the possibility of the Christian interpretation of sin and redemption. Sin is possible because we are not God but relatively autonomous; and sin is destructive because "we are made by and for God," that is, absolutely dependent on God. Correspondingly, redemption is necessary because we are estranged from God, and it is possible because, again, we are made by and for God. Augustine first wove all this together into the fundamental symbolism of our common tradition: the transcendence of the unconditional and eternal God, the immanence of God in creation, the consequent goodness of time and of the world (of nature), and yet the possibility and the actuality of the Fall due to freedom, and hence both the need for and the possibility of redemption in time. A junior edition of this synthesis, showing the interrelations of creation, divine transcendence, world affirmation, sin, and redemption, appeared in my own earlier work on creation. One may well ask, therefore, If all this was good enough for Augustine, and if a modern revision was possible, why should we suggest a further and even more radical rethinking?

Before we turn to that point, however, let us note the important interrelations between God, the human, and nature that the symbol of creation implied. Through the mediation of God the Creator of both, nature and humankind are implicitly and deeply related to each other. Both have value as God's creation; both reflect the divine life, order, and "glory," if not the divine image; and both participate in the divine purpose of redemption and reunion. The human is, to be sure, distinguished if not separated from nature: As spirit humans are creative and responsible to be obedient to the divine law through their freedom, just as nature is obedient through its regularities. Implicitly in this vision, nature in its own ways shares with humans the creativity, order, life, and value for itself that the infinite power and purpose of God have given to it. Unfortunately, however, much of this remained at best implicit, at worst forgotten and overlooked. The relation of life and fertility radically receded (almost as quickly as the Baalim did); the role of nature as merely the theater for redemptive history came to the fore; and the predominant relation of the human being to nature was at best that of responsible steward and at worst that of a dominating sovereign. The clear affirmation of time, world, and history — of the rationality of nature and

the meaning of history—involved in creation remained as one of the predominant assets of the Western inheritance; and the high evaluation of the
human as rational, responsible, and creative, as therefore of infinite value,
represented perhaps the most precious part of this inheritance. But both of
these assets (history and the human) eclipsed the admittedly subordinate role
and value of nature in the symbolism of creation, leaving us with the question, How can we reevaluate radically the status, role, and value of nature,
which we have overlooked, and yet preserve the affirmation of history and
the human, on which most of our culture's real values rest?

THE APPARENT NEMESIS OF
GOD AS ABSOLUTE BEING

I turn now to the reasons that this traditional interpretation or reading of the
symbol of creation—both vis-à-vis God and the world God made—
currently seems unsatisfactory, in need of if not rejection at least radical
revision. No symbol or set of symbols represents the most fundamental
causes of an epoch's major dilemmas; the actuality of what we term sin,
expressed through greed, aggression, hostility, dominance, and exploitation,
does represent that fundamental cause. But symbols channel and encourage
estrangement and self-love, or they can break, criticize, and reshape them.
Thus do they have a creative or destructive, healing or disintegrating role
in history. If, then, creation as an interwoven gestalt or cluster of symbols
has seemed to have gone awry, in what way has it done so?

My suggestion may be put as follows: The belief in creation resulted in
an undialectical and thus an unqualified affirmation of being, first with
regard to God as Creator and then with regard to creation, to the world, and
especially to humans within the world. Let us begin, as this history does,
with regard to God. That God transcends the creation that has its sole source
in the divine being, life, and purposes is, as we have seen, intrinsic in the
symbol. This has led in part to a sense of the intrinsic mystery of God. God
is not a being among the beings of the world, and thus God cannot be
experienced or thought of as those other beings are. Since all our words and
categories come from such experience of the finite, none of them can apply
directly (univocally) to the divine that transcends the finite; all must at best
apply symbolically or analogically. In this sense, among others, God remains
essentially mysterious: the more God is revealed, the more the divine is
veiled; the more we understand God, the more we understand that God's
mystery is quite beyond our understanding. Hardly a major theologian has
denied this implication of transcendence; and the greatest have made it
central.

Another implication of transcendence, however, has tended—so it seems
now to me—to overshadow this first one. This is the transcendence of God

expressed by means of the absoluteness of God's being. Here the creative being of finitude is not transcended in a mystery that, so to speak, transcends even being; rather the relative being of finitude is transcended in terms of an absolute degree of being, namely, the absoluteness of God's being. This is, of course, by no means an unequivocal error: God is or exists in a different way than creatures are, if God is their source and ground. Nevertheless, if the emphasis is put here, on the transcendence of finite being into absolute being, then God's nature becomes defined by its unconditional and absolute character rather than by its mystery, and the dialectical nature of the relation of that mystery to the being that is God is lost, as the continual relatedness of God to finite being is also sacrificed. God becomes, so to speak, un-equivocally absolute in being: *a se* or independent, necessary, changeless, timeless, actual, unrelated, or, as in Protestant orthodoxy, undialectically sovereign in absolute power. The divine nature comes to represent, in other words, the transcendent glorification of being rather than the transcendence of being and thus the principle of being's transmutation. In turn this undialectical glorification of being contradicts rather than buttresses other important elements of the Christian vision.

In the first place, the God who is undialectically changeless, necessary, impassible, and hence unrelated comes soon enough to contradict the God who creates, preserves, and guides a changing world, the God who comes into and participates in that world, and above all the God who shares in some mysterious way in the suffering, vulnerability, and even the mortality of all creatures. But these latter aspects of God — God's presence in temporal being and changing experience, God's participation in the ambiguity of our existence, and God's revelation of God's self in and through weakness — are the basis for our knowledge of God, even God as Creator and so as tran-scendent in the first place. Without God's presence in and through time and change, God would not have been known as eternal and changeless; without the light of God's participation in weakness and death, God would not have been known as the eternal giver of life and of glory. Thus (as both Barth and Rahner saw), in such an order of knowing, it makes no sense at all so to define the divine order of being as to preclude both the divine participation in finitude and the divine sharing in vulnerability and nonbeing. The church's twofold answer to this — namely, that such relations of God to change and finitude are not "real" relations and that it is only the creaturely nature of Christ that shares the weaknesses of temporal being — is no answer at all. In both cases the divine nature has been defined so as to contradict other fundamental aspects of that nature: namely, as one capable of revealing itself in time and one as present to our world in redemption. Small wonder that most twentieth-century theologians have followed Barth in questioning the priority of this extrachristological definition of God as absolute being and have empathized with Moltmann's effort to understand the divine nature also in terms of the divine suffering present in and revealed through the crucifixion.

These intrasymbolic tensions within the Christian doctrine of God are, however, by no means the end of the story. With the Renaissance and especially with the Enlightenment, the affirmation of the reality, goodness, and potential meaning of the world, grounded on the confidence that it had been established by the good God, grew apace: More and more it was commonly apprehended that the real is located here, in the midst of temporal change; that goodness alone inhabits that temporal world, its tasks and vocations; and that fulfillment is increasingly possible in historical time. For such an apprehension or self-understanding a persistent sense of deity is in any case precarious; but a fortiori in such a situation any sense of the reality, goodness, and relevance of a deity quite transcendent to time and change tends to erode. And erode it did. The categories of aseity, changelessness, and necessity became mere words, inapplicable and empty in real experience. Moreover, whenever the absolute deity reappeared, through orthodox proclamation (Catholic or Protestant) or in cultic memory, it seemed to many only to threaten the waxing and deeply treasured sense of autonomy in modern culture. The God who was originally experienced as the principle of the establishing, undergirding, and fulfilling of an ambiguous creaturely creativity, had now become the heteronomous negation of all such creaturely creativity. The absoluteness of God was not the sole cause of the deity's reported death, but it surely did nothing in the eighteenth and nineteenth centuries to put that event off.

The story goes on. I have suggested that the definition of God as absolute being represents an undialectical affirmation of finite being applied to God and thus transmuted into unconditional being and that this move did not fit the major emphases and themes of Christian belief. Now, the point is that as the reality and relevance of the divine receded from modern Western consciousness, this undialectical affirmation of finite being did not recede. In fact, with the growing autonomy, knowledge, and power of God's human creatures (at least Western ones, but then they were sure they stood for all humankind), this self-affirmation only increased. As a consequence, as Marx might have put it, the undialectical affirmation of finite being moved down from heaven to earth, from the sacred to the secular, worldly realms. The autonomous self—the cognitive self as scientific knower, the emotive self driving toward fulfillment and happiness, the deciding self legislating its own values—this autonomous self is now undialectically affirmed in relation to a world whose potentialities for value are also undialectically affirmed.

Such an unqualified affirmation possesses (as Augustine saw) an infinite dimension; it sees itself as innocent and benevolent, but in fact it is driven by the powers of alienation, domination, and infinite thirst, by concupiscence. It sweeps, therefore, without limit across every previous horizon. Western thinkers gloried in this descent of infinite power and purpose onto earth and into their hands. It was the fitting reward, so they reflected, to peoples blessed with an absolute God, an absolute revelation, and (later) an absolute civilization. Looking at this process from the inside, our history books continue to speak glowingly of newly "expanded" horizons, of the "opening up" of whole new regions and realms of possibility: of geography, knowledge, techniques, goods, experiences, fulfillment.

From the outside, however, from the perspective of those who were overrun, this was not so much an expansion of horizons as an expansion of the imperial ego. Those wider horizons meant in historical fact newly achieved and newly organized empires, a conquest, possession, and exploitation that soon encircled the globe. The glory of the infinite God, harnessed to this lively creaturely ego, meant that crosses accompanied gunboats and traders to every corner of the earth.

The empires have now receded; the West is proceeding to pay the bill. But concurrent with that political expansion, and gaining momentum in our century as the empires have waned, has been a corresponding imperial conquest of nature, which, as we now see, will in the end present us with an even more devastating bill to pay. Once undertaken, this unqualified affirmation of ourselves, equipped with ever more efficient knowledge and techniques and so holding out ever more alluring promises of satisfactions, is almost impossible to stop. It presents us, therefore, with a particularly clear disclosure of the self-destructive possibilities of intellectual, scientific, and technical creativity if that well-armed autonomy is driven by what the Buddhists call desire. Expanding selves, united in a community of self-love and driven by concupiscence, present a vivid image of historical nemesis. Finite being, unqualifiedly affirmed and transmuted into absoluteness, results in the imperial and so the oppressive, not to mention the self-destructive, ego. Was God flattered by this name we gave to God: absolute being? Was not the very point of the revelation we treasure that an affirmation of being is ambiguous, that the first shall be last and the last first? One suspects that an undialectical affirmation of being represents, from a Christian perspective, an overaffirmation of being, an expansion of power, interest, and will untrue to the gospel and a nemesis for both self and world.

THE DIVINE MYSTERY:
POLARITY OF BEING AND NONBEING

The positive thesis of this chapter is that creation can more coherently and faithfully (adequate to Christian sources) be understood as also the disclosure of the divine nonbeing. Put more precisely, in the act of creation God revealed God's self as a polarity of being and nonbeing rather than as absolute, unconditional, and necessary being. In our tradition the nature and will of God are disclosed through the divine activity: creation and providence, incarnation and atonement, resurrection, justification and redemption, and so on. In all of these, I suggest, this polarity of being and nonbeing is disclosed. As one moves from one divine activity to the other, however, the relations of being to nonbeing seem to change. The proportion, so to speak, of being is greater in the act of creation, less in the "kenotic" event of incarnation, and least of all in the act of atonement. Correspondingly, as one moves through this series of revelatory actions to their center—incarnation and atonement, where weakness, vulnerability, and even death are paramount—the presence of nonbeing increases in intensity, apparently contradicting (as we have noted) the divine power of being manifest at creation. This apparent contradiction has long baffled church theology: How does God as being share in the weakness and suffering of the Son? If God does not share in this, are these events of redemption—and they are central—then not revelatory of God; and is not the divine redeeming love on which all of Christian faith depends even more intimately related to these acts disclosive of nonbeing than it is to those other divine acts more disclosive of being, such as creation and providential ordering?

I suggest that these fundamental puzzles of Christian theology—and of the texts on which that theology is based—are more appropriately understood if we view the divine mystery as a polarity of being and nonbeing rather than as a mystery of absolute being. A full discussion of the divine nature as manifesting such a polarity, and of the ways this mystery is unveiled in the full scope of divine activity—providence, incarnation, atonement, resurrection, and sanctification—extends far beyond the limits of this chapter. My concluding task is to show that even within the activity of creation, God reveals God's self as a mysterious dialectic or polarity of being and of nonbeing.

As we noted, modern experience and so modern reflection on experience have become more and more aware of the reality and value of the finite, creaturely, and historical realms we humans now inhabit. This is, again as noted, in part due to the Christian heritage. One effect of this increased awareness has been a new appreciation for, even celebration of, change, potentiality, and novelty, on the one hand, and of human autonomy, freedom, and self-direction, on the other. In fact, these two, change and autonomy, represent the foci of modern culture, its fixed points of concern, its lodestars. But as philosophy has always understood, change and autonomy bafflingly represent nonbeing as well as being, a mixture, as Plato put it. As a consequence, in other epochs they were frequently disvalued and even feared. Concentration centered on the "being" aspects of finitude; and, despite incarnation and atonement, theology separated God as radically as it could from these "negative" elements of creaturely existence. Unfortunately, however, the being and the nonbeing aspects of finitude are quite inseparable. Above all, the reality and goodness of creaturely life is as essentially interwoven with these elements of nonbeing as they are with the elements of being. There can be no finitude without nonbeing; finitude as both real and good is a paradoxical union of being and nonbeing, a creaturely polarity of these two apparent opposites.

Nothing is so essentially characteristic of finitude, of the creaturely, as temporality (actually spatio-temporality) and change. Both are also disclosives of nonbeing: Temporality represents the vanishing of the present and of all that inhabits the present; change represents the replacement of what is by what is not, a present actuality by future potentiality. These "negative" aspects of finitude dominated pre-Christian consciousness: Time and change represent continual loss and ultimately signal death. How could they characterize the divine as well, even if God had entered them to share in them and transform them? But these elements of nonbeing also represent the reality and the value of finitude: Temporality is the possibility of the new, of a new birth and a new life, and change can represent growth, growth in grace and wisdom. Being and nonbeing dialectically penetrate one another in temporal and changing finite or creaturely reality: neither can be or have value without the other. The question is, Is this polarity of being and non-being a disclosure of the nature of God?

The same baffling polarity of being and nonbeing characterizes spirit or personhood as this dimension appears in creaturely life. It, too, is character-ized not so much by changeless continuity as by temporality and change, by a continual openness to the new as well as the continuation of character. Above all, each self, to be itself, must achieve distance, relative separation, relative otherness—from its own past, its present self, its community, its world—if it would become a self, knowing itself in its world, constituting and directing itself, and relating freely and intentionally to others. Essential to this process of transcendence of self, community, and world is a continu-ing presence of alternatives, of genuine possibilities, of "not yets" that may nevertheless be. Such real alternatives or possibilities are the necessary condi-tions for authentic decisions, and so for the possibility of self-constitution and self-direction, for the reality and value of the person. Also, the self is hardly a changeless substance, if it would be a self, that is, authentic and autonomous; thus, these possibilities cannot be already actual if they would be genuine possibilities for decision. In sum, nonbeing appears in every crucial interstice of finite being: in temporality and spatiality, in change, self-transcendence, and decisions for the future—precisely at the points where finite being possesses both reality and value. Again arises the question of the relation of God to the nonbeing essential to the reality and goodness of creaturely existence, if God is the sole source and ground of that existence.

We can push this argument one step further, namely, to the implications of the mysterious act of creation itself. God, we say, brings the world into being out of nothing; or more precisely, as Irenaeus and Tertullian put it, God establishes the world in being, positing it into existence, and positing thereby a real, autonomous, and yet dependent "other" than God's self. Creation is not a part of God, *de Deo;* nor is the ground of its reality separated from God, *ex materia.* It is of God and so absolutely dependent; and yet it is also real and self-constituting. This is an almost fiercely paradoxical set of relations. Not only is ex nihilo paradoxical. So are the assertions that follow from ex nihilo: that creatures are dependent and yet real, dependent yet over against, dependent yet autonomously rational and autonomously respon-sible, dependent yet self-constituting and self-directing. All these are equally paradoxical, or at least dialectical or polar, apparent opposites that mutually sustain each other. True creaturely life is neither ruled by an alien sovereign nor is it self-sufficient, *a se;* it is theonomous, constituting itself as spirit yet constituting itself in an Other, as Søren Kierkegaard put it. We are not our own, as Calvin reiterated; yet we must ourselves so choose, if we would be God's. Every generation of theologians has puzzled out these paradoxes and reexpressed them in its own terms.

However we choose to state this central relation established by creation, between the real creature and its Creator, this relation necessitates room of some sort alongside its Creator. The creature is there in and of itself as well as of God. Thus is the absoluteness of the Creator qualified in creation. Creation represents not only the positing of being but the self-negation, the self-limitation, of God in order that authentic, finite being be. God steps back in creation, as Kierkegaard put it. Or, set in terms of our images, creation reveals or discloses a polar aspect of nonbeing as well as being in God, a dialectic of being and nonbeing.

Modern theology since Schleiermacher has, as is well known, had difficulty in distinguishing creation from providence. Although there are interesting and valid reasons for this, I think the distinction is still important and have implied it in this account: Creation concerns the bringing of a dependent yet real, finite existence into being solely by the activity of God. Providence, by contrast, represents the divine relation to the creaturely so constituted, the continuing relations of God to God's creatures as dependent yet real: preserving and ordaining or directing being the main elements of the classical doctrine of providence. This relation, however, as we have noted, is to a self-constituting finitude in passage, a finitude laced with elements of nonbeing as well as being. Again, therefore, the divine creative activity, in preserving and directing such a creaturely world, must make increasing "room" for the aspects of autonomy and possibility, of genuine self-constitution ushering into novelty, in order precisely to create and preserve the creaturely creativity that characterizes the reality and the value of that world. Again, in providence the absolute power of deity is radically limited; the relation of God to possibility as possibility should be asserted and the responsiveness of God to novelty in history acknowledged—all of them polar aspects of nonbeing, of divine self-limitation, balancing the traditional aspects of being, of divine self-assertion.

Both as Creator and as providential Lord of history, God limits God's self in relation to a dependent yet real creation, and that self-limitation is a disclosure of the polar nature of God as a mysterious dialectic of being and of nonbeing. These "negative" elements, moreover, increase in intensity and in significance in the deeper revelation of God through incarnation and atonement; here the contrast to the absolute, changeless, and necessary God becomes itself almost absolute. God "comes" to an alienated and desolate world; God manifests the divine in and through finitude, weakness, vulnerability, and suffering, and God even shares in the final negations of anxiety, lostness, and death, in order precisely to refashion and transform God's creatures to what is neither pure being nor pure nonbeing but the divine unity of both.

CHAPTER 7

THE MEANING OF JESUS
THE CHRIST

The figure of Jesus the Christ is almost perversely enigmatic and many-sided. But then so is the God who presumably sent him and so are the communities or churches who seek to follow him. Amid this variety, how are we to think with any intelligibility of the meaning of any of this? The Christ who represents God, acts for God, is God — this is the divine Christ who for some saves us from hell, for others whose sacred body we share, or who rescues us from the tomb. But he is also the merely human Christ, the master, the way, the ideal, the new authentic possibility, who teaches us wisdom, gives us life's rules, and in our day presents us with our true selves, an open future, and urges us on to liberation from landlords and cartels, from bigots and tyrants, from the oppressive "-ism" on the other side of the world. Alongside the Christ who denies life is he who affirms and celebrates it — and he who (via Norman Vincent Peale and Robert Schuller) shows us how to master it. Is there any thread of unity here? Can these apparently stark antitheses be given enough coherence so that some sort of consistent vision of this figure and his role for Christians is possible? To say that such will be presented here would be wildly presumptuous; everyone, especially every colleague, will disagree with my summation. But still my aim is to be as inclusive of these different emphases as possible and yet to bring them together into a picture that is both faithful to that many-colored tradition and also relevant as a possibility to a contemporary person. I shall not prove this figure; but I will try to make this picture of the Christ relevant for modern commitment and contemplation.

To me the unity amid all of this obvious diversity comes from two inter-related structures or characteristics of Christianity as a religious form of life.

101

One I shall call the dialectic of affirmation, negation, and reaffirmation; the other, the polarity of the sovereign preeminence and the self-giving of God combined with the dependence and yet the autonomy and initiative of human beings. These two, both the dialectic and the polarity (or paradox) have their origins in the Hebrew Scriptures; but, and this is why they are central to us, they receive for Christians their paradigmatic expression, their clear and definitive manifestation, in Jesus the Christ, that is, in Jesus of Nazareth and what he is taken to mean by his community. This dialectic and this polarity represent, it seems to me, both the fundamental structure of the meaning of the Christ and the fundamental structure of the faith that has ensued as a consequence of his life.

THE AFFIRMATION OF THE WORLD

I begin with the first moment of the dialectic: In what way does Jesus the Christ represent the paradigm, the vivid, central, and definitive expression of the affirmation of life, the affirmation of world, history, and human being? Two aspects of the figure of Jesus express this affirmation, one of them appropriately pointing to God's action in him, in his appearance and destiny, and the other, his human grandeur as the model for us of human and of history's possibilities. Let us look at these in turn, beginning with the way Jesus the Christ represents and has represented God's affirmation of the world.

Two of the most familiar, and puzzling to modern people, aspects of the Gospel stories about Jesus are, first, that his coming represents the act of God to save the world and, second, that in fact he who is now born among us helped to create the world. For Christian piety, the appearance of the babe in the manger represents the definitive expression of divine love for the world God has made: "God so loved the world that he gave his only begotten son" (John 3:16). As countless carols sing out, Jesus' birth, his entire coming is received as the primary sign of God's love for God's creation. Correspondingly, Jesus, now the sign and seal of God's love and care, is in turn identified with, in fact, in some strange way identical with, the divine power and wisdom that created the world: "In the beginning was the Word . . . all things were made through him . . . he came unto his own . . . became flesh and dwelt among us" (John 1:1–14). These two stories about Jesus — God the Creator's descent in the appearance of Jesus to save us and Jesus' (the Logos or Son) presence in power in creation — are charming but baffling to modern persons. They can be seen, however, to be myths representing the divine affirmation of the world. God in and through Jesus expresses God's care for the world. The Jesus who calls us to follow him is not an alien or enemy of the world leading us out of it but at one with its own deepest creative forces, and thus with ours, and so in reestablishing our relation to God — this Jesus reestablishes our true relation to the world. Here the divine even "became flesh"—the most worldly of matters—to bring the world back to itself. God does not rescue us from the world but rescues the world and ourselves from what both have made of themselves, from a distortion of their true natures. The initiating aura around Jesus, his preexistence in creation, and the divine meaning and character of his birth thus identify him and the world in which he appeared with the divine creation of all things. At the start, God, the historical figure Jesus, and his world are neither separated nor alienated but precisely united in harmony. No more resounding affirmation of world— matter, space, time, history, society, and persons—could be imagined; Jesus shares the divine creation of the world and so represents the divine affirmation of it. In Jesus the Hebrew theme that God cares for and affirms the world God has created is brought into sharper focus and wider extent: God now loves the world as God had already shown love for Israel.

The second major affirmative theme evident within the figure of Jesus the Christ is not so puzzling to us because it stems from his human excellence— we moderns understand this, even if we do not begin to possess or achieve it. In him what is taken to be the highest human possibility appears in fulfillment, in actuality. What we only might be has in him become, an existence fully like ours but without the distortion, frustration, meaninglessness, hostility, and destructiveness that dominate our own lives and tear us apart from ourselves and from one another. Jesus represents, therefore, *true humanity, essential humanity,* or *authentic humanity.* The conditions of human existence are the same as ours: flesh, temporality, anxiety, loneliness, weakness, dependence—even temptation and fear. But here these conditions do not prevail; that is, they do not distort or warp his possibility of magnificent humanity. He lives fulfilled under the same conditions within which we live so terribly unfulfilled. Thus, he represents not only a final definition of human perfection, although he does—and this is a great deal of his definitive significance because here we see who we really are. But, even further, he represents hope, a real possibility for this life unknown and unrealized by us before. The flesh is weak, to be sure, and life in it is risky; but that weakness and that risk are not lethal, nor is participation in them fatal to excellence. As Jesus shows, life in the flesh, in community, and in history does not hinder salvation but may become itself a means to it. On another level, as a human enterprise, life and its creative possibilities are here deeply affirmed.

This affirmation of life in the world, among men and women, in society and in history, is, moreover, strengthened and deepened by the character of Jesus' excellence: the sort of model of authenticity he represents. His excellence is not that of the controlled and unattached ascetic who withdraws from the relations of the social world in order to relate himself only to himself and to the divine. On the contrary, while clearly his existence is moment by moment rooted in his relatedness to God, this is an authenticity of outgoing love—of caring and concern for all around him, even (or especially) for the least among them, and of active healing and restoration of all the wounded, hurt, dismembered that he met. He was, as Barth rightly emphasized, for others — and not just "as God" but as a human among other men and women. Thus, surprising but by no means contradictory is his teaching that humans should love their neighbors and serve them, and further that the neighbor to be loved includes all whom they encounter, even their enemies who seek to do them in and even the unacceptable whom it is quite normal to shun. Not only did he teach this; he did it in case after case. Thus was the truest love redefined not merely as sympathy or fellow feeling but as *agapē*, love of those apparently unworthy to be loved. As God had first loved us who are unworthy in Christ's "coming," so we are to love others whoever they are. Because of the Christ, a new vision of both God and the human appears: of God as "grace," the fullness of overflowing, unmerited love, and of the human as potentially loving — and therefore also just — to his and her neighbor. Finally, there dawns the notion of society as a kingdom of such love, God's kingdom ruled by this figure representing all three: God, human being, and a fulfilled society. Even though the harmony of these three — God, the human, and the social-historical — did not characterize the world yet, still such harmonious fulfillment was to come in its own time. As far as we can make out, Jesus himself clearly looked forward to the final divine affirmation of this same world in the full appearance at the end of God's love united with God's power.

Jesus thus presents new affirmative possibilities, a new set of ideals, a new future for humankind and the world. This we moderns can well understand, and we tend to see Christianity and him as the teacher of superlative ideals — although his possibilities turn out to be more impossible than we like to think when we say we understand them. Still, two elements remain embedded here in this affirmation that are difficult for modern persons, yet are necessary to the power and effectiveness of Jesus' role. The first is that these ideals represent not only possibilities, but that in him, in a genuinely historical figure, this authenticity or perfection was itself actual, realized, historical. That is, Christianity begins with and is dependent on an actual historical founder, a concrete person, one who really lived in some such way as we have described. Otherwise, faith is merely offering us noble but unrealized ideals: a new vision or a new law that no one has yet fulfilled. The requirement of the historical actuality of Jesus in Christianity runs deep: not only that its Gospels are true in some meaningful sense, or that the crucial events — birth, atonement, and resurrection — happened. Even for those humanistic Christians for whom the ethical possibilities he presents are central, this historical requirement is there: Unless he was actually loving, committed, self-giving, serene, in a word "authentic," all this remains merely a hope, an impossible possibility. Also, if he had not been actual, the important confidence that God loved the world in him would remain merely an idea or a dubious wish. One of the major assets of Christian faith among the religions has been its undeniable affirmation of life, human being, and history, and its confidence in the possibilities for fulfillment, now and in the future, for all, here in history. All of this dissipates if the historical actuality of Jesus dissolves. As Tillich put it, then the New Being has not yet come—and we have an entirely different gospel. How this historical actuality is either established or defended is a complex matter; but its centrality is undoubted.

Much Christianity, especially in its modern forms, views this affirmation of life's possibility, and this presentation of a new vision of authentic humanity, as the essential center of Christianity, as nearly all there is in the Christ for moderns—although this epic is surrounded by stories about God that give it emotive force for us. This view is, I think, questionable. The affirmations of the moral and of human possibility, and the ethic that goes with them, are crucial. But all too frequently those affirmations of universal goodness become incredible in the face of evil outside us; and even more often these new possibilities are frustrated in the face of the evil inside us. Then, as the level of darkness rises, this picture of God's world and of ourselves can become misleading at best—Do not worry, you can do it if only you try—and hypocritical at worst—Evil is unreal, the world is good because God is in it and loves it. Because experienced reality is as complex as this image, we must proceed beyond this first level or moment of affirmation to the next moment of negation.

THE NEGATION OF THE WORLD

As we have seen, Christianity can be interpreted as an essentially optimistic, world-affirming religion, with its founder Jesus the Christ declaring the love and care of the sovereign God, the possibilities of human and social perfection if we adopt God's way of love, and the coming kingdom of God, a transformed social world. Needless to say, it has more than once been interpreted that way, especially in times of waxing cultural growth and especially by the more comfortable classes in such times. Yet Christianity can be and has been interpreted entirely differently; namely, as a world-denying faith, as the negation of ordinary life in the world, and as providing, therefore, few grounds for worldly hope and confidence. Such was certainly the way much of the Renaissance, the Enlightenment, and the nineteenth century (for example, Nietzsche) regarded Christianity when they looked back on the medieval Christian inheritance. Much of the modern world has interpreted classical or orthodox Christianity this way: as radically world denying and so as opposed to modern optimism. Thus, for them the orthodox Jesus Christ appears as one who detested the flesh, who called us to a life of abstinence void of normal relations, who pointed us beyond history to eternity, and, while we yet tarried here, who extolled pain and suffering as more blessed than even the simplest natural pleasures. Whatever one thinks of the macabre excesses of such orthodox interpretations—and they are as much an excessive distortion as is the sunny confidence of Christian liberalism that all is right with God's world—there is no question that the negation of the world is an aspect of Christianity and so an essential element, if only one, of the figure of the Christ.

The story of the Passion—the persecution, trial, condemnation, and death by crucifixion—is there, dominating the recorded narrative of his life as it dominates the extraordinary images of that life in art. Remembering and preaching the cross have been central to the church's word and its sacraments alike and to its music and piety. A refusal to adopt some of the world's dubious ways has characterized most of the vital renewals of Christian history. What, then, is genuine in this negative moment of the dialectic? What is there of world and self-denial, of world and self-condemnation, world and self-transcendence—if not of flight from world and self—available in this figure that is authentic and credible to us? How does the dying figure on the crucifix fit with the loving and loveable master of the Galilean hills? Needless to say, a careful assessment of this negative moment in the dialectic is crucial to any comparison of Jesus' way with that of the Buddha, of Christianity with Buddhism, and of the Christ with the Bodhisattva ideal, for throughout Buddhism very significant negations (of the suffering of the world, of the self, of all attachment, even of the power and reality of the divine itself) surround and so permeate and shape every motion, even that of the Bodhisattva who vows to save the world.

As my remarks have already made clear, the story of Jesus' coming, as well as his own teachings, underlines the desperate need of the world for rescue: The world is darkness (John 1:5); it is perishing in sin and disobedience (Romans 1–3); Jesus could save the world but it would not (Matt. 23:18–19), and so its "house" is desolate. Things are said to be in desperate shape as Jesus appears. Now, it is a mistake to regard this negative assessment of the world—as bathed in error, bound in sin, and desolate, headed for death—as simply the result of the Genesis story of the Fall. Quite the reverse. That story itself was there and respected because it provided an explanation of the experience of otherwise nameless evil, suffering, and death in Israel's life. Correspondingly, the New Testament is suffused with this sense of need, of helpless lostness and yet inescapable responsibility, not because of an authoritative doctrine but because of the character of common human experience, interpreted and rendered meaningful by traditional faith. Such an assessment of experience as estranged and so in desperate need was presupposed in all of Jesus' teachings and was made inescapably vivid by his own capture, persecution, and death. The world was so lost that even he, the ideal and authentic human, was condemned by it! Even more, it was not simply the wicked in the world who did it, which would have made the situation intelligible, but precisely the "good": the scholars, the holy and devout, the respectable, the sacred and noble law (both Jewish and Roman) itself. All that stood for power, life, and value in that world condemned him, named him sin, as Paul says, an outcast hated by God. No wonder, once one recognized and admitted him as authentic, recognized his transcendent virtue and true obedience to God, that in turn the world is now, from top to bottom, itself condemned as lost. The story of the Fall, of a fallen history and a fallen race, was set in the center of Christian interpretation not because of the authority of Genesis or Paul but because their experience of Jesus' rejection and death required that it be set there.

Nothing in contemporary experience seems significantly different from this. Our epoch finds itself surely as much lost in self-love and so apparently bound to self-destruction as that ancient world was. Its "progress" seemingly has only given it renewed power and so added ability to destroy itself more thoroughly. As the bringer of salvation, Jesus presupposes the desperate need of the world and so of all of us in it for rescue, and thus he represents the sharpest sort of negative assessment of our present situation, just as the Buddha's promise of Nirvana, of rescue, presupposes that "all existence is suffering."

Although, as noted, the coming of Jesus the Christ and his frequent words about the world's need represent the negation of the world's ways—in more familiar language, the judgment of God on the world—the cross (that is, his death by crucifixion) both in Scripture and tradition expresses and represents that negation most definitively. The importance of this event for the story and so the meaning of Jesus the Christ cannot, therefore, be overestimated. The Passion represents the climax of each of the Gospels, the inexorable *telos,* as he knew, of his teachings and the life that embodied them; and it represents as well the epicenter, of which the resurrection is the other balancing epicenter, of the apostolic reflection on who he was and what he had done for us as redeemer.

What sort of negative moment, then, is the cross? How does the figure of the dying Christ represent the condemnation of the world? First, the separation of God from the world, the loss of God, the absence of God is here deeply represented: Why hast thou forsaken me? The chosen one of God is starkly abandoned; the presumed purposes of God utterly defeated; the identity of God with creation and the fulfillment of creation is shattered. A world that crucifies Jesus is darker than dark, empty of meaning, suffused with pointlessness and death, and even the disciples flee. God is here effectively dead: on the cross, to be sure; even more in the heavens themselves. No sharper negation of harmony, coherence, meaning, fulfillment, promise or hope could be imagined. The world here is deserted, void of order or significance. We are near to the level of negation represented by "God is dead" or "all existence is suffering."

Just as sharply are human ways, institutions, and character negated. The fickle crowd and the rough soldiers mock him; the distinguished, the respectable, the righteous, his closest friends and his most faithful follower, all pass by on the other side; no good Samaritan appears. The entire race seems here to join not in praising its fulfilled and authentic representative but in seeking to eliminate him. He who was declared sin and so killed in turn here reveals, by becoming their victim, the deep lostness, error, and estrangement of all others; he uncovers or discovers their sin, that is to say, their overriding self-concern and hypocrisy, their defensiveness and consequent cruelty. Ironically the church continued this even in celebrating it. In forgetting Peter's own continuing betrayal, it revered Peter unambiguously, congratulated itself as sanctified by grace, and blamed the Jews, as if the community that followed Jesus itself escaped this condemnation! Jesus the Christ represented in his teachings and his life the love of God for all and the saving grace of God to all; but in his death, which also represents his teachings and his life, he incarnated the deep judgment and condemnation, the "wrath," of God on all who are sinners, that is—as this story makes plain—on all of us.

The whole point of this moment is misunderstood if it is thought that it was the wicked not the good who crucified Jesus. Thus is the normal revealed as in fact abnormal, as deeply askew, the respectable, who see themselves as fully righteous, as dominated or bound by sin. Jesus had said this about respectable people over and over again; and he had called repeatedly for the strange, even abnormal, denial of self, the loss of self, the giving up of place, security, and power if one was to be whole. All this the world, and we, do not do; nor do we have any intention of doing it! Thus did he, who gave up his own self-concern, his own attachment, who did "die to self," in turn have to die. His sharp critique of self-love, of making yourself the center, of taking thought for the morrow is here in the cross intensified: He dies because of the world's self-love. Thus do these two pivotal negative elements of the figure of Jesus the Christ—the requirement of self-giving and the denial of self, on the one hand, and the death on the cross, on the other—coincide to express the negation of the world and of our human being in the world, which out of self-concern eliminates him who comes not only to save us but represents as well our own authentic selfhood. Usually holy figures are at worst ignored; actually most are admired and revered. This one is killed ("his own knew him not"). The negation of ordinary life and its ways is very heavy here. No wonder Christian doctrine has consistently insisted that Christ has revealed to us with a new clarity that "history is fallen." The relevance of this point to the situation of modern men and women seems unquestionable.

One final implication of this negative moment that the tradition has not wished to draw is the presence of negativity within the divine itself. Because of its strong affirmative assertion of the being of God as Creator, as therefore necessary and eternal, omnipotent, giver of life, the church has refused to ascribe any nonbeing, any essential principle of negativity to God. God as being is the opposite of nonbeing, as life is the opposite of death, as necessary and changeless being are the opposite of vulnerability and suffering. Yet the church has also maintained that in Jesus God is fully revealed, and that, as he said and as we have noted, in the death of Jesus the meaning of his messiahship, that is, of his relation to God, whatever that may be, becomes finally plain. This strange incongruity, not to say contradiction, has been questioned in our day: Many have insisted that the divine itself—even the Father, to use the traditional term—participates through the death of Christ in suffering, estrangement, and even in death, in all the signs of nonbeing. In our experience precisely of negation, and in our suffering from it, we encounter there the divine and can thus have hope. Just as at his death the

"Godly" denial of self is manifested by the Christ, so there, too, the nonbeing within God and the divine participation in our own nonbeing reveal themselves. If the cross, as well as the incarnation and resurrection, is a true symbol of the nature of God, the omnipotent power and being of God manifested in creation and redemption must be qualified by and integrated with the nonbeing within God visible in Christ's death. Thus does the dying Christ bring the Christian perspective within range of much that is essential to Buddhism — as in the Mahayana, the paradoxical identity of samsara and Nirvana and the apparently contradictory (to *anatta*) category of "suchness," or the "true self," bring Buddhism close to affirmative aspects of Christianity.

In sum, the negative moment in the figure of the Christ is of the utmost importance. It gives realism and so relevance to the message of the Christ and vast revealing power to his life and death. For our existence, too, seems barren of God, void of hopeful significance, and doomed to common self-destruction. Only a figure that recognizes, deals with, and participates in this reality in our life can aid either our ethical or our contemplative struggle — as it is basic to "doctrine" that only through his death could the Christ save. The death, as noted, negated the teachings of Jesus as simply fulfillable on their own, just as it also validated their negative implications. Now we shall see how the next moment, that of reaffirmation, negates this negation and reestablishes on its new level the initial creative moment.

THE REAFFIRMATION OF THE WORLD

In describing the figure of the Christ as representing first the affirmation of the world and its human possibilities and then as the negation of the world and its inhabitants, we have in each case spoken of God and of human being. This is appropriate since this figure is traditionally taken to be both divine and human, and so to reveal both to us, to show, as Irenaeus (ca. 190 A.D.) said, God to the human in a new light and the human to God in a new light. This polar emphasis — on the divine and the human — continues even more markedly in the culminating moment: the moment of reaffirmation or re-creation, the fulfillment of redemption or salvation as this figure incarnates, represents, and offers salvation to us. As the first polarity of the divine and the human embodied what was the traditional mystery or puzzle of the two natures of Christ, so the present one embodies that other mysterious puzzle of Christian reflection, the paradoxical relation of divine grace and human freedom, for both must be actively present for redemption in Christ to take place. The meaning of salvation is to be understood most helpfully in relation to that from which salvation rescues us, what in effect it conquers or negates. In the Christian tradition, Christ has been experienced as Savior first in rescuing us from our bondage in sin, second in liberating us from domination by fate, and third in bringing us eternal life in his conquest of death. Christ, then, is savior (as opposed to model and judge) as the victor over sin, fate, and death.

In both the Catholic and the Protestant traditions, the central role of Christ as Savior has been in the conquest of sin. Here a theme that appeared early, that of the divine concern for the lowly, the divine love for the unloveable, the divine mercy for the culpable, so prominent in Jesus' teachings and action, reappears in the culminating significance of his death. In this death, so states the gospel, Christ, the innocent, takes on our sin, makes it his own, releases us from it, and so sets us now justified, forgiven, and reestablished back into relation with God, as "children not servants or slaves in the Father's house." What can this strange transaction mean to us? Set in the mythical terms of an exchange through sacrifice, this story is a symbol of the persistent, accepting, reinstating and re-creating power of the divine love, and Christ is the prime if not the only manifestation of that love. In his death we experience ourselves not only as judged and purged but as re-accepted and reinstated, and a new life with God replaces the old life on our own.

This experience has given rise, I should judge, to the strange theory of the transaction. This experience was continued in the life of the community as its living center: in the preaching of the word, in the sacrament of the Eucharist, and in every form of Christian liturgy, prayer, and contemplation. It is called the experience of justification leading to sanctification, of faith in forgiveness leading to the power of a new life. It is the way in which, to use Luther's phrases, Christ is both "for us" in his death and "in us" in our rebirth and subsequent life. It is central to the psychology, the spirituality, and the contemplative implications of Jesus the Christ. Without this dimension of the Christ as Savior, the new possibilities presented by Jesus as model and teacher remain only a new law misleading us to an illusory sense of virtue or condemning us to frustration. But in turn without them—that is, the new possibilities of authenticity defining the new life or, put another way, without Christ as model—this experience of salvation in Christ can become itself abstract, taken for granted, dead, a mere doctrine; and neither salvation nor new life ensues.

Let us note how inextricably the action of God and that of the human—present paradoxically in all ordinary events—are also creatively present in this central Christian experience. We have seen how crucial for the role and meaning of Christ this "divine side" is: the appearance of the love of God into the world to rescue it, the manifestation of the wrath and judgment of God on the world's inordinate self-love in order to awaken its transformation, and finally the revelation of the accepting and renewing grace and mercy of God to reestablish, reempower, and redirect the self in a new life. The Christ event is mainly an event in which God comes to us: as creative love, judgment, and grace. But equally essential to all this are our human desire for rescue, our repentance in the face of God's judgment, and our responses of faith and determined obedience, of our own outgoing love, as we encounter grace. Law and gospel incite our repentance and trust, just as new possibilities and promise encourage, make possible, and guide our free self-direction. We choose and re-create ourselves, as Kierkegaard said, in the light of God's judgment and love in Christ, and we choose our path in the light of the authentic model Christ gives us. Thus he is at once savior and model, redeemer and teacher-guide, "of God" and "of the human."

Christ is not only the savior from sin, however; he has also been celebrated as the liberator from fate, whether the cosmic fates represented by the stars or the more contemporary experience of the historical fatedness of oppressive and unjust institutions, such as slavery and patriarchalism or the crushing fatedness of class and racial tyranny. Cosmic fate seems unreal and irrelevant to moderns, partly because we believe so fervently in progress away from such nightmares of the "childhood" of the race. Have not our knowledge and technical skill freed us from such impotence and a sense of the inexorable determination to suffer? And yet, as the experience of the bomb indicates, scientific knowledge itself can become a threatening fate over which we have no apparent control, not to mention modern historical forms of colonial, capitalistic, and communist determinisms. Whatever we moderns seem to will to do, new dangers of endless suffering and meaningless death seem only to mount. Christ as liberator remains a necessity, one who liberates not *from* history, like most other religious liberators, but *within* history, as the presenter of new possibilities, as a continuing challenge to the injustice of what is, and as the bearer of the promises of God's future, of a kingdom that transcends the unjust and determined present.

Needless to say, this aspect of the figure of Christ, as liberator from fate, is the one to which present liberation theologies have appealed. One thinks of that immensely powerful sculpture of the Brazilian Christ with raised fist smashing the oppressors and persecutors, a union, incidentally, of Christianity and Marxism that would astound conservative Christians. We note again how crucial the human Jesus here is as issuing a call to new possibilities of historical action and being in the world; but equally vital is his representation of God's providential rule over history, a rule that looks to and is sovereign over all of time and so over a new future. Without that faith in cosmic order conquering fate, as a correspondingly Marxist faith in the material dialectic shows, modern persons as well as ancient ones have little heart for historical action.

We come now to the last—in some ways the first or earliest—aspect of the figure of Christ as Savior: as the savior from death, the conqueror of the tomb. Even more than with the other two—the savior from sin and fate—Christ in this role is first of all the resurrected Christ, he who led the way from death to eternal life. For many this is the central meaning of this figure, and frequently—especially in times of cultural breakdown and frustration, as, for example, in the Hellenistic period—this has been received as the greatest gift of God in Christ. As we have seen, however, in the Gospels and tradition alike it is more than balanced by other facets of this multivalent figure. Still, the victory over death remains basic, even for moderns, although one wonders why this need be said. We die as frequently, if not as soon, as the ancients did; and death even for us surprises and truncates life.

If values reside, at least in large part, in life and because of life—in human love and affection, in relations and actions in the world, in prospects for the future—then death represents the negation of value, and final death its final negation. For us moderns, however, life beyond life is apt to seem both incredible and irrelevant, until it comes near us and ours. Life's transcendence of the power of death is central to all continuity and permanence of value and so to all meaning; if all die in the end, time becomes finally a destroyer and space becomes devoid of ultimate meaning. Only God and life in God can provide the reaffirmation embodied in the promise of salvation and so vindicate the other affirmative facets of Christ's work and transvaluate its negative, judgmental facets. Only with the victory over death does the dialectic come to its reaffirmative term. As is evident here as at the beginning, the polarity is qualified. While our participation through faith and obedience of some sort seems essential, still—as the symbol of the resurrection of the body itself has emphasized—all now depends on God to give us each life out of death as all depended in the beginning on God to give us life out of nothing. The ultimate ground for this faith is the known power and love of God revealed in this way in and through Jesus the Christ; but what is revealed to us here is an infinite love that is, so we believe, the basis for God's saving and redeeming relation to all of God's creatures, to all beings everywhere. This is one point of light amid great darkness; a point of light particularly bright and luminous to those of us who are Christians— it is one point, but the light seen there is a universal light, the light of an infinite and universal love.

THE QUESTIONS OF EXCLUSIVENESS

This has been a long story, in part because the figure of Jesus the Christ, as the variety both of Scripture and of church history show, is complex and multifaceted. I have sought to make that variety coherent via a dialectic of affirmation, negation, and reaffirmation and a polarity pointing to a union of both the divine and the human. I have not sought to prove to modern sensibilities the validity of this picture; however, I have tried to make it credible, to present it as a genuine possibility for modern commitment. We have seen Christ as the affirmation of the world and the human: in God's rescuing love, in creation, in the actuality of a concrete life with human possibilities and a promise for the future—the "liberal Christ." We have seen him as the negation of the world's evil ways (and ours); as the uncoverer of the universality and pervasiveness of sin, even among the righteous (even among us): the human victim and sufferer (as we are) from the fallenness of historical life, and so the bearer of the judgment of God on all. Finally, we have seen him as the savior, reaffirming creation, ourselves, and history, the savior from sin, fate, and death. In each, his role as human (as Jesus) is central and necessary; in each, his status or rank as embodiment of the "acts of God" is essential. In order to describe this figure, we have had to rehearse almost the entire spectrum of Christian faith, which is no surprise since he has been and remains its center, shaping everything that is said.

Two modern questions remain, questions illustrated by Buddhist-Christian encounters and the dialogue they assume. They are modern because they have simply not arisen in this form before, and yet they are inescapable for each of us. They are: Is the salvation he brings exclusive, given only to the relatively small company of his followers in history? And, granting he represents a decisive manifestation of the divine power, truth, and grace, is he the only one—are other religions and viewpoints here excluded? These are baffling, paradoxical questions, not easy to answer, especially briefly at the end.

They are paradoxical because any answer seems to contradict itself. Most modern theologians have denied the dual destiny, that some are eternally damned in Christ and only a few saved. This duality seems to many of us to deny precisely what Christ reveals—namely, the universality, width, and openness of the divine love and above all its transcendence over our own errors and sins to redeem the unworthy. Yet we know this about God's love and can hope it for all precisely because we take what Christ reveals to us to be true. Our confidence in the universality of God's love seems dependent on our confidence in Christ as revealing this love, which in its own way represents a paradox. Correspondingly, most of us cannot but recognize the truth and grace—to put it in Christian terms—in other religious traditions and that we can learn from them as they have from us. Thus does Christ, and with him all other "saviors," seem to be relativized, to become merely one among many. But not fully, for this recognition of truth and grace in the tradition of the other does not require the Christian's or the Buddhist's abandonment of his or her religious commitments or perspectives nor the repudiation of its truth. Nor especially does it imply—in fact it denies—the adoption of some nonreligious perspective from which each faith is now viewed and to which all faiths are relative and in fact false. This does not solve but merely shifts the problem. That new humanism in turn becomes its own dogmatic center, and, above all, it is one that grants eternal salvation to no one! Each of us, Christian or Buddhist, believer or unbeliever, cannot escape but has to deal with both the validity and the plurality, both the absoluteness and the relativity of any final position we may hold. Perhaps all we can say is that Christ reveals the mystery of God, a mystery that transcends, though it does not negate, even the clarity and reliability of what is even there manifest. But that sense of the mystery of the divine beyond all we can say or know is hardly as new as it sounds.

CHAPTER 8

HISTORY, PROVIDENCE, AND THE PEOPLE OF GOD

The general theme of this chapter is the relation of the church, the people of God, to history and especially to the trends and so to the general patterns of events of contemporary history and thus to our impinging future. This chapter does not, therefore, let me say at once, propose any complete or full-blown ecclesiology, a doctrine of the church; I shall not concentrate on the church as word and sacrament, on the meaning of grace within the church's life, or the problems of justification and sanctification, of the Christian life or the character of the Christian community. My theme is the church's relation to the world, to the social and historical process in which the church lives, and in which we live, and so the role of the church in the public life of men and women in our social present and future.

I shall begin in this first section, in fact, as theologians should begin in logical dependence, with the Scriptures, with the "biblical view," so far as I can discover it, of God's activity in history in relation to the people of God. I shall then in the second section discuss some of the pressing issues of our historical and political present and our immediate future. In the last section I shall combine the two into a view of the church's role in the events of contemporary history.

PROVIDENCE AND THE PEOPLE OF GOD IN THE OLD TESTAMENT

Anyone who knows me, has read anything I have written, or attends carefully to these words will know at once that I am not a biblical scholar. Still, I can read. In addition, fortunately, there is Gerhard von Rad's great Old Testament theology to be read, and there is the Old Testament itself, which (perhaps appropriately) I reread while traveling across Russia on a train.

The choice of the Old Testament was not accidental. The New Testament is of minimal help with our problem; namely, the relation of God—and so our task as God's people—to the historical and political events of our time, or, put in the language of doctrine, the symbol of God's providential action and our responses to that action. As almost all contemporary New Testament scholars agree, providence—the work of God in nature and especially in historical passage—is of little moment in the New Testament. There the concern is about the eschatological action of God in the events of Jesus Christ's life, death, and resurrection or, alternatively, that future eschatological action promised in and through those events and the work of the Spirit in the community of the church. It is difficult, if not impossible, to develop a view of providence out of the reflections of Bultmann, Kümmel, or even my former colleague Norman Perrin on the writings that make up the New Testament, although one can (I think) find clues to it in some of the sayings, a bit more in Matthew and Luke, and even more in the letters of Paul.

There is no question, however, that the conception of God's action in history—that is, in and through the political events of history, in the rise and fall of history's social institutions—is utterly central to the Old Testament. The main object of witness and reflection in Israel's writings (histories, prophets, and psalms) was God's action in history in that sense, an action in special relation to Israel's founding and life—and possible demise—and thus not explicitly concerned with God's universal action in general history. Nevertheless, that action in relation to Israel presupposed God's "hidden" action in her social and political life and in the groups and nations surrounding her. Such action in and through the social events of history (providence) is the presupposition for the words of promise, judgment, and renewal that dominate Israel's religious life, that provide the clue to her understanding of the events of history in which she participated, and so that shaped her view of herself and her destiny. Because the Old Testament concerns itself with this special relation to Israel *(Heilsgeschichte)*, the Old Testament witness can provide only analogical symbols for our own understanding of our place and role in general history. But because Israel's faith is precisely that a divine plan and sovereignty expressed in promise, judgment, and care lie behind and work in the events of historical life and control them, the Old Testament is (1) the place for us to look; and (2) what we find there functions probably as a presupposition in turn for the eschatological action witnessed to in the New Testament (and is not its antithesis), as the whole Old Testament is a presupposition for the New Testament.

DIVINE CREATIVITY IN HISTORY

How, then, does God act in history according to the Old Testament—that is, in and through history's events in relation to the people of God? We shall find this a dialectical action, a paradoxical one, one with varied aspects both positive and negative. I shall suggest that this double, dialectical action establishes and shapes the unique Hebrew sense of history. I shall discuss what we may call the positive or creative side of this divine action first.

God Establishes and Sustains Israel

God's action in history is clearly constitutive of Israel's existence as a people: of her being as a community, of the norms and standards of her life, of the fundamental symbols with which she understood her task and role in history, and even of her major political institutions. As Israel understood herself, she represented a community called into being, and sustained throughout subsequent events as a people, by the divine election and promise, ratified or embodied in the gifts of the covenant and its law. Subsequently she knew that the judges who early on ruled her and in various ways saved and maintained her existence were established by God's action. Israel also knew, although there were variant traditions here, that through a new significant divine action, the institution of kingship had been established by Yahweh. The structures of Israel's existence as a community and their sustenance were gifts of Yahweh's activity in history. Even in the Old Testament, therefore, social forms have a sacral character, and social tradition is sacred, a possible reference for and meaning of Romans 13:1.

Let us note (as Pannenberg has emphasized) that here the symbol of election, and the providential activity that helps to effect it, do not refer merely to individuals, to their personal, inward faith and their salvation beyond history. Rather they relate to the constitution of social, economic, and political forms and so to the social structures of a people's historical and public existence. Any interpretation of the later category of the kingdom—surely an extension and reinterpretation of this seminal work of Yahweh with God's people—must take account of the social and historical meaning of God's election and action and not privatize, individualize, and "inwardize" that category too much.

God Offers Israel New Possibilities

In the interpretation of the Prophets, especially the later ones, this creative role of Yahweh becomes more complex. Certainly every prophet called Israel back to its sacral origins in Yahweh's founding and sustaining activity, back to the covenant. But, as von Rad emphasizes, the really new note in the prophetic literature was the witness to new acts to come, a new constitution of the people in a new covenant. Israel's betrayal of the sacred gifts of her constitution and life as a people had abrogated these traditions; she could not count on them any longer, she could (and let us note the difference here with later Christian views of election) be rejected. But a new relation, a new creative constitutive act, was coming in the future, and more than anything else it was this of which the great prophets (Jeremiah, Ezekiel, Second Isaiah) spoke.

Here then we have two actions of providence in the constitution of Israel's life and the new possibilities offered to her. Traditional structures, on the one hand, have a sacral origin and role; and new possibilities, on the other, possibilities beyond and even antithetical to these given structures, have a sacral origin and character. Out of the interrelation of these two effects of God's providential work (the nemesis of what had been divinely given in the past [a strange idea!] and the promise of future divine possibility), the Hebrew sense of history arose and not out of either past covenant or future eschatology alone. Moreover, as von Rad suggests, the unique prophetic sense of individuality arose from the same dialectical relation of old and of new in concrete history—two important aspects of the modern historical consciousness that (ironically) arose against this symbol of providence.

God here institutes the new in history and thus constitutes social existence in new forms, the conditions of social existence. God is thus the ground for the sacred that is old, for tradition—in social and political, as in religious, life—and the sacred that is new. The issue of understanding the relation of these two (the sacred that is old and the sacred that is new) is the prime issue of understanding both history and politics and so of understanding our task in each situation. In any case, God has here, as God's creative work in history, a constitutive, cultural, and renewing role, a role constitutive of our given tradition, our present freedom, and of new possibilities. The forms of our social existence have a sacral character; social life is not possible or meaningful without them. Yet the new forms are also sacral, a demand on us and the basis of our confidence and hope.

DIVINE JUDGMENT IN HISTORY

But history, as we have already noted, is also seen as deeply estranged in the Old Testament. Almost from beginning to end, it is the story not only of the divine creative and sustaining action but also of Israel's continuing betrayal of the covenant and her relation to Yahweh. Thus, another aspect of Yahweh's activity in history appears: that of judgment, an "alien" work of God that leads to destruction and ultimately to nemesis, to tearing down the very structure of social systems that Yahweh and Israel had together built. There was hardly a historical moment when Israel, her leaders, or her people did not "do what was wrong in the eyes of Yahweh" and so when divine judgment was not experienced or expected. The Old Testament is imbued with the consciousness of the estrangement of human freedom, of a freedom *within* the sacral covenant (an interesting point for the church to remember). It is also suffused with the conviction of the historically self-destructive character of that distorted freedom and of the nemesis of history's creativity that it effects.

This is also characteristic of our present experience of history, as I shall repeatedly note, not the least of America's present experience and that too of the church. Both, church and America, manifest divine gifts of new possibility and, in the case of America, creative social and political forms, technology, and so immense proficiency. Yet each one also manifests a strange estrangement of that freedom and those creative possibilities that seems to be able to lead to destruction, loss, tearing down, and, possibly, to a new world beyond ourselves.

There are two further points to the Old Testament view of evil or estrangement that are important for our understanding of both the divine judgment and the character and effects of sin in history.

The Social Fate of Estrangement

According to von Rad, the "early view of sin" insists on a social "fate," a series of evil social consequences following almost by necessity from the sinful deed, consequences that are mortally dangerous not only to the doer but also to the community. Most liberal commentators regarded this view of evil as primitive. It seems to me, on the contrary, to be empirically obvious and very important: Sins do have social consequences and for our children and their children.

At the beginning such evil consequences could be prevented, it was believed, by Yahweh; the community could be rescued by the right kind of expiatory deed. We may note here that only later was Yahweh seen as the agent of the consequences. As the sense of moral offense against Yahweh in any act of sin increased, Yahweh's role changed. To the prophets and the histories written from their perspective, Yahweh was the agent of retribution. God, says Hosea, is the raging lion that we will meet. With the later prophets the sense of sin is so great that even the sacred tradition that Yahweh has constituted must be torn down. All in the community will suffer (Isaiah 24:1-3); Israel's institutions will be laid waste, and the people will be, so to speak, unconstituted. In Isaiah 34 and Jeremiah 4 the divine judgment represents a return even to primal chaos, an undoing of God's originating—as well as God's historical—creative work. Surely this sort of deep nemesis of society and culture, of a social dwelling place for humans, is frequently experienced as well in our history as a culture and so all "creation" seems to disintegrate; and universal suffering, not-at-homeness, and desolation characterize all of experienced reality.

In understanding our contemporary task, it is important to ponder carefully this biblical emphasis on the social consequences of sin, the "fate" that sin in a community has for the community, for the children and descendants, and to seek to understand it in terms congruent with our own modern consciousness of history. We experience this fate or fatedness, too. This fatedness comes to us through the warped, oppressive social institutions initially established by human creativity and divine constitution—family, economic and political structures, relations of communities. These warped social institutions stifle the freedom of people caught within them; they must be dealt with politically, by political liberation. Without this they create universal nemesis. The concept of fate following out of sin clearly implies this, as does the prophetic word of divine judgment on the injustice of Israel's life.

The Judgment of the Powerful

In the Old Testament view of sin, the mighty in particular are brought under judgment, and, as noted, the sins of the mighty have cataclysmic consequences for all people. There is a special biblical distrust, one may say, of achieved power, whatever form that power may take: political power, the power of wisdom, or the power of virtue. This theme is obviously continued in the Magnificat and, one may suggest, emblazoned in the cross, where it is the powerful, the good, and the religious who crucify Jesus and where, therefore, powerlessness alone represents the divine incarnated in history. One thinks of Isaiah's prophecy of doom for all that is "high and lofty" (Isa. 2:11–13) and Ezekiel's condemnation on all who "seek to think the thoughts of God," who are "blameless," who have "beauty and wisdom" (Ezek. 28:6–19).

The point of this special critique on the mighty, as Reinhold Niebuhr wisely saw, relates to the social and communal consequences referred to earlier. The mighty are not said to be more sinful than others. Nevertheless, their position and power make their sins more effective. This greater effect or consequence of their sin is not only manifested directly on those under their power; it also has an indirect and so wider effect because it is they who establish the forms of society, in large part for their own interests and therefore reflecting those interests. It is they who establish its norms and principles. Their decisions, whether right or wrong, affect multitudes. Their responsibilities for suffering, for the evil social consequences of our common sin, are thus greater, and so a more severe judgment is theirs.

A biblical interpretation of God's action in history thus does not, as much radical social thought does, accuse the mighty alone of sin. It recognizes the sinful propensities of weak and powerful alike, of oppressed along with their oppressors. Nevertheless, it directs a particular word of warning and judgment on the mighty, the wise, the good, and even the holy for their sins: Because their privileges, power, and security are greater, the consequences of their betrayal are greater and so their responsibility and guilt for suffering are greater. It is well for an affluent and powerful nation to remember this biblical word — and this meaning of providence. It is well for a comfortable middle-class church to remember it, too.

The Old Testament histories and the prophetic interpretation present us with dramatic irony. First, Israel experiences divine election and gift, promise and covenant, the constitution, sustenance, and protection of their social being, interpreted and reinterpreted according to new possibilities creative of Israel's life. Then rebellion, rejection, and betrayal are followed by destruction and catastrophe or nemesis. But then (the continuing surprise) is offered the promise of a new act to come, a gift of new possibilities from the divine creativity. This cycle of creative gift, destruction, and new gift or new possibility is not a necessitating cycle: Israel can always repent, and there is, even more, the assurance of new mercy and new gifts to come.

Let me say that this strange, convulsive, dramatic, cataclysmic view of history as interlaced with meaning and mystery, meaning and meaninglessness, creativity and tragedy, hope and hopelessness is true also of our experience of history, especially American experience. We, too, have felt our history and its characteristics as gift, new possibility, creativity, sustenance, and protection; and now we are vividly aware of it as characterized as well by warping and the possibility of self-destruction. Perhaps, however, the main message for us, besides the judgment on the mighty and the affluent, is that in a situation of apparently inevitable destruction, new social and historical possibilities are there, a new synthesis of old and new is possible, a new covenant. To believe in divine providence is to expect such a *kairos,* such a new creative possibility even in the most desperate of historical situations, even in a situation of apparent nemesis. We in America never thought this sort of faith arising in the valley of the shadow of despair would be necessary. Perhaps it will be and is what we should now preach. What that possibility, that *kairos,* is depends on the situation, as was clear in Israel's history. It may be the preservation of the structures and norms of the community as given to us in our tradition; it may be the refashioning of that tradition into new forms; it may be the overthrow of a hardened and oppressive tradition—all these alternatives have biblical warrants. One crucial task of theology and proclamation is, thus, to discern the signs of the times, to be "without the law" in this sense, to enact the prophetic role: to see what it is that the Lord's creative and judging action in history requires of us now.

There is one final implication of this account of God's action in history, of providence as seen in the New Testament: Providence—even as gift, constitution, sustenance, judgment, and then new possibility—is not enough. It represents neither the whole of the divine action nor even its culmination. History is ambiguous in spite of, really because of, its creativity, through both its sacral traditions and its new possibilities, as our own history shows. There are thus two levels to the problems of historical life and so two levels to the divine activity and to the church's task.

As we have seen, in the Old Testament view sin has its social consequences. Put in terms of our modern understanding, as a result of our greed and self-concern, oppressive institutions are created that exploit and oppress people in this and in the next generation. Each age bequeaths a social situation of unjust institutions that are unbearable to their children and to the children of others, a kind of "fate" that can oppress and stifle the freedom of multitudes there. With this, the inheritance of oppressive institutions, political activity is necessary to enact the new sacral possibilities that providence gives to us. A new social covenant, according to the Old Testament model, is always a possibility and a demand in history. This is most important for us to realize. The church must support the new social possibilities that lie before us. To deal with the fate of oppressive social institutions is the task of political activity — and it is essential for the divine providence in history.

But, and this is my main point in concluding this section, because inward sin — that is, the betrayal of the covenant, the break in the relation of the self and the community to God, and so its resulting injustice — forms the main problem for the Old Testament, new social possibilities and even new institutions, however important, are not enough. Sin continues even in the midst of these new possibilities. Thus, as the culmination of the biblical view of history, an inward redemptive divine activity supplements God's providential and judgmental action. This is a universal divine activity — as is providence — appearing throughout the religious and cultural life of men and women. But for Christians its center and testament, its criterion and sure sign appear in the new covenant in Jesus the Christ and in the church.

As I shall argue repeatedly, these two aspects form one history: the inner life of men and women in its creativity and sin, and the outer public life of events and continuing social institutions. The two main characteristics of history, its creativity and its nemesis, arise from the inner — from creative new projects and from sin. In turn, the character of our inner life — our anxieties, temptations, and calling to service — is shaped and determined by the outer public life we lead in community. Insofar as the consequences of past sin are a fate for others, creating warped and destructive social institutions, the Christian task is political, and liberation is its genuine biblical goal. Insofar, however, as the fundamental problem is inward, the relation of the self to self, of self to others and to the divine, political liberation is not the final solution to the problem of history. Redemptive forces acting on the universal life of men and women are also necessary, and this is the main concern of the work of Christ and of the witness to him in the New Testament: the role of word, sacrament, and Spirit in the community of the church. But also insofar as inward affects outward and is in turn reflected back in inward suffering, loss of dignity, and humanity in fatedness, the call to eradicate the social forms of fatedness is absolute.

The redemptive forces are universal as God's action in history is universal; but they are centered and manifested in the covenant and in the Christ. The task of the people of God, whose mission is established there, involves these two roles: the conquest of fate through political liberation and of sin through grace, and thus the spreading of these redemptive forces to all. The church is for history, not history for the church. As the promise of the Old Testament makes plain, the goal of the church is that all nations may be brought to human fulfillment, through liberation and grace. Thus, the Kingdom is the goal alike of political acts of liberation and of the witness to grace. The Kingdom represents as a symbol the new and redeemed form of social existence of God's community and people, established by a new inwardness in relation to God and characterized by a new social covenant and so by new social institutions. Only thus can God, who rules both history and the human heart, find fulfillment in the divine Kingdom.

PRESENT CRISIS, DEMAND, AND PROMISE

We live in a time of vast change, a kind of rupture in history. Matthew Arnold's words are even more true of our era and its future than of his own: "One world is dying, another is struggling to be born." Change is all around us and in us.

Change is an old theme in modern life. It was a pervasive consciousness in the Renaissance, and it became explicit in theories of development and progress in the Enlightenment and the nineteenth century. It has also been an intrinsic part of the American experience. But, if I may put it so, our present experience of change, or of impending radical change, is a changed, a new experience of change — and of great theological relevance. We experience change as potential menace, as a threat to our ways of life and their ideals; we experience the future as radically uncertain and the new as perhaps the utterly unwanted. As Robert Heilbroner says in his grim little book, "I assume that the reader shares with me the awareness of an oppressive anticipation of the future."[1]

This sense of a potentially oppressive, menacing future is new to our culture and recent theology. Liberalism encouraged and welcomed change as bringing in a brighter day, closer to the Kingdom. Neoorthodoxy recognized change, denied the progress, and sought to opt out from it in inward existence and the covenant community, but to my knowledge never conceived of the future as more menacing than the past or sought to deal with that problem theologically. Of course the recent eschatological and liberationist theologies have looked forward in hope to the future as God's realm where the divine will, the divine intentions, and so the divine being in all its glory will be manifested within history. Thus, I am not sure how relevant any of our contemporary theological options are to what appears to be our actual historical situation and its real possibilities.

However new and uncomfortable this situation is to theology (or to the academy) — a *novum* we don't quite like! — it is surely true that theology cannot avoid it, nor can preaching and meditation evade it. Social changes and the historical events that accompany, divert, direct, or encourage those changes form together our world, the world in which each of us as persons comes to be and exists. This social situation constitutes in large part the mode of our personal, ethical, and religious existence. Our deepest anxieties arise out of our historical situation; our most lethal temptations to sin come to being there. Correspondingly, from our historical situation and its changing face comes the clear call to our creative action, for our courage, serenity, and the capacity to sacrifice and love. We *are* as personal, ethical, and religious beings *in* our historical situation. This is the deepest meaning of our historicity. We exist, as afraid or courageous, and we decide and choose in our changing history, in the face of our common future. No separation of

---

[1] Robert Heilbroner, *An Inquiry into the Human Prospect* (New York: W. W. Norton, 1974).

personal, existential, inward existence and the process of social and historical change is possible. Individual and community, person and society, soul and history dance together down the corridors of time.

Thus, historical change and the common social future that impinges on us pose religious as well as political and economic issues for us. The historical situation shapes in part the way we *are,* our anxieties and courage; in turn, the way we are will shape through our response the future we bequeath. Religion must speak to and of the facts of our historical situation and the direction of social change or be irrelevant to our personal existence. At times the couch and even the temple are swept away in social flood, and even meditation may be interrupted. This is crystal clear in the Old Testament, where historical events shape directly Israel's religious existence and in turn are themselves determined by Israel's relation to Yahweh. This is in large part what we mean, or should mean, by calling Christianity a historical religion.

History has both an outer and an inner side, both objective social changes and human responses, both, so to speak, sociology and politics. Thus, changes are prepared subjectively, inside humans in their anger and frustration, their interpretations and judgments, their longings and hopes, all together leading finally to determined action, to a reshaping of all that is. Changes are also prepared objectively in trends in our world. Usually both go together to create historical transformation, though not necessarily so.

SUBJECTIVE CONDITIONS FOR CHANGE

Only two decades ago in this country, we were more vividly aware of the internal, subjective conditions of change than we are now. Vast numbers of our youths longed for change, for a new day in time and a new, withdrawn space in which to live. They felt deeply an alienation from what was around them, from the present culture of their fathers and mothers and sought to change or leave it. Lest any of us think this all has passed, we should now speak to anyone in an oppressed group in this country—the poor, blacks, women—or to anyone from the Third World. There the subjective conditions for radical change, for the transformation if not the overthrow of the dominant structures of our social present, burn like fire and can at a signal ignite our history. Change is in part the result of political decisions, of freedom as well as destiny in history, and the conditions for it are omnipresent elsewhere in our world.

But radical change is not wholly dependent on these subjective conditions. The reality of change is not merely a matter of what we think, talk about, or even want. I can imagine that as one reaction to the appearance of the last Ice Age, men and women stopped talking about the weather! Change also has objective roots in the destiny of the present, in the shape of its dominant trends. It is these as well that we must look at and ponder theologically.

OBJECTIVE CONDITIONS FOR CHANGE

There are, I believe, four areas of major change in our present, trends that portend a new sort of world for us all within the proximate if not immediate future. Because this world, I believe, will be new, it has vast possibilities of promise, of new justice and liberation. But it is also a world that has possibilities of menace. The latter, as it slowly develops, may well feed our anxieties and tempt us deeply; but it may call forth our confidence, serenity, trust, and virtue. It is here that our "ultimate concerns" will make their appearance, take their shape, and so form our existence for good or ill. There is a sociology of feeling or of awareness about history as well as a sociology of knowing within history. To those on top, who are secure and privileged, change or the threat of change always means anxiety. It means fear, and it may result in panic. To those on the bottom, who suffer from the structures of the present, the possibility of change means hope, the promise of new fulfillment.

Technological-Industrial Society

The first area of change concerns the steady development of a technological, industrial society. This development has been the result of human creativity, intelligence, and freedom; but, strangely, once it has embarked on its career it seems to have a life of its own, to force continually deep changes in both personal and communal existence, and in the end possibly to threaten the very freedom that has created it. At first—with Francis Bacon, the early scientists, and with the beginnings of technology—technological development provided the great ground for hope in the future, and until very recently most modern utopias were based on the notion of a technological paradise from which all these forces that oppressed and determined human life would be banished. This optimism was not all wrong. New technological developments do bear the promise of more comfort and security, and they are unquestionably necessary for our common survival. But now technology and the society it spawns wear different faces. With all its promise for more food, comfort, goods, and services, a technological culture seems to bring about a deterioration of the quality of life and to threaten what is human about us.

Our environment becomes more and more overlaid with rows of similar homes, Dairy Dips, shopping centers, factories. To care for humans, we seem to dehumanize everything into an endless series of meaningless developments. But inside the home, we say, there is humanity, freedom, creativity—a human world. Inside there is the television set, and often merely consumption—a passive way of being human. Things satisfy our needs but not us; consumption is a condition for being human, not its secret. A technological, goods culture both forgets this truth and establishes it empirically! Inside there is also emptiness; a loss of self appears in our dehumanized world.

Furthermore, in our public life of work and of community, we find ourselves parts of ever-larger and more rationally organized systems: of commerce, industry, academy, government, even of church. Correspondingly, people become parts whose individuality, originality, conscience, and taste can, if fully expressed, only impede the smooth running of the organization and so who must "cooperate" or cease to participate. The danger of technology is not that we become slaves to machines but parts of a machine, of value only if we keep the system going smoothly. Again aspects of our essential humanity are threatened: our individual conscience and judgment, the quirks that make us who we are, in ideas, capacities, and style. In feeding and clothing men and women, technological culture cries out for defense of the very humanity it supports. All of this is felt deeply in our culture, in its lostness, its suppressed anger, its hunger for meaning, community, and inwardness. Western women and men have learned to manipulate the world, but they have lost their sense of the reality of their own inwardness, and even of their own bodies. And, ironically, it has in many cases taken Eastern religions to help rescue us historically here. This problem will increase; and every aspect of our tradition must be retrieved, treasured, and brought to bear personally, socially, and politically in order to preserve the inward, the personal, the original, and the unique about humans in a technological culture—else we will be in history lost.

Economic and Social Life

The results of technology and industrialism on the structures of our society have been drastic. As Marx would put it, changes in the means of production have effected changes in the relations of production: in patterns of work, community, of the distribution of goods, of the relations between people. Our cities have grown and grown—and deteriorated into jungles of violence. Our standards of living have risen—but so has the proletariat and the ghetto. Goods are plentiful—but so is poverty. As we have produced, so inexorably we seem to pollute as well. As the quality of our world and our humanity seem threatened by what we once took to be progress, so the "development" of our economic and social life seems to breed as many social problems as it solves. Instead of resolving our dilemmas, our growth seems to exacerbate them.

These new crises arising unexpectedly and suddenly—consider how recent is the radical deterioration of the American city and the massive pollution of the environment—demand new solutions. The older resolutions of more expansion and development have caused the problems. New approaches, economic, social, and political, are therefore required, else both cities and nature, and much of the population, die. But new answers, if they are really new, require new ventures in planning, corporate solutions, shared responsibilities, and shared rewards. We need to speak again and in new ways of the common good, not just the individual good. These new ventures in turn require new conceptions of society, of its economic order, property rights, priorities, and responsibilities. There is to me no question that a technological society, grounded in increasingly communal participation and communal work, representing an increasingly organized and interlocking system of work and distribution, requires more corporate, communal, "socialist" approaches to our common life. As each of us is more and more a part of a community of labor, so our responsibilities and rewards should be communal. Only then can a technological society avoid an increasing maldistribution of power, reward, and standard of life.

All of this — although obviously true — runs into many of our historically treasured social symbols: self-made persons, the rights of individual work, the rights of property — in sum, the "right" to individual and personal well-being in a sea of poverty and want. New responses to new problems are not so easy, since they are not merely a matter of rational or even of pragmatic policy. They require also that we reconstruct in effect our social world and so many of our most fundamental values and convictions. This is difficult and also very frightening, and thus it meets radical political resistance. If a society is constituted by its symbolic structure, the security and meaning of life within that society is likewise there constituted. To change radically that structure, therefore, is both to threaten to dismantle that society and to render insecure the basis of major groups, particularly affluent, ruling groups, within that society. Many of the anxieties about the future among an established American middle class stem from a deep fear not only of change in habits and standards of living; but it stems even more from a fear of the irrelevance of the familiar world of American social ideas and values and its replacement by an utterly alien world of values.

Social change — a necessity if we are to survive — betokens promise to those who suffer in a given society. But it spells anxiety for those who are established. The possibilities of such a situation are explosive: the possibility of violent upheaval or of oppressive reaction. Only confidence on the part of the oppressed that they can initiate change, and courage and serenity on the part of the established that they will accept change, can save us. We must initiate changes if we are to respond to changes we cannot prevent. For American middle classes, maintaining courage and serenity in the face of such changes will be a difficult spiritual achievement. Serenity and objectivity are difficult in the face of social changes that may lessen our own security. Most of our church people will experience diminished social position and power. The achievement of a deeper confidence in history is utterly necessary if a time of great social change is not to be a time of violence, oppression, human tragedy, and grave sin. Social change forces upon an affluent American middle class issues of justice and injustice, choices of personal well-being or corporate sharing, choices of private versus common good. If we make idols of our own affluence and the symbols that support it, our future will be oppressive and violent. This is a moral and ultimately a religious issue that a changing history sets before us. It is again the issue of the relation of the sacred that is old, but now possibly demonic, in relation to the sacred that is new and demanded of us for justice.

Loss of Western Power and Dominance

Looking abroad, we find even more crucial issues for us appearing on the horizon of our future. These portents are again filled with promise and possibility but also menace and the temptation to grave sin. What is portended in this case is the West's and thus America's loss of relative power and dominance in the world. This process is well underway, but it is bound to proceed much further in the next decades. How far it proceeds and what shape it will take in, say, twenty or thirty years will depend greatly on, among other things, how we respond to this process. A communal response to the loss of relative power is a tricky, demanding, and explosive enterprise fraught with the greatest of temptations.

For roughly two hundred years, the West has dominated the entire world. Where it wished to dominate and rule, it did; what territories and resources it coveted, it took; what governments defied its will, it upset and replaced. When it so willed, the West could determine events to its liking, form the kinds of peace it wished, and establish orders favorable to its own norms and desires. The world was dominated by the Western powers and thus by Western symbols and norms. These powers, to be sure, fought against each other. Nevertheless, no alien power representing an alien culture has appeared as a fundamental threat to their world since 1456, when the Turks threatened Vienna. No wonder the European intelligentsia decided that history was "progress."

This dominance lasted through World War I for Europe, since then briefly for an America that inherited this role. It is fast slipping away. For example, of the four present major powers, none is European and only one is Western. Two of them—Russia and China—represent styles of life, norms, and goals diverse from, if not antithetical to, the bourgeois, liberal European culture of the eighteenth and nineteenth centuries and so to us. Few in the Third World, except petty tyrants whose remaining power we hope is short, remain "vassals" to our will or even half-hearted adherents to our symbols. Increasingly the members of that world will represent other interests, other styles, other goals than ours, and their voice will be continually stronger. The future marks surely this loss of Western and American dominance and values. It will be a strange world for us in which our way of life will not be the standard for all. It may in fact be that in the end our civilization and its values will be isolated, disliked, detested, dependent in part, I would suggest, on how we respond to this challenge.

The temptations will be vast indeed. In this sense of impending loss of control over one's own destiny and security will lurk the temptation to seek through one's remaining power to stave off that loss: to unseat governments unsympathetic to us, to prevent the rise of new orders, to support tyrants who will lick our corporate boots. I need not point to our sorry track record on this matter in Vietnam, Chile, Greece, and now in Africa—and I do not yet know that we see the point. We can lose influence, isolate ourselves, divest ourselves of power—because we thus betray and so weaken our own powerful symbols and stance — if we wish by these methods. In the end we can help to pull down around us the whole noble house of our tradition and the shaky peace of the world, leaving to that tradition only the tarnished symbolic structure supporting the remaining tyrants of the world. This is a fate the revolutionary founders of 1776 — whose words and hopes rang round the world of their time to better the world — would hardly credit or applaud.

Let us recall that like language itself the meaning of sacral symbols is in their use. If they are used to free the oppressed, they will — as ours once did — ring around the world as powerful and creative symbols for all. If they are used to support privilege, they will die with these forms of privilege.

Again these are political and economic issues, but ones fraught with moral and religious content, with temptations to national pride and idolatry, to the sin that follows from anxiety about one's own strength and prestige, to possibilities of dominance, exploitation, and tyranny, to the rise of aggression and conquest and infinite cruelty. America — and the whole West — will be tempted by precisely these changes that open up genuinely new possibilities for other peoples. Our spiritual strength, religious convictions and integrity, courage and serenity, and capacity for justice will be determined here, in this arena. The meaning or the meaninglessness of our social and theological symbols will here be tested, established, and enacted. History and religion are correlated, intertwined, because our existence and our tasks are historical.

The Ecological Crisis

There is a fourth area of change, the deepest and most serious of the crises, where we and all those with affluence and power will be spiritually tested as none have before in history. I refer to the ecological crisis in its broadest extent; namely, the all-too-probable collision course between expanding population and expanding industrial production, on the one hand, and the depletion of the resources of the earth and the thermal limit on energy usage, on the other. This is a complex issue. Nevertheless, it can be said simply that we cannot keep increasing production at the present rate, and yet seemingly we must do so if an expanding population is to be fed and standards of living around the globe are to continue to rise. (Those standards of living must continue to rise if social peace is to be maintained in the capitalistic, the communistic, or the Third world.) The result of the first imperative to conserve resources is that almost certainly rates of production will have to taper off. Thus affluence in the developed nations in turn must decrease, preventing our available resources from being quickly and completely depleted. The world to come will be a world more crowded, less affluent, more frugal at best for us all.

The second imperative — that rising standards are a condition of well-being and social peace — means that if the social results of such relative scarcity are not dealt with, it will be a world of increasing poverty and despair and so of social tension, rivalry for goods, and unbearably authoritarian governments. Probably our present affluence and liberties will seem in fifty years aspects of a paradisiacal time. It is not a pleasant prospect that science and the social sciences together picture for us. Its first effects are already appearing in the energy problem, the mounting food crisis, and runaway inflations.

In such a developing situation, the temptations for those with power and affluence will be enormous. Can any politician, whatever the relevant system of political rule, promise a decrease in standards of living for her or his people and long survive? Yet if we do not control ourselves, we will be driven to grab resources that become short and to strip nature ever more ruthlessly. The gravest danger is a concerted effort on the part of the great powers—an ironical result of détente—together to corner for a time the world's remaining resources and so to retain for a fleeting moment their present standards by imposing their will and so their tyranny on the rest of the world. To muster the self-control requisite for a just distribution of depleted or depleting supplies will take great virtue, as on a raft or in an internment camp when the supplies run short. Human nature does not suddenly become more selfish under such stress; but, by the same token, it surely does not become more virtuous. With increased anxiety comes greater temptation, and so we all, almost against our will, find ourselves acting out a self-concern relatively invisible amid security. Here is a stark moral and religious challenge to the churches of the affluent world.

To establish in all of us (in preparation for this new, probably unaffluent world) a sense of meaning in life not based on material goods, and so to bring to prominence criteria of concern for community, justice, sharing with others, there appear other vast spiritual challenges. To foster respect for humanity and personal freedom in a world that almost certainly will come under increasingly centralized, possibly authoritarian control—for without new forms of authority no response to this crisis of redistribution will be possible—is another spiritual and religious task. The challenges of the future are such that without confidence, serenity, and courage, without justice and compassion, without responsibility and community we and our race may well be lost in violence, tyranny, hunger, and death. It is almost as if the day of judgment—a kind of "social moment of truth"—not a technological utopia, were coming with the future that is rushing at us. Religion and religious faith must be historical if we are to survive. Mere practical intelligence and objective technological know-how have together almost killed us. Ironically, they are apparently liabilities not assets in the race's survival. What a calling lies before us!

It is in the process of historical change and our march into our common but unknown future that issues of ultimate concern are raised, questions of our being and nonbeing are posed, temptations to sin appear, and the call for courage, love, and justice is heard. Here, in history, in community, it is that we exist, that is, decide and become what we are, as persons, and incarnate our faith or betray it. The present shape of social change, history in that sense, is not at all irrelevant to gospel or faith, church or theology. It sets the "world," the situation within which each of these (faith, gospel, theology, and church) come to life or die, take on meaning or fade away in meaninglessness. Social praxis is where historical destiny calls forth, where church and theology *become,* become real, redemptive, and effective. God's word becomes incarnate in our world through our social praxis in the present and for the future of that social world. History is the outcome of the polarity of destiny and freedom, of situations and conditions, on the one hand, and of our responses to them, on the other.

I have in broad outline attempted to give the probable situation or destiny that future days will present to us and to our children. Our and their responses will make all the difference. These responses reach for their own conditions inward into our commitments, values, norms, and hopes; and, if religious faith has any relevance at all, these latter in turn are formed, strengthened, and refined by preaching and theology. Our role is plain in a changing world.

It is here, finally, that we see one role of theology, of theology of history, in the human future. To be in history, I have said, is at once to be immersed in its pervasive stresses and changes, to be and to become oneself in that process. Yet to be humanly in history is also to transcend that process so as to respond to it, to direct and divert it. History is an overwhelming fate for those who do not seek so to understand and to deal with it. This transcendence is necessary for response, judgment, decision, and action, for politics. Such transcendence requires awareness, "political consciousness" as Marxism puts it, the consciousness of trends in the past and the present, of dislocations, injustice, and suffering in the present, and consciousness of threats and possibilities and their demands in the future. Thus are we led inevitably in our historical existence to conceive symbolically the structure and the dynamic factors of the history in which we swim, to set that structure into dominant and meaningful symbols, to create a philosophy or to acknowledge a theology of history on which our judgments, confidence, and hopes may be based and through which our lethal anxieties may be conquered and overcome. To be human in history is in part to transcend history so as to be in relation to the total horizon of history, to its dynamic structures and operative factors, to its promises and threats, and its ultimate norm and final goal.

The relevance of the Old Testament view of history under the divine providence and of the "calling" of the people of God, both of which we traced in the first section, are obvious when one surveys our world. The modern situation — of technological development, social change, changes in the balance of power, and the issue of our relation to nature and her resources — bears promise but also menace within itself. Thus, the modern situation, born out of scientific, technological, and industrial developments, has not made religious faith, commitment, and existence nor a deeper understanding of history and its grounds of confidence irrelevant. These developments have made each more necessary to our life than ever. In the following section, I shall essay, however inadequately, to draw these two discussions together and so attempt to conceive the role of the people of God as it responds or may respond to the divine providence in relation to this situation.

THE CHURCH'S ROLE IN A CHANGING WORLD

Two major conclusions have come out of the preceding discussions, besides the feeling that we are living in an explosive age. Let us draw them together in order to discuss the role of the church in such a world.

THE CHURCH'S TASK: MINISTRY OF GRACE AND LIBERATION

The first issue was to specify as clearly as possible the intimate and essential interrelation of inward, private, "existential" human existence — our "historicity" — to the social history in which we are immersed. The situation of our souls, to use the older term, is correlated with the kingdoms of this world and their dramatic changes. We saw that within human inwardness in its estrangement and sin, the most fundamental problems of social history gestated and arose. The objective "fate" that is experienced in social situations — oppressive institutions, wars, injustice, exploitation of people and the earth, radical inequality of power and distribution, and so on — is, we noted, ultimately the result of the self-concern of dominant and affluent groups that shape institutions and events in favor of their own interests. Inward sin is the fundamental cause of the fatedness, the lack of liberation, freedom, and integrity of life that characterizes history.

Correspondingly, we saw that it was in the social situations brought about by social changes — by historical passage as well as by situations in individual life — that issues of ultimate concern arise: deep anxiety, the temptation to sin and injustice, new possibilities for creative action, and the demand or call to active life in creative service. Historical change, and so events in history appearing from the future, raise religious as well as moral issues for us as individuals and as members of our communities. Here the integrity and reality of our faith and commitment are challenged and tested, and the reality of a new life disclosed or found wanting and empty. The two separate kingdoms — so familiar to Protestant tradition all the way from orthodox Lutheranism through evangelical piety to contemporary existential-eschatological interpretations — of individual versus social, private versus public, inward, subjective, existential versus outward, political-historical, cannot be separated. The Old Testament understanding of Israel in her relation to history makes this point plain. The church is in the world, as are we, and cannot be herself inwardly unless she also serves the world.

Since the inner and the outer cannot be separated, the roles of the church are both dual and inseparable. Without the one the other is inevitably ineffective and possibly demonic. In the outer realm, the political and social sphere, the realm of institutional structures and political events, the church's role is that of liberation: the freeing through constructive political action of men and women from the fatedness of distorted, unjust, and exploitative institutions; and the encouragement of new possibilities in social existence. Without such creative responses — and that means political concern, decision, and action — to the crises of its time, this moving, historical life, and the individuals in it, will be dominated by fate: conflict, oppression, and the loss of the human. But clearly the church is also the medium of the redemptive forces of history, those aspects of grace communicated to us through word, sacrament, and community that minister to the inward personal relations of self to itself, of self to neighbor, and of self to God.

Both are necessary, liberation and the ministry of grace, if there is to be reality and healing in the other. If liberation alone is taken, that role loses its Christian basis, its principle of judgment, normative criteria, and grounds for repentance, and the promise of real renewal is lost. If the inward, redemptive role alone is taken, then — because we live in the world, are anxious, tempted, and called there, and act there — the reality and meaning of that redemptive role evaporates into matters of external piety and empty phrases. As a medium of divine grace, the church, if she ministers alone to her own "spiritual" needs, will have not only an ineffective but, worse, a conservative, oppressive impact on actual life. Church people and church institutions are still there in society, profiting from and secured by society's institutions, as middle class, white, and American. If they do not criticize and seek to transform those institutions, their very piety serves to bless those warped institutions.

THE CHURCH IN GOD'S HISTORICAL ACTION

The reality, power, and task of the church are to be understood in relation to God's action in history. The church's self-understanding in both its outer and inner roles appears in relation to its understanding of God's providential and redemptive action in history, of God's relation both to the outer secular world of social change and historical events and to the inner world of sin and grace, to the covenant community, the people of God. As modern history has made abundantly clear, even a creative culture cannot make it alone. It, too, as in the Old Testament, seems to face the possibility of nemesis and must look beyond itself for any hope.

In both the world and the covenant community, the divine action, as we saw, was one of the constitution and support of social forms and symbols, of the social conditions of human existence in time. It consisted of judgment on both the distorted character of those structures and symbols and the use our freedom had made of the gifts of providence in covenant and law, and so in the dismantling of an unjust and inauthentic world. It also consisted of the further gift of new possibilities to each situation, of a new covenant in actual social structures in the world, and of new interpretations and expe-riences of grace in the covenant community of the Spirit. It is in relation to these three moments or aspects of the divine providential activity that the church can achieve a deeper self-understanding and a truer appreciation of her dual role.

The definition of the character and goal of this divine action (in constitution and creation, judgment, and new possibilities) is given to us in God's revelation of the divine purposes and promises, although how we are to recognize the divine work in outer history, hidden as it is in the ambiguity of social events, distorted institutions, and selfish acts, remains a continual problem for us as it did for Israel and the prophets. This definition is disclosed primarily in the symbol of the Kingdom as the final fulfillment of the covenant and the promise, and that symbol in turn finds its definition through the person, teaching, and destiny of Jesus. As it has throughout theological tradition, the eschatological goal of God defines and controls God's providential work in time and history. The character or shape of that goal is centrally manifest through the person, teachings, and promises of Jesus. Here it is, we believe, that the mystery of historical change, of the hiddenness of God amid the strange works of men and women, is disclosed so that the promises of historical life, the principles of its judgment, and the grounds for its hope are seen, and our task in the world is now understood and made plain.

That divine work—as all the biblical symbols pointing to the divine activity in time indicate—involves three aspects: (1) the creation and sustenance of our being—our security and identity as existing human beings, the major concern of justice; (2) the creation of structures of common life that are meaningful, in which meaningful life, work, and existence are possible for all, in which participation by all in what is creative and valuable is possible, another major concern of justice and of liberation; and (3) the encouragement of community, of relations of respect, tolerance, and affection among persons in a community. Being, meaning, and love are the major aspects of God as we experience the divine; they are the fruits of God's work in our lives and history: Through God we are, we find meaning, and we establish community. Thus is God's kingdom, insofar as it relates to history, a social order where security and identity, meaningful work and activity, and real community are formed. Through the nature and work of God in time, as manifest to us in Jesus and the kingdom he preached, the goal of time is seen, the criteria wherewith our judgments can be made are given, and the form of new possibilities given to us is known. Thus does what is known and experienced of God in the covenant community, in God's redemptive work in history, disclose what is the shape and ground of God's "secular" work as providence in the outer, public world. The kingdom of grace reveals the true aim and the true possibilities of the kingdom of the world. As in the Old Testament, these two make up one history, the Word disclosing to the prophet, through covenant and promise, the meaning and goal of God's action in wider history and through its events.

THE CHURCH AS CATHOLIC SUBSTANCE AND PROTESTANT PRINCIPLE

As the accounts of the people of God in both Old and New Testaments make clear, the church does not exist from itself alone. As I have shown, neither its own autonomous activity nor even its innate capabilities provides the secret of its life, although such activity is necessary. Rather, it is the activity (providential and redemptive) of God and the presence of God's grace in its midst as word, sacrament, and the bond of love that give to the church its grounds, norms, and promise. Thus, as Tillich insisted, the church is a theonomous reality; it has and must have what he called a Catholic substance, a relation to God's calling, to God's word and God's grace, to the Spiritual Presence, if it is to do its task, if our autonomous freedom, our decisions, and our acts are to be rescued from ineffectiveness, from duplicating the empty and self-concerned life of ourselves and of others in the world.

But Tillich also insisted as do the prophets that this substance, this spiritual presence, is only creatively, and not in the end destructively, present if there is also what he called the Protestant principle. This principle involves the realization of the fragmentary character of even our own Christian existence, the realization of the distortions we effect on the gifts of grace and the call to service, and the possibly demonic use we can make even of our own holiness, truth, election, and the promises given to us. Thus, the church must be aware of judgment on her life and must practice a living repentance for her own sins. Both the inner life in community of the church and its role in the world as servant church are impossible without these two elements: the holy that is present among us in the gifts of grace and the realization that we ourselves are not that holy but only its fragmentary and wayward media, and thus under continuing judgment and in need of renewal. Repentance for the church's own sin is the condition of the presence of healing grace, as the latter is the sole condition for the creative mission of the church to the world.

Nothing illustrates this so clearly — and the relation of inner existence and outer public life in the church — as the relation of Christianity and the church to the Holocaust, the most demonic historic event of our time. Individual Christians and some elements of the church courageously protested against this eruption of the ultimate in evil in history, and suffered accordingly. But many more individuals and much larger elements of the church participated in that demonic event or remained quite silent. In order to preserve its "spiritual substance" and often merely to preserve its numbers, its "effectiveness," and its position, the church as a whole chose to remain aloof and indifferent and manifestly lost thereby whatever religious substance it might have sought to preserve. Only self-criticism, repentance, and a calling to serve in the world would have manifested and saved any real holiness. Correspondingly, only repentance and self-criticism and a renewed sense of our mission of justice can redeem in our present our own fragmentary holiness and reestablish the covenant. Thus, the same requirements apply to us all in our social crises and situations: in race relations, in relation to sexism, in problems of economic injustice, in issues of our national imperialism, in relation to social liberation movements. The substance of the church's life can be there — and can be there even in an affluent American church — only if repentance for its aloofness from suffering and a new call toward justice are also there. Concern for the world's justice, and in the end for our own justice, is the sole basis for the reality of transcendent grace in the church's life. Like outer and inner, world and transcendence, social existence and the sacred cannot be separated or both are lost in emptiness.

THE CHURCH'S DUAL ROLE IN PUBLIC LIFE

In this concluding discussion, I would like to extend this formula of Catholic substance in union with Protestant principle into the understanding of society and the role of the Church in the public world, in order to specify further what we are called to do there. The basis for the extension of this model from *ecclesia* to social community has already been given in my discussion of providence. God acts in the world, in social and historical change, much as God acts in relation to the church, amid the covenant people. God's providential activity and the divine redemptive activity are diverse but parallel, each directed by the same eschatological goal, and the former is to be understood and guided by what we know of the latter. Consequently the church's task in the world is to preserve and foster the Catholic substance of society's life and to express and enact the Protestant principle within the body politic as well. Without both forms of ministry, the church's mission is incomplete and abortive.

Prophetic Role

In the Old Testament, as we saw, Yahweh constitutes and sustains Israel's social existence, through the establishment of its institutions and the giving of its fundamental symbols, norms, and grounds for hope in time — its vocation in history. This is an aspect, I suggested, of God's providential role in all of history and in every social community, as we can see in Amos 9: "Did I not bring up Israel from the land of Egypt and the Philistines from Caphtor and the Syrians from Kir?" We know, both from our common experience of public life as well as from sociology's inquiries into the structures and characteristics of that public life, that a living, meaningful community is possible only if it has a "religious" substance, a sense or awareness of unconditioned significance within the securities, meanings, and community embodied in its daily life. It must possess in common a commitment to these, its participating forms of social existence, and to the symbolic forms that communicate these meanings and so structure the community's life. An awareness of ultimate being, meaning, and justice must permeate the life of a community if it is to function. By contrast, when a community believes its existence is ruled by fate, and thus lacks the hope of security, when work is experienced as meaningless and empty, and community relations appear barren, political action becomes ineffective or demonic and the community itself dies. The individuals within it die as well. A community disintegrates through spiritual alienation, when its meanings and values evaporate and life is left isolated, empty, and barren of security, significance, and community. Such is characteristic of much of our life. The religious dimension of a community's life is essential to its being and meaning; the presence and sustenance of this dimension in each society is an aspect of the divine providential work in history making human existence in society, a dwelling place in the world, possible. The demonic results of the disintegration of this spiritual substance of community were evident in the Germany of the 1920s and the 1930s. They are a danger whenever injustice and poverty make security a myth for many, where work is meaningless, and where nonparticipation in worthwhile activity is widespread, and where people are through social disintegration isolated from each other. Then a new national or racial religious substance, providing in demonic form security, meaning, and community, will arise (once in Germany, now possibly in America) to threaten our humanity and all who share the world with us.

Priestly Role

Thus the church has not only a critical, judgmental role in relation to communal life, it also has a constitutive, priestly role, supporting, encouraging, and helping to reshape the fundamental symbols and social institutions that make possible a community's existence. This priestly role has, I believe, two aspects.

It means, first, the task of recovering or retrieving the religious dimension, now almost lost, of our public life. This dimension is embodied in the meanings and the norms—the fundamental symbols—that guide and shape public life and contribute to the common good. "Religion" in the form of this sacral dimension of public life constitutes as well as criticizes and transcends a community's structure and life, and so should the church. Ideally (or eschatologically), one may say that this social symbolic and constitutive structure is characterized by justice and love, and so that in the end it takes the form of the Kingdom. In practice civil religion, as well as the *ecclesia* itself, is far from this ideal form. Nevertheless, the forms a society's civil religion does take are constitutive, sacral for its life, and where they are creative, their support and encouragement is one of the major roles of the church in the world. The church should be positively concerned with the religious substance of its culture's life as essential to the creativity of that culture and to the quality of all human life within it.

This priestly role means, second, that part of our task of reflection, study, and preaching is to disclose within our public, communal tradition those symbols and meanings that are especially significant for our present and our immediate future. In our case these are, I believe, those aspects of the liberal and the American tradition that lead to more secure being, more meaningful existence and work, and more community. Much in our social tradition is, to be sure, now useless, anachronistic, and even negative, according to these criteria, for times and social situations have radically changed. But much is extremely valuable. Part of our task is to make that discrimination and so reinstate the significance—and their relevance to ultimate significance—of the creative elements of what has been given to us. No prophet discarded or repudiated the whole covenant. He recalled people to it, even though he spoke also of new possibilities; he never denied, in social or religious terms, the value of sacral tradition as constitutive of human existence in time.

As we well know, however (and the Old Testament is here also clear), there are demonic possibilities in the sacral traditions of secular life, in civil religion, as there are in any ecclesiastical sacral tradition. That which is ultimately significant in a community's life, its being, its meanings, and its levels of community, can become the basis for its fanaticism, cruelty, imperialism, and oppression of others, as the religions of nationalism, racism, of class and group amply show. It is because communities have, in order to be at all, a sacral foundation—a "Catholic substance"—that they are so dangerous and history is so full of catastrophe and suffering. Without that substance, they disintegrate into emptiness and meaninglessness, a terrifying void that calls for demonic answers. With it, however, they are capable of idolatry, of making the sacral gifts that establish their community life into the divine itself and into the center of the meaning of history.

Such pride—and its inevitable result, injustice—is for the Old Testament, as for history itself, the source of nemesis, catastrophe, and the breakdown of history, the source of the appearance of the divine judgment—illustrated in this century, as noted, by the careers of the church, of the "Christian nations," and of our own nation. My analysis of the present situation revealed the danger of this idolatry as we face a darkly unknown, contingent, and insecure future. The sacred dimension of life is ambiguous; it is *of God* but it is *not God*. Thus, a principle of criticism of the very values we cherish, of the sacral elements of our common life, is as necessary as is the support of those elements. The Protestant principle must apply to our role in the world in union with the Catholic substance, as both must apply to the church's own life.

Judgment on its world as well as on itself must be part of the church's word to the world. This judgment involves especially a warning to those groups and communities with power and affluence since it is their idolatry, more than the errors and the sins of the weak, that is responsible for more suffering. There is neither covenant nor church without this word, of that both Scripture and history assure us. Somehow the American church has thought it could have grace and hope without judgment either on itself or its culture. The Scriptures should all along have shown that this was wrong; but now, as in the Old Testament, current history has shown it.

As judgment is not the final word for Israel, however, so it is not the final character of God's providence in history. This is important to recall in a day when the menace of the future is particularly plain, a menace brought upon us by our greed, indifference, and our callous search for power and security. The deepest note of the prophetic word was that although Israel had betrayed her covenant, and although she was encountering or was about to encounter an apparently endless doom of nemesis, of the breakdown of all she valued, still a new covenant was to come. History remained open, a realm of promise. The future as well as the past was ruled by the sovereignty of a God whose final face was neither judgment nor nemesis but the promise of new possibility.

This word, set now into the understanding of our own social future, indicates the promise of new possibility in each historical situation, a new *kairos* arising as possibility and as demand out of our present, however dark that present and however limited its possibilities may appear. To have faith in providence and so in history is confidently to expect such a new possibility and to work for it. But, let us note, to be given a new chance is at the same time to be challenged to justice, to be faced with a new demand, and to accept the appearance of a quite new social covenant. We cannot see the historical form of this new possibility, and what we expect will not be what comes. But history is not fate, it remains open, and new possibilities unguessed in the opaque present are there. To hold this faith is to believe in providence. To proclaim it is thus to give grounds for confidence and hope. Such confidence is necessary for any communal life, and its inspiration forms our present major task in an increasingly anxious world.

PART THREE

Christian Symbols
of Praxis

CHAPTER 9

THEOLOGY OF CULTURE AND CHRISTIAN ETHICS

What does a theological analysis of cultures—a look at culture with regard to its religious dimensions—have to offer Christian ethics? Made more specific this question means, In what ways do norms and obligations of behavior shift with fundamental cultural shifts? That the consequences of action change as the cultural situation changes has long been recognized; thus does a prudential or pragmatic ethics insist on different policies for different situations. Recent developments have clearly shown that important cultural shifts uncover new ethical concerns: in genetic ethics, medical ethics, business ethics, and so on. But do fundamental patterns of obligation— natural laws or covenant requirements—shift? These are familiar and long-debated matters that I shall surely not settle here. Possibly, however, these reflections on the fundamental cultural shifts we are experiencing will lure us to ponder again this interesting question: What does happen to ethics and its principles, or to theological principles, in periods of vast cultural change?

I shall reflect upon three fundamental cultural shifts in our time, continental shifts one might say, shifts that are not only immensely significant but that in rather strange ways have been part of my own personal experience. I am convinced that while these changes require a technical, economic, political, and social analysis in order to be comprehended fully, in the end they can be understood only if they are also viewed theologically. Whether they change the shape of our obligations or merely of our ways of enacting our traditional norms, I leave to others to decide. Certainly they will affect what we find on reflection we should do, even as on a deeper level they will affect our sense of who we are, who we are called to be, what our life and history are about, and what the power is that rules us all.

I am speaking of fundamental cultural shifts in our time, changes in the shape of our cultural-historical existence. These are related to but distinguishable from the fundamental ethical issues of our time. Changes in the cultural situation help to set our ethical issues, to pose the demands that require responsible action. Still, the cultural situation and the ethical-political issues within it are significantly different. The three overriding ethical issues in the immediate foreground of our common experience are, it seems to me, nuclear control and disarmament—in short, peace—social justice, and the preservation of the environment. I have written on all of these, and many wiser heads have done much more. Omitting discussions of them here does not imply that they are secondary. It only represents a change of focus from the foreground of our present being in the world to the wider background of that action and reaction, to the changing shape of the cultural epoch in which we find ourselves and in which we must act. This changing shape sets the stage for our responsible action; it is the situation in which we act, and, as noted, that situation must also be understood theologically, in categories appropriate to the understanding of religion and theological affirmation.

THE ESTABLISHMENT OF SCIENCE

The first new factor in the second half of the twentieth century is what I wish to call the establishment of science. By *establishment,* I mean the category as we use it in religious history when we speak, for example, of the establishment of Christianity at the heart of Roman and later of medieval culture. In turn, this means that the spiritual tradition so established—be it Christianity, Islam, Confucianism in China, or Shinto in Japan—is universally regarded as completely essential to the life of its culture. It is regarded as necessary for the society's material welfare, health, defense, and harmony, as well as necessary for its spiritual well-being. The existence of the community is considered utterly dependent on its relation to this knowledge, these rites, this law. When a spiritual tradition is thus established, immediately it is given (or it appropriates) immense authority and dominance, its expenses are happily borne, its preeminence in intellectual and aesthetic life is guaranteed, and its functionaries, usually priests and theologians, draw to themselves immense prestige, even adulation.

Establishment, however, brings problems as well as vast advantages and honors. As one essential center of cultural power and dominance, an established religion draws to it dubious as well as sainted characters, as the church discovered. The pure doctrinal motifs, behavioral standards, and modes of personal being maintained when the community was outside the social matrix now get muddied by mixture with the worldly world; doctrinal confusion and imprecision, even heresy, as well as corruption set in. Moreover, since it now dominates the whole society from top to bottom, the spiritual tradition in question penetrates into every cultural level, and so it appears in a wide variety of unexpected forms, on a popular as well as on an elite level and with bizarre and even demonic results. For example, once established, Catholic Christianity mixed with Mediterranean paganism in Spain, Italy, and Greece, and the evangelical gospel mixed with our own mountain culture in the Alleghenies, not to mention Chicago and New York. In each case types of Christianity widely deviant from its original shape, and often abhorrent alike to the Council of Bishops and to the National Council of Churches, appear on every side. Let us also note that only after the church was rudely disestablished by the Enlightenment revolutions did it realize all of this, not only that it had once been established but also establishment's baneful effect on its Christian life. Thus did self-criticism, self-examination, and purification become possible.

That this category of establishment now applies in analogy to science and technology in most modern cultures has become increasingly apparent since the Second World War. Gradually science has become the utterly necessary theoretical basis for every essential aspect of our common social life: for agriculture, industrial production, communication and organization, medicine, scholarship, and above all defense. Our physical existence, security, economic and personal well-being, and modes of understanding are made possible and dominated by science. Thus is it established: financially by the resources of the society, intellectually in the budgets and curricula of our educational institutions, and spiritually by its clear dominance as ruling queen among all other intellectual and practical pursuits. No modern society, whatever its cultural and ideological forms, does not intend in this sense to establish science at the heart of its life, as Japan in its recent history has so clearly shown.

All this about the domination of science we in the humanities have realized for some time. Still, it was involvement in the creationist controversy that alerted me to some of the other consequences of the establishment of science. There we encounter the new reality of what can only be called popular science — a deviant form of science, in fact one allied to popular religion, and so a possibility only when science has become thoroughly established on every level of the culture. Creation science is a form, even if a deviant form, of science: Its perpetuators and defenders hold Ph.D.'s in science, and many have tenured positions on scientific faculties or laboratories (for example, four at Purdue and about ten at the Westinghouse Laboratories in Pittsburgh). The well-endowed Center of Creationism in San Diego, the Creation-Life Institute, is staffed solely, as claimed, with M.A.'s and Ph.D.'s in the natural sciences, not by theologians, biblical scholars, or ethicists. If Jerry Falwell is to be called descriptively a Christian (and how can one deny it? he is hardly a Buddhist), albeit a somewhat dubious one by some standards, so these are scientists in this common descriptive sense. However mistaken, they claim their views of origins to be science and therefore themselves not to be at all against science. I have debated four creationists, each one with a Ph.D. in the hard sciences. Each time my opponent has made the point that he speaks "as a scientist" against myself, whom he termed graciously "only a theologian." We can understand all this only by recognizing that science and technology have now penetrated the culture so completely that they appear at all the culture's various levels. As popular gospel religion now uses the latest technology as effectively or more effectively than elite religion does, so literalist religion has entered the laboratories and universities of our land—in fact formed its own universities—and established a form, albeit a strange form, of popular science, a new and bizarre union of science with the cultural and religious forms of Protestant Fundamentalism.

This union of Fundamentalism and science has not always been so. The Scopes trial represented the sharpest sort of antagonism of science and literalistic religion. The reason was that science, technology, and modern forms of education had then by no means penetrated to the rural, literalistic, and fundamentalist levels of our cultural life and thus were confined to the sophisticated, urban life of America. As opposed to this sharp antagonism, the present trials have represented on both sides two sorts, two very different sorts, of union of science and religion: on the one hand, a union at the popular level of creation science and fundamentalist religion; and, on the other, a union at the elite level of the membership of the American Association for the Advancement of Science with the major theological schools, university departments of religion, and the members of the National Council of Churches! Paradoxically enough, the main proponents for the 1981 Arkansas Act 590 (a law requiring the teaching of creation science in Arkansas public schools) were trained scientists; the main antagonists *against* the law, both the plaintiffs and the witnesses, were church persons and students of religion.[1]

Not only did the creation scientists represent degrees in science and in that way witness to science's domination of the whole culture. The creationist movement itself had been and continues to be bred by this same domination. As they all witnessed, in public and in private, the creationists objected mainly to the dominant scientific community's "teaching" that science is the only form of knowledge. As a consequence, because science refrains and must refrain from speaking of God, they concluded that science represents an atheistic position, a denial of God. Those of us who have long countered that claim of science alone to know can hardly fault that complaint, although we can well fault its understanding of scientific method. Nor would we fail to empathize with the angry assertion of a creationist mother that she joined the movement when her child came home from school and said, "The science teacher told us today that science now knows that Genesis is wrong." Creationism is a response to the arrogant claim of science that it represents the only mode of knowing and so that only what it speaks of is real. In that sense one can see here how every newly established religion, in this case

---

[1] See the account of these trials and the author's role in them, in Langdon Gilkey, *Creationism on Trial: Evolution and God at Little Rock* (San Francisco: Harper & Row, 1985).

scientism, seeks through its mythical self-understanding to eliminate its older rivals, a familiar enough process in religious history (in this case science calls religious knowing pre-science).

These strange unions of science and religion bear watching. They are a function of establishment. As when any religious tradition penetrates to the heart of a culture, it becomes shaped and reshaped by that culture (although it never thinks it is), so when science has entered any one of the wide variety of cultures in the twentieth century, it has found itself in turn reshaped by each of them. We should long ago have noted this. When Nazism took over German culture, it took over as well, almost without a whimper, the science and the laboratories of that advanced scientific society and formed the bizarre and frightening Nazi science. The same, with interestingly different modifications, took place in Stalinist Russia, and much of that reshaped science, I presume, still dominates the University of Moscow. Had Maoism lasted, that would have provided another sort of union of science and ideology, science and the religious, and again it would have been science that was reshaped by ideology, not, as we had once expected, the reverse. My own bet on the most bizarre candidate of all will be Iran's Shiite science when it develops. Considering the number of Shiite students we are training in the universities of the West, this will soon happen. We may be sure that these students will not return to Tehran, or the Sunnis to Saudi Arabia, to reestablish there the social and intellectual patterns of the Charles River Basin, Philadelphia, Morningside Heights, or Hyde Park.

For some time theology has stated what we are seeing, perhaps with less empirical conviction; namely, that every active culture represents a unity, a unity of the cognitive and meaning, of science and its own fundamental mythical structure, of knowledge and the spiritual substance of the culture. Thus, every culture seeks and finally represents some form of unity of science and ideology, of scientific knowledge, technical know-how, productive and organizational techniques, and its own cultural substance. Japan, for example, has now appropriated and integrated modern science, technology, and industrialism into its cultural and spiritual tradition. It is evident that in this process it has transformed these imports into something Japanese and not Western. China will do so even more markedly. We did not expect this because we were bedazzled by the image of the universality of our own Western culture and by the power of science and its method to effect the transforming operation. To us, therefore, Western culture as a whole represented the development ordained or destined for all alike in the bright new future, namely, the goal of history's progress, the "modernity" that was guaranteed for the future. When other cultures became scientific and technological, they would become, as we said, Westernized, as if all the rest of their cultural substance would slowly dissipate or be transformed into our forms of life. This was an arrogant dream and utterly illusory. It was not based at all on historical experience but rather upon our own progressivist eschatology. The fact is that when powerful cultural traditions import intellectual, cognitive, and spiritual elements from other cultures, they reshape them into their own forms, as Rome did Christianity, China and Japan Buddhism, and as Italy did with the spaghetti it once imported from China. Every modern culture will become scientific, technological, and probably industrial; but it will shape these into its own cultural forms, as Germany, Russia, Japan, and now San Diego have already done.

The obvious and important lesson from this is that science and technology are not autonomous or self-sufficient but dependent elements of cultural life, dependent for the forms of their embodiment on the institutional, legal, moral, and spiritual substance of their culture. If science can unite as it did with Nazism to form Nazi science, it should not surprise us that it can unite with Protestant Fundamentalism to form creation science and the Moral Majority. But it should disturb and possibly frighten us. As both examples show, the health of science and technology, that is, their benevolent rather than their demonic and destructive consequences, are now seen to be utterly dependent on the spiritual health of the larger culture into which they are appropriated and by which they are reshaped. I mean by this the political institutions, the legal structure, the educational system, the social habits and customs, the ethical norms, and finally the religious convictions. If these form an alien, oppressive, or demonic spiritual substance, the science that unites itself to them will become in turn infinitely dangerous. In sum, a scientific culture does not so much call for more science and technology if it would be healthy; on the contrary, it calls precisely for a renewed emphasis on the humanities, ethics, and religion. On its spiritual and cultural matrix science depends, if it would not be lethal.

A TIME OF TROUBLES

Our question has been, What kind of interpretation does a theology of culture offer that can help ethics and religious ethics in its deliberations? Recall that theology of culture is understood here as the analysis of a current socio-political-cultural situation with regard to its religious dimensions and issues; that is, with regard to those aspects to which a theological analysis or description might contribute. The first continental shift within our cultural situation was the establishment of science with its many unexpected and bizarre consequences. The second is closely but paradoxically related to it — namely, the "time of troubles" in which Western culture as a whole now finds itself. These two are closely related because the thorough establishment of science in our cultural life has been in part, if only in part, responsible for our time of troubles. They are paradoxically related because the last thing the Age of Science, as the Enlightenment and post-Enlightenment worlds happily called themselves, expected was that this new age would, through the establishment of science, usher in such a turbulent and precarious era as our own.

"Time of troubles" is a category taken from Arnold Toynbee's massive and helpful *Study of History*. This category does not refer to or postulate the necessary decline of a culture or of what he calls a civilization. There is always the chance, says Toynbee, that new and creative responses will prolong the life of the civilization in question. This category does, however, refer to a period when the possibility of collapse or radical decline appears on the scene for the first time. It is a period when forces within the culture seem to reveal themselves as more and more out of control, when solutions to important problems seem more and more elusive and ineffective — that is, when problems mount at a much faster rate than do any hints of their resolution. A time of troubles is, however, not only a period of growing dislocation, "out-of-joint-ness," and conflict. Even more, the culture now, precisely through its most creative factors, seems to have turned in on itself and to be embarked on the process of destroying itself. The institutions, customs, and beliefs that in the waxing of its life had been creative in developing the culture's power, security, and well-being now appear to change their character and role and to become destructive, creating new dilemmas and contradictions that threaten to pull the society's life apart. The feudal system in Europe, for instance, had been a creative vehicle of order at the start and became a destructive vehicle of radical injustice and oppression as it neared its end.

It seems to me clear that Western culture now finds itself mired in such a time of troubles. The institutions that have been creative of our modern civilization — those which once not only established the unchallenged power of the West but which were also exported across the globe — are now the source of its own deepest dilemmas. I refer to science, technology, and their offspring, industrialism, and one can add the creative social theories that accompanied their rise, namely, capitalistic democracy and socialism. The modern West has, of course, many aspects other than these and roots far deeper than these elements penetrate. Nevertheless, the military, economic, and political power, the expanding well-being, and the moral authority that, despite its manifest arrogance, cruelty, and greed, the West exhibited during its rise and dominance had their sources in these elements. Science, technology, industrialism, and democracy — these four have constituted the spiritual substance of our culture, the basis for its most important self-understanding, its sense of uniqueness, its awareness of vocation or task in history, and so its confidence in itself and above all in its future. To us and to those outside the West that envied, admired, or detested us, these have represented the West and with it modernity. In fact, as our school textbooks illustrate, advances in science, technology, industrial capitalism, and democracy have in effect defined civilization for us. They have defined what my own textbook complacently called the March of Civilization, and with this the entire meaning for us of the story of history.

The point is that precisely these same elements, once constitutive of our culture's substance, success, and glory, are creating rather than resolving our deepest and most important dilemmas. I need not outline in detail the ways that scientific and technological developments and industrial growth, on which the life and welfare of the culture utterly do depend, seem all too inexorably to be leading us toward possible destruction. The new weapons, the inhumanity of technological systems and of the society they spawn, the despoliation of nature as a result of industrial expansion—all of these pose those mounting dilemmas that seem to brook, within their own terms, no solution. Without science, technology, and industrial growth, we perish; but with them, it also seems, we perish. Knowledge is power, said Francis Bacon, and modern culture has obediently devoted itself to the accumulation of both empirical knowledge and worldly power. In fact Bacon was quite right about these two. But to our horror and chagrin, the power that knowledge has created has turned out to be the power to destroy as well as to build. Here the solutions that built modern culture are of no avail. Modern culture, as a consequence, has become uneasily aware not only of its own possible mortality but also of its significant one-sidedness and limitation, its unheeded and yet newly evident partiality.

This emphasis on scientific knowledge, technical know-how, and industrial and military power, which is what other cultures saw in us as the magical secret of our dominance, was in our liberal eyes more than balanced by the humanitarian thrust of the West, by its emphasis on individual rights, democracy, equality, and the worth of persons. In fact, to most of us liberals, this is the West, not the military and industrial power the Republicans worship and other cultures have both hated and envied. We were not completely wrong. The Western conquest of the globe in the eighteenth through the early twentieth centuries was as much the work of its social and humanitarian ideals as it was of its technology, industry, and guns. Between them, Western democratic and socialist ideas and goals have toppled nearly all the traditional tyrannical regimes and unjust social orders that had inhabited the world prior to the Enlightenment. Since then, both wings of Western culture have endeavored to spread democratic or socialist revolutions along with scientific and industrial revolutions in order to create a world civilization on its own pattern. This image, or dream, of a universal modern culture, modeled on our own version of it, is still held in most of the power centers— industrial, political, and academic—of the contemporary West.

Power, however, corrupts social ideals as well as it does scientific knowledge and technological development, something this Pelagian culture had no possibility of understanding. As the social theories created by the West (democracy and socialism) came to dominance, their revolutionary zeal abated and their ethical content waned. Like many religions before them, in being established both became united with the status quo and thus conservative rather than prophetic in their intentions and meanings. The ideas of democracy (one thinks of free elections, for example) have become, as Marx rightly prophesied, slogans for the privileged, even for tyrants, around the globe, mouthed in country clubs and posh resorts rather than shouted in the streets. Correspondingly, which Marx did not predict, official Marxist doctrine now rationalizes and defends the oppressive power of the Kremlin and little else. In our own period of the waning of these systems, most of those really committed to the radical ideals of democracy or of communism are mainly found in the prisons of the other. Thus, on the level of its ideologies, the West is also in a time of troubles, a period when the creative solutions of its own past seem to have reached a term, a point where each of these ideologies seems to create as many problems as it resolves. The clearest manifestation of this is that the ideological conflict — nay, the religious one — that threatens to engulf us and to bring the culture of modernity into disintegration, and possibly all of life with it, is a conflict between two creative social theories so formative of Western culture and so patently the center of its human worth. Over and over, our most creative achievements seem to tempt us to self-destruction, a theme incomprehensible to the liberal culture that illustrates the theme so elegantly.

I add one further note usually omitted from analyses such as this. This is the sudden and radical loss of power and dominance the West has undergone in this half century. When I went to China in 1940, this supremacy still prevailed. The whole of East Asia, India, and Africa, not to mention South America, was owned, exploited, and explicitly ruled by the West, as were the main port cities of China. This dominance, if not actual rule, had long been the case. Since 1520 or so no non-Western power had been able to challenge, much less defeat, a major Western power. For four hundred years we entered, robbed, and took over wherever we wished, so long as we could deal with the other competing Western powers. By the end no remaining rival cultures were left. All were completely conquered and, as we like to say, "pacified." No wonder we thought, on the one hand, that they were primitive and, on the other, that history represented progress! Although we took this power for granted, others felt, resisted, and resented it during these four centuries. As a consequence, the last 150 years have been characterized by a series of increasingly violent reactions against this dominance, beginning in nineteenth-century China and India, continuing in the twentieth century not only with the Indian revolt but exploding wildly with military and Shinto Japan, reaching an even more resentful climax with Mao, and at present ablaze in Tehran and possibly in the entire rest of Islam. In our half century, the epoch of this absolute dominance is now largely gone. Whereas in 1914 all the major world powers were European, now not one is Western European, and only one major power is in any sense a representative of the Enlightenment West; the rest (Japan, China, the Soviet Union) represent very different cultural traditions. We and Europe still think that America has inherited Europe's power. We have not. That power, as well as the spiritual dominance that accompanied it, is now a mere fraction of what it was as recently as 1940.

This is a vast historical and cultural shift, a dramatic turn in historical fortune: from dominance and superiority on every front to what is at best a precarious equality or parity; from a supreme confidence in our fundamental institutions to radical doubt about them if not fear of and for them; from confidence in history and the future to a vast anxiety about the meaning of the historical continuum and dread of what is to come. Unnerving as this is for us, let us remember that all of this has been good for the world as a whole. The word *liberation* — in all its most recent nuances — refers to one or another facet of the breakup of this once-dominant culture: Victorian, European-colonial, capitalistic and multinational, white, male, "square." With the mention of each of these epithets of our culture, another liberating facet of this breakup has appeared in our time. Thus, new possibilities for creative political and moral action abound in this time of troubles.

New crises for action, however, also appear. In such a time, problems, dilemmas, and contradictions tend also to mount. Perhaps most significant, the ethical — and back of that the religious — suddenly strides center stage as the most important ingredient of social and personal health. When the culture is waxing and growing, the ethical seems relatively unimportant, a matter for soft rather than hardheaded intellectuals. At the forefront in optimistic times is an increase in relevant knowledge, expertise, and know-how, the development of appropriate social institutions, and possibly more education and training in "objectivity." When, however, each one of these creative aspects or functions of culture reveals, in turn, its own deep ambiguity (that science, technology, industrialism, and even democracy can be used destructively as well as creatively), the ethical comes center stage. Now the creative results of action are not so much dependent on the accumulation of knowledge, instruments, or institutions as on the character of the human users thereof and so on how they decide to use them. Thus, the norms and the moral constraints of a culture become determinative, as we earlier found they were in relation to science and technology. As I discovered to my surprise in an internment camp during the Second World War, a moral disease can threaten the community's life as effectively as can a physical one or a shortage of material supplies.[2] All the way from issues of medical and genetic ethics to the vast problems of nuclear arms and nuclear conflict, this newly apprehended ambiguity of science has uncovered a host of new ethical dilemmas, and above all it has revealed the supreme importance of the ethical for the possibility of continuing human existence.

Our recent experience has been that the power to know, invent, fashion and refashion, to organize — all that goes into creative intelligence, all that characterizes *homo faber* — is not solely adaptive, the key to survival, as our scientific culture had thought. It also reveals itself as potentially self-destructive, as we never dreamed. Perhaps creative intelligence is our fatal flaw, unless it becomes more than intelligence, unless it becomes wisdom. Again, even intelligence is dependent on its use; and, again, the moral appears in a difficult cultural epoch as before it never had appeared for us.

The religious appears as well in such a time. Such periods, vulnerable and precarious, with broken meanings and threatened hopes, are times of great anxiety — personal and communal. The decline of a culture breeds new hope for the oppressed and is therefore "good." It also breeds, however, vast

---

[2] See the account of this experience in Langdon Gilkey, *Shantung Compound: The Story of Men and Women under Pressure* (New York: Harper and Row, 1966).

anxiety in the dominant classes, in the oppressors, and is therefore dangerous. Reinhold Niebuhr was right. Anxiety is the temptation that leads to sin, and thus a time of troubles is a time sorely tempted: to panic, to fanatical self-defense, renewed aggression, oppression of rival points of view, to a host of acts that a moral community, peace loving and fair-minded in its own vision of itself, would never consider in less precarious times. Religion, as well as dangerous politics, appears in all its wild variety. This sets just as serious a set of problems for responsible ethics as religion's disappearance did. But most importantly, the issues, subjectively of commitment and objectively of the symbolic structure to which commitment is given, emerge as of equal importance to the ethical, since the nature of ultimate commitment is fundamental to the health of ethical decisions. In such times unconditional allegiance is always given to some god. Thus, the question to which sort of god—to which ideology—it is given is paramount. The deeper questions (first, How is it possible to be critical of even such required allegiance? and, second, How is it possible credibly to speak of hope in a cultural and political situation such as this?) become predominant theological issues every bit as important to ethics as to systematic theology. Issues of theology thus accompany issues of ethics out of the wings and back onto the center of the stage of communal existence.

THE PARITY OF RELIGIONS

One final shift in our cultural situation has immense ramifications for ethics as well as for theology. This is what we can call the new sense of the rough equality or parity of religions. More specifically it represents the acknowledgment on the part of persons in each religious community of the presence of healing grace and truth in other communions. This recognition of parity is, I think, new. To be sure, a significant number of religious communities (Hindu, Buddhist, and liberal Jewish and Christian, to name a few) had recognized that other religions are neither completely false nor malevolent and thus had acknowledged in them a relative measure of truth and grace. They represented "other ways," so to speak, to the common goal of all religion. Each of these relatively tolerant traditions, however, understood itself as representing that common goal and as embodying the superior or supreme way, as being itself the measure of the truth and grace present in other religions, or, as the Christian liberals liked to say, the absolute religion.

This may be about as far as we can get at the moment, and it is certainly better than the more traditional Christian understanding of other religions as simply idolatrous or false. Still, it does not fairly represent our present existential situation. This is one of rough parity, or of the mutual assumption of parity. That is to say, the other represents not merely an imperfect or undeveloped form of my own religious consciousness but embodies a genuine alternative, one that enjoys a measure of truth and of grace not even found in my own tradition. The other, then, is a dialogic partner that can supplement, deepen, and enlarge my own vision, in effect challenge and reshape it.

The causes of this new situation among the religions are multiple. On the large scale, the major cause is the devaluation of the authority and supremacy of Western culture. It was as the religion of a clearly superior cultural matrix, not on its own dogmatic grounds, that liberal Christianity called itself absolute. Now that the supremacy of the West is radically questioned from all sides, however, the sense of the clear superiority of that culture's religion has dissipated both in other cultures and here at home. Another cause has been the appearance on our own turf of other religious alternatives, converting our friends, spouses, and children to some non-Western form of religious faith. No one who has experienced either of these quite new phenomena can assume the absoluteness or perfection (even in principle) of his or her own traditional faith, as our dogmatic grandparents and even our liberal parents might well have done.

No one, it seems to me, has yet been able reflectively to articulate and thematize this new situation theologically. This represents the most interesting single set of problems facing theologians today, presented to us by shifts in culture and articulated by a theology of culture. However, our concern is ethics as well as theology. Frequently philosophers of religion and ethicists assume that the problem raised by "other religions"—the problem of the particularity of this or that viewpoint—represents issues only for dogmatic or systematic theology and not for philosophy or ethics. It is assumed that this particularity is theological, stemming from christological or revelational claims alone, and so a particularity not equally relevant to so-called metaphysical or ethical principles. This is an illusion, fed by the confidence that the philosophical and ethical principles that undergird or animate our cultural life are universal, universal because they represent the established principles of a universal modern culture—much as formerly Christians assumed that their gospel was universal because it represented the definitive revelation of the universal God. On the contrary, we now know that other religions and cultures represent genuine alternatives to Western metaphysics and Western ethics as much as they represent alternatives to Western theological doctrines. As we have already noted, science, technology, and industrialism characterize other cultures as well as our own; but it is illusory to think that this means or will mean a universalization of the Western cultural substance rather than the appropriation and transformation by Japanese, Chinese, Islamic, and Marxist cultures of these facets of modern culture generated historically by Western life. Thus, the issue of the genuine plurality of fundamental viewpoints faces Western philosophy, social theory, and ethics fully as much as it does Western theology. None of these represents a universal standpoint. Each has to reinterpret itself in the light of pluralism—that is, in the presence of genuinely alternative ways of looking at and responding to existence. Many ethicists interested in comparative ethics, especially comparative religious ethics, recognize this new issue. I wish the university as a whole, in its medicine, psychology, social sciences, and philosophy, did as well.

In each of these areas (theological, ethical, philosophical, and scientific), a new sort of paradox confronts us. On the one hand, there is the devaluation of Western culture, which has introduced a new and deeper level of relativism into our social, intellectual, and spiritual life. Relativism has, to be sure, long been experienced, known, and absorbed by the modern Western consciousness. In fact the relativity of scientific conclusions, of historical and cultural creations, therefore of moral and even theological points of view, has practically defined Western consciousness. But we have not absorbed the relativity of that consciousness itself! In some sense we must also understand ourselves on this new level as relative, as representing in the whole of our cultural life only one perspective on the whole of things, a perspective limited, finite, partial. This is deeply unsettling, not only to our religious faith but also to our faith in science, democracy, human rights — in the whole panorama of social, ontological, ethical, and religious principles that make up our common life.

On the other hand, this relativity cannot become a total relativity: standing nowhere, affirming nothing to be real or to be of worth, embodying no ultimate principles of criticism, renewal, or hope. Then, of course, all dialogue ceases, since we have no viewpoint anymore, and we become inwardly bores and outwardly ineffective. Even more, our time of deep relativity is also one of vast existential, political, and cultural uncertainty, anxiety, and possible despair, as we have noted. Because of this, it is also a time tempted to panic and aggressive idolatry. Clearly, such a time calls for affirmation, trust, confidence, and hope, if we are to be serene within this newly precarious temporality. The same relativism and uncertainty about our culture that challenge our native assumptions call as well for the reaffirmation in renewed form of the strongest sort of faith, of an unconditional commitment, an unwavering hope. In the most relative of times, we must discover ourselves grounded in something quite unrelative. To comprehend, recognize, and articulate this paradox (on the one hand, this new consciousness of relativity and yet, on the other, to be firm and creative about our theological and ethical principles) is no small achievement, a challenge to the most ingenious of ethical associations. But, in a time of troubles, it is precisely this mixture of the relative and the absolute, of criticism and affirmation, of humility and courage that we are called to embody.

CHAPTER **10**

ETHICS IN CHRISTIANITY AND BUDDHISM

Ethics as a subject for reflection has usually been construed as concerned with questions of moral and immoral action both in one's personal life (virtues and vices) and in the world, either in intimate or broad communities Ethics in this broad sense has more and more concentrated its attention on questions of public behavior in relation to the wider community — professional (as of doctors, scientists, and technicians), political, and economic behavior, behavior between social and national groups, and so on — and less and less on issues of personal virtues and vices, although no one in our day can forget these latter issues. This social concern has shown itself in religious as well as secular ethics. Questions of social justice, liberation, unemployment, poverty, racism, sexism and patriarchalism, economic and political exploitation, colonialism, militarism, peace, and so on dominate — and rightly so — the present horizon of theological and religious ethics. My intent in focusing on this broad but central field of ethics is that this field — and I include here questions of morals — be sharply circumscribed; namely, by speaking of ethics and morals not so much in themselves as in their relation to religion and especially in their relation to Christianity and Buddhism. Although I will concentrate on the former, I find it useful to keep an eye on the latter as I proceed.

RELIGION AND ETHICS

Of course discussions of such moral or ethical matters can be carried on independently of religion, as most of the field of present philosophical ethics attests. Even when religion is added, ethics can be taken as the central content,

157

the main point, of a reasonable and useful religion. Here religion at best provides aid if not succor to ethics: its cosmic legitimacy, its ontological background, or its ultimate warrants through promises of fulfillment or reward. Ethical ideals stand here in principle on their own; religious beliefs provide at best the security of cosmic importance and permanence, on the one hand, and incitement, emotive power, or hope of reward to autonomous ethics, on the other. Several times in Christian history such a view of religion as merely the horizon of ethics has surfaced: in some of the early apologists, in the eighteenth century, in some modern forms of rational religion, and in some forms of liberation theology.

If this view of ethics as virtually independent of religion, or of religion as in effect the handmaiden of ethics, fails to satisfy us, and we wish to give to religion a more essential role in ethics, still generally we have considered ethics as the fruit or consequence of religion. I do not mean here ethics as the fruit of theology — an implausible claim at best. I refer to religion, the deepest religious relation and commitment or centering of the self, the self's religious existence. In this context we ask how religion issues in ethics, how religious commitment or faith, religious existence, and the principles derived therefrom ground, guide, or reshape our moral judgments and make possible our enactment of those judgments, our moral labors in the world. In all these cases religious ethics concerns itself with personal and social praxis, behavior in the world that fosters or accompanies religious faith as its most important, in fact its justifying, fruit. If the relation of religion to ethics is so defined, in the modern context Christianity, which has for a number of reasons emphasized this aspect of religious ethics, seems to come out well ahead of Buddhism. As Americans who invented baseball and basketball generally win in these sports, so Christians win in this contest that their own emphases have helped to nurture.

Although this represents, I hazard, our main contemporary emphasis in religious ethics, it is important to recall that this has not been the only way that religion and ethics have been related, both in our own tradition and perhaps especially in other religious traditions. I refer here to the "ethical" behavior or action preceding the religious, action making the religious more possible and/or aiding in its development. Here we can view ethics as preparation for the religious; moral action, personal or social, as nurturing the possibility or the capacity for the religious or for the reception of the religious. Such ethical behavior can, of course, be various: It is represented in forms of self-discipline and self-relatedness (for example, ascetical practices); in attitudes and forms of self-control (attachments and nonattachments); in patterns of "religious practice" (*Zazen,* meditation, yoga, Scripture reading, prayer); in modes of communal relatedness and activity (in monastic communities, in serving others, and so on). These represent patterns of voluntary, intentional, and self-directed action that encourage — or are held to do so — a richer, deeper, more solid, and more effective mode of religious existence. In this sense regular participation in liturgy can be added to such patterns of self-discipline nurturing religion. Generally these have not been considered ethics; they are usually called religious practices. I am not sure why, except for the modern bias referred to earlier. They are self-directed, voluntary, and self-initiated: "self-power," to use a Buddhist term; they represent patterns of inner and outer behavior; and they concern what is taken to be the good and the bad. In any case, let us recall that ethics in this general sense can be related to religion not only as consequence but also as preparation. This point may help us to give a more balanced estimate about the relations of ethics to religion in Buddhism and Christianity.

ETHICS AS PREPARATION
FOR RELIGION

With these preparatory remarks in mind, let us now look at the tradition of Christianity — and, however nearsighted I may be, glance once in a while across at Buddhism. How then has ethical action served as preparation, as a mode of nurturing in Christianity? Here it may be helpful to mention two categories familiar in Christian history but not frequently used today, except in the nostalgia of Lutherans and Methodists. I refer to the law and discipline. By discipline, I do not mean the parental or educational usage, namely, punishment; I refer to moral and spiritual practices relevant to the religious life.

The Law

The law — the prescribed, in fact the divine pattern of ethical and religious behavior — has functioned as preparation in two very different ways and in two enthusiastically antagonistic traditions.

Guide to Goodness

The law has been for many — shall we call them liberals? — the authentic guide for helping us to become good, good enough inside and out to be worthy of a religious relation and so worthy of the fruits of that relation. Here the law leads to the religious, not the reverse. Whether in this view the law represents an innate law of nature, a directly revealed law, or an ecclesiastical or canon one, in each case it has been believed that following this law, or seeking earnestly to do so, represents a large part of the essential preparation for the status of genuine believer or member of the community and thus legitimate recipient of the treasures promised to faith. Much of patristic Christianity so regarded it; and the entire merit system of medieval piety combined such obedience to canon law with assent to the creeds and participation in the sacraments to define a Catholic in good standing. In the modern period, Deism and most of liberal Protestantism certainly viewed Christianity in this way; and even much evangelical Protestantism — despite its frequent disclaimers — has regarded only those who practice the evangelical law as holders of true faith. I think, moreover, that this represents the dominant form of Christianity today, whether one looks at popular evangelical piety on the right, at mainline Protestantism in the middle, or at liberationist Christianity on the left. They may disagree thoroughly about what the law urges them to do, but all seem to agree that following it represents the supreme condition or prerequisite for religion in any meaningful sense.

Schoolmaster to Repentance

In direct and conscious opposition to this tradition of "works" has been another which has seen the preparatory work of the law in a very different light. To this tradition moral works of the law, even were they possible for us, could not in any way really provide the conditions for either faith or justification or even for the reception of sacramental grace and certainly not for eternal life. Only God's free and unmerited—by any sort of works— grace can do that. The religious relation comes only as God's gift—what the Shin tradition and its recent advocate Tanabe Hajime call Other Power—and not as a result of our moral or religious efforts, however strenuous.[1]

Still, and paradoxically, the law for this second tradition does have an important preparatory function; in fact it is, as Saint Paul said, the schoolmaster that leads us to Christ. In this role the law reveals to us our moral and spiritual inability and thus uncovers to us our estrangement and bondage. The law persuades us, or elicits our assent, voluntarily to repent in humility, to despair of our own powers, and to depend entirely upon the grace of Christ for our soul's health. For this view, the ethical, if followed with seriousness, ends in a nemesis; but realization of that nemesis can—if we so will—lead us on to the religious level. Thus, as Kierkegaard once said and Tanabe has repeated,[2] repentance represents the fundamental form of ethics for those who find themselves unable to follow the law or to break the bondage of sin. Here repentance is an act of ours, an act in which we voluntarily, consciously, and deliberately participate, and must do so; an act that begins or initiates the religious. Clearly, for this tradition, grace is also involved; but so are we, if it is to be genuine repentance. After all, the same combination of grace with our willed participation holds equally for the other, more familiar role of ethics, namely, as referent to the ethical fruits of love that may follow.

SPIRITUAL DISCIPLINES

When we turn to the category of discipline or, perhaps better, spiritual practices, we come to the heart of the preparatory role of ethics in most profound

---

[1] Tanabe Hajime, *Philosophy as Metanoetics,* trans. Takeuchi Yoshinori (Berkeley: University of California Press, 1986), 190.
[2] Ibid.

religions. The range of practices here is immense, and it characterizes the behavior patterns of the serious participants in the major religions of the world: the monastic or ascetical patterns of life that dominate vast communities of Buddhist and Christian religious; the vows characteristic of most powerful religious communities; the important spiritual practices of meditation, yogic exercises, *Zazen;* and so on. As a result of the combined influences of Reformation and Enlightenment, all of this has been generally regarded in the modern West as delusive, escapist, and irrelevant; as failing to do what these "works" claim to do, namely, to nurture the soul or even to prepare for the religious; and as diverting proper attention from the real business of religious ethics, namely, creative action in the "real world."

At present this judgment, so it seems to me, shows itself to have been seriously premature. One cannot but feel that Western Christianity is weakest in its spiritual content, in the depth and reality of its religious existence, of its interior, personal relation to God—ironically exactly what the Reformation sought to reestablish in a world dominated by defunct spiritual practices. Present Christianity's theology is surely muddling, its ethics faltering, but where it is really at a loss is in the realm of inner piety, and here it suffers from a dearth of discipline, of spiritual practices.

Correspondingly, most of the lure of non-Western religions—Buddhist, Hindu, Sufi, and Sikh—lies here: not in theology, not even in liturgy, certainly not in their religious ethics for and in the world, but here in the wealth and crucial relevance of the spiritual practices they offer that nurture the soul, nurture identity, and make possible an experienced touch with the divine. One further point: Even in Protestantism this spiritual barrenness, if I may so describe it, was not always the case. Puritanism, Pietism, and nineteenth-century evangelical life emphasized the role of moral law. They also emphasized their own sorts of spiritual practices: daily Bible readings, daily prayers, regular—in fact almost endless—church attendance, moral self-discipline, and all those things they considered good works. Evangelicals did not relish thinking of these things as "merits" or as "ascetic" practices, although these practices may well have looked that way to their skeptical or fun-loving neighbors! But despite their evangelical theory of sheer grace, they pursued spiritual practices diligently. I am confident that nothing is further from the intentions of the Christians reading this chapter, including the author, than reviving these practices of Victorian evangelical piety, and thus most of this for us now is only a part of history. But the hard fact is that, as a result, the inner "religious" element, the element of piety in Protestant Christianity, has had immense difficulty ever since. One sign of this is the strange fact that while spiritual practices clearly dominate most of serious religion, the study of this side of religion has been noticeably absent from our schools of divinity and seminaries. We study Scripture, theology and ethics, church history, counseling, preaching, and church administration, but hardly any curricular, intellectual, or spiritual effort is spent on the center: the nurture of our own souls and their relation to God. Have we turned over all of this side of religion to the analyst?

In any case, there can be little question that in this crucial area of religious ethics, where ethics represents a path to the religious, Buddhism has at present infinitely richer resources to offer than Christianity has. It is this side of Buddhism, the capacity of its various traditions to prepare the soul for enlightenment, that rightly makes it so attractive to us all—to those of the West who have become Buddhist and to those who wish to be helped by it. To be sure, the mystical and monastic traditions in Catholicism are themselves exceedingly rich resources, and it is no accident that these have quite recently been rediscovered and restudied by Catholics and Protestants alike with an intense and new sense of their relevance. Nevertheless, here we have the most to learn from our Buddhist colleagues.

This does not mean, I wish to urge, that by borrowing new forms of their traditional modes of self-help we are reembarking upon the path of "merit," as our Reformation forefathers might well have thought. The latter, too, as a matter of course undertook regular spiritual practices considered appropriate for spiritual nurture. In using those practices (prayer, Bible reading, and the like), they were certain not only that these practices alone were insufficient and could be dangerous but that without them faith, or better, grace, would find only parched and barren ground. This is in fact more or less Tanabe's position: Salvation, the religious relation to Absolute Nothingness, is utterly dependent, he says, on Other Power and received only by faith. Nevertheless, without the strenuous effort of self-power, in serious ethical striving and repentance, no mediation of the Absolute is possible for us.[3] As self-power must for him unite with Other Power, *jiriki* with *tariki,* so, for even Reformation Christians, the law and discipline must accompany the gospel if the latter is to be heard effectively.

ETHICS AS FULFILLMENT
OF RELIGION

Let us now turn to ethics as the fulfillment of religion. Here a number of very important traditional words or symbols come before us: obedience to the law; *caritas,* the love that perfects faith; love as the "deed" of faith; the third role of the law as a guide rather than a condemnation—and so on down to the moral ideals, the social gospel, and the liberationist movements of modern Christianity. This has been, as we noted, generally what Christian ethics has been taken to mean, and it is a many-faceted tradition. Ethics in this tradition was largely, though not exclusively (as medieval Catholic good works show), personal and individual in character: being good or holy and striving to keep the relevant Christian community holy. But since the eighteenth century significant shifts of concern have occurred, and the focus has latterly been on action seeking to build moral community in the world:

---

[3] Ibid., li, 4, 7, 9, 17, 30, 86–87, passim.

tolerance, succor, justice, liberation, and peace. As Buddhism is far richer on ethics as preparation, so, as many Buddhists have long recognized, Christianity seems to be richer here, especially in questions of social ethics. Among a number of factors that might be cited, four have been, I think, especially important: (1) the Hebrew prophetic and rabbinical tradition in which moral obedience to Yahweh is central to the religious covenant; (2) the clear emphasis in the New Testament on love and service to the neighbor as the test as well as the fruit of real faith; (3) the presence throughout the tradition of the symbol of the Kingdom, signaling the rule over social relations, and with that the moral rule, of God; and (4) the Western concentration, largely due to Christianity and Judaism, on history, on this life in social community, and so on the ultimate responsibility of the Christian and the Christian community for justice—in all the many interpretations of that word—within the wider historical community.

Clearly any interpretation of Christianity that does not recognize and make central these ethical fruits that accompany faith is inadequate on all four counts. From Paul to liberationist theology, all agree that without love all else is vain. Faith must issue in works, else it is not so much barren as completely lacking! In this sense, although Paul may be the "official" theologian for most of Protestantism and latterly of Catholicism, to me the Epistle of James represents the closest scriptural norm of most modern theology: Faith without works is dead, or, put in our current idiom, any theory without praxis is abstract if not ideological. Now, if I do not here enlarge much further on this theme, it is not because of lack of interest in it. I thoroughly agree with modern liberationist theologies that praxis in the world for justice and liberation is the heart, as it is the test, of Christian faith. There is more to religion than this, to be sure, but there is nothing of ultimate importance to all the rest of religion if this is lacking. It is the most necessary of all the necessary "hither" conditions of true faith.

What is more, much of modern Christianity—and a good deal of modern Buddhism—has discovered that love enacted in the world's life must, like most things that enter the world, change its form. It must appear as an aim, a striving for justice, justice compounded of differing amounts of equality, freedom, and order, one of these three being more called-for in any given situation than the others. What is even more startling, action here for justice must frequently, if not always, take the form of political action and thus use—and seek not to misuse—some of the worldly instruments of power.

The reason for this necessity of the political is simple. As both of our traditions hold firmly, evil in human history does ultimately stem from the human heart, from our inward parts: from sin and ignorance, hubris and ego, concupiscence and desire. These are, to be sure, in a sense subjective, inward, spiritual. But their effects in the world—through the mediation of the human creativity that fashions the cultural world—are to be seen objectively, out there, in the misshapen, alienated, and oppressive institutions that dominate history: institutions of slavery, economic privilege, overweening political power, patriarchal dominance, social, class, and racial hierarchy. These warped institutions channel behavior from generation to generation. As warped in favor of the dominant groups that helped to fashion them, they encourage sin, give free rein to it, and perpetuate it. They thus mediate the sins of the strong into the lives of the weak and cause the untold suffering of the latter. Such institutions must be refashioned if love or compassion is to become realized, embodied in the actual world. Love is spiritual, but its work in the world is not merely spiritual. As Berdyaev said, the work of love is also the material action of breaking and sharing bread, and that means political and social action.

Contemporary Buddhism, if I may hazard a couple of judgments on this point, has also recognized this, and compassion, enriched by the twin concepts of justice and *agape*, has recently been much more clearly and centrally articulated than before, and practiced, even into the political arena. To me the largest reflective problem for Buddhism in the region of social ethics is the difficulty within the Buddhist perspective of a philosophy or theology of history and so of a philosophy or theology of historical community within history. These two (philosophy of history and of community) provide — and have always done so — the necessary ontological base for any social ethic, as a philosophical or theological anthropology provides the necessary theoretical base for ethics as a whole.

We return then to Christianity. As a consequence of its most fundamental structure, it has been an essential aspect of Christianity to look forward to redemption and to the redemption of the world — now understood explicitly as the world of history, of communities in space and time. This vision of a redeemed community, of the Kingdom, has motivated most of the creative works, such as they are, of Christians; and this vision, secularized in any number of forms, has given all of modern life perhaps its peculiar flavor of political intensity, of impatient expectation, and yet of social seriousness and responsibility. To those of us whose life experience spans the tragic contours of twentieth-century history, any simple expectation of a redeemed human future seems difficult and precarious indeed. We feel we will be lucky to survive through the next century, far less establish a new kingdom at its close! Nevertheless, recognizing how precarious our own personal redemption has been, and how even more dubious has been our personal growth in grace over time — in both of which we still retain confidence — let us not despair about the power and intentions of providence with regard to communities or about the possibilities of ethical action in history, if that action is grounded in genuine religious transformation. We do believe in the possibility of that transformation, both for individual persons and communal history. We can, therefore, also believe in the possibility of greater grace, wider justice, and so of deeper community and peace in the human future. But that hope for the future, fundamental to our faith, sends us back to our theme for the present: How are religious transformation and ethical action to be fruitfully combined?

Let me in conclusion, therefore, bring together these two elements I have discriminated within the ethical in its relation to the religious. I have sought to argue, first, that the ethical fruits of the religious—being for others in the world and so praxis for liberation—are central. Further, I have claimed that the religious, the relation to God, is neither dispensable nor subordinate. On the contrary, in the entire Christian tradition—and in Buddhism—the ethical behavior I have described presupposes an important inner transformation of the self, a return to its authentic self from its inauthentic one, and thus a loss or negation of self, a recentering, a rebirth, a *metanoia* of its attachments, loves, goals, center of security. On the basis of this religious transformation, the self may then act creatively for others in the world. Hence there is in both traditions a prior and inner negation of self in order that there be an outward rebirth of the ethical. Unless this is so, the ethical hardly follows from the religious but tends totally to dominate it, as we have seen.

If this is granted, if the religious is central in some way to the ethical as its source and ground (and recall, I do not mean by the religious the theological), if an inner change is necessary in order for new outer action to be possible, the question of the spiritual conditions for that religious reality becomes important precisely for the ethical in the world. To "transcend the world and the world's ways" in order to serve the world creatively is hardly natural, nor is it a result of ordinary educational procedures, even at the Ph.D. level. It does not even follow from hearing or studying good theology. It comes through concern, effort, and practice, by passing through and not avoiding the ethical, as Kierkegaard insisted. As I have suggested, it especially requires some consistent and serious modes of spiritual practice— if the religious is to be the serious and indispensable partner to the ethical that both our traditions insist it is. Again, we return to Buddhism's value to Christians in this dialogue on the existential and religious levels, as well as on the theological, and its rich tradition of practices. At first reflection, ethics seems to represent a Christian game that Christians play (at least in theory and articulation) better than others do. But the daily practice that makes possible excellence at this game is possibly coached best by our colleagues from South and East Asia.

CHAPTER 11

THE CHURCH AND PUBLIC POLICY

Should religious institutions concentrate solely on the spiritual health and moral guidance of their members and alone through them influence the directions the wider community will take? Or should the institution through its constitutive leadership and administrative structures seek to influence public policies in whatever ways are available to us in a democracy — through education, pronouncement, argument and persuasion, protest and lobbying — as, for example, the American Catholic bishops have done in their pastoral letters, as Jewish groups have done, or as the various communities of the National Council of Churches have done for some time.

I take it that a third alternative for us is out, namely, to seek any directly constituted authority and power of a religious body or persons — open or hidden — over legislative, judicial, or executive processes. We would all repudiate this, I presume, both on constitutional and probably on religious grounds as well, whether we mean the authority of Rome or of a bishop or a set of bishops or, most bizarre of all yet unfortunately most likely, of a self-chosen set of Baptist preachers. If I opt for the second alternative, as I shall, that is, the explicit effort on the part of religious bodies to influence public policies — through means available in the democratic process — this is not because I dream of a "Christian America" or even of a Christian party, and through either one the establishment of Christianity as the preferred and so guiding religious influence in American life. When religion thus seeks through political means to dominate the world, whether an empire, a nation, or a party, it becomes in turn dominated by the world; it may gain the world, but it loses its soul; it literally takes up the sword and dies by it; and, correspondingly, as Roger Williams and William Penn argued, the souls of all those within its orbit are endangered.

Clearly if we repudiate both inaction in the public realm (and concentration alone on the religion of individuals) and direct political action (the effort of a spiritual power to rule the political realm), we are involved in a fairly tricky balancing act. The academic name for such a saunter down a tight rope is *dialectic:* neither this, on the one hand, nor that, on the other, but both-and, and only so much of this and only so much of that. My teacher Reinhold Niebuhr used to love such a run between opposite extremes: He always avoided "the Scylla of spiritual domination," on the one hand, and the "Charybdis of religious withdrawal," on the other. Each of us, too, is aware of this dialectic in his or her own experience of this issue, for there are even at present twin dangers that face us. When Protestant liberals urge suburban churches to get their churches involved in economic, political, and social issues, meaning justice, peace, and racial equality, down at the end of the same road they meet Jerry Falwell, and they turn around. When Catholics applaud, as they should, the bishops' letters on nuclear deterrence and economic justice, down that same road they meet Archbishop O'Connor— and the ghosts of McIntyre, O'Boyle, and Spellman—with their quite different Catholic agenda for the public realm. Each one seeks to bring religion to bear on public life; each has a significantly different agenda to propose, and the two sides have significantly different means of exerting that influence. As a consequence, since we do not recommend their interpretation of the role of religion in politics, we must be at once persuasive and careful in putting our point. In an epoch when social anxiety expands and so religious fervor waxes strong, a great deal, a very great deal, is at stake in this debate.

REASONS FOR THE CHURCH'S PUBLIC ROLE

Let us begin positively, with the fundamental theological reasons religious institutions must, within certain limits to be clarified later, take on an active, persuasive role in public policy. One of the most fundamental theological propositions in our tradition is that there is and can be no individual Christianity, a religion of self-subsistent individuals. All Christianity—as all Judaism—is communal in character. We are created by God in community, male and female, the prototype of the community; as both human and religious—and the two are in the end identical—we are members of community: of the covenant people, the people of Israel, the people of God, the church. Correspondingly, the goal of our faith is both communal and individual together, expressed by the two great biblical symbols: the messianic reign of God and the kingdom of God. We may enter as individuals, although even that is questionable, but what we enter is a community of faith and obedience. Moreover, all communities in history are also institutions, with institutional and therefore political and social structures of authority, decision, and implementation. As our psychological and sociological self-understanding tells us, persons and community are polar, each essential to the other, each creative of the other—and destructive! Correspondingly, our religious faith assures us, however personal, individual, and inward our faith, it is at all because of and in a community and its tradition, and it expresses itself outwardly in the common, shared, ongoing institutional life of that community.

Religious institutions, however, are always themselves in a wider community, the political, economic, social, and cultural community as a whole. They may be in it in various ways: They may dominate it, avoid it, protest against it, quietly be one part of it, ignore it, or seek to influence it. But all alike are in it, willy-nilly. Only if they and each of their members cut all of their essential ties with the world — as in certain monastic communities and sectarian groups — are they in any meaningful sense separate or independent. But if their members and leaders are in the world and participate in it, if their homes, vocations, and recreation are part of the world, certainly the institution also is a solid part of that world.

This participation in the world is fundamental, determinative, and total. It is not just that the wider community allows and supports the churches — tax breaks and so on. The interpenetration of church and world reaches far deeper into the spiritual and ethical being of the religious community. Religious institutions reproduce the culture religiously: in their modes of liturgy, their thoughts about their beliefs, most of their norms and goals, in their social relations among themselves, in their hierarchies of authority. Roman Catholicism here is America in Catholic form, as are the Presbyterians, Episcopalians, and especially (ironically) the Baptists. Ask a European, and the answer will be unequivocal. Thus, unless it works at it — and this is real work — the church is segregated in a segregated culture, nationalistic in a nationalistic culture, materialistic in a materialistic culture, class conscious in a class culture. The sins of the world quickly enough affect and contaminate the life of the church. Since the church's life and especially that of its middle-class members profits from these worldly social structures, the church has a responsibility to deal with them. To be in the world (and our churches are certainly there) is to be ruled by the world, unless . . . Without an explicit criticism of and protest against these cultural sins, therefore, the church is itself swamped by them and guilty through them. We saw this clearly with Germany and we see it in South Africa. Unless these churches concern themselves deeply and actively with public policy, they quickly become Nazi or racist and are so judged. There is no choice here: You either deal with public policy or else you sink because of it. A church that ignores public policy is determined by it and is rightly blamed for it.

We are, then, as religious communities in and of the wider community, the world — and we have no intention, laity or clergy, of getting out. What then are we to do? How is the church to be in the world and yet neither swamped by the world and so useless nor a danger to the world and so demonic? Let me suggest that we have a positive and a negative role in relation to the world, to culture, if you will, a priestly and a prophetic role. The church also has much the same relation — of affirmation and criticism — to herself, and that complicates matters endlessly, as Falwell and O'Connor teach us. But for now, let us speak of our supportive and our critical roles in relation to society, that is, vis-à-vis our public policy on important social issues.

PRIESTLY ROLE IN SOCIETY

As the communal character of Christianity — and of Judaism — issues from the deepest theological level of both, so does the positive relation of the church, the people of God, to the creative cultural life of women and men. Biblical faith has always insisted that men and women are made in the image of God, and this has been universally interpreted in the tradition as the culture-creative powers of the human spirit: reason, both practical and theoretical, freedom and self-determination, the sense of beauty, and the *eros* toward value. It has emphasized, in fact originated, the reality of each human as *person* and the corresponding value of community as potentially just and caring. This sense of the human as creative of culture and of culture as the locus of human values is not confined to our biblical tradition, but it is forcefully expressed there; we are at a very deep level a humanistic faith.

We can go even further. Let me suggest that wherever the church's public policy ceases to represent an alliance with secular forces in support of secular aims and ideals (civil rights, peace, economic justice), we become uneasy about it. That is, whenever it is, so to speak, purely religious, most of us now tend to step aside and even to disapprove. When the churches in Germany defended against the Nazis the "freedom of the pulpit" or the "sanctity of church property," and not the Jews, we saw them as inexcusably remiss ethically. When Protestants seek to teach biblical creation and to conduct prayer services in public schools, we resist; when Catholic leaders seek to implement their views on abortion in terms of public law, many feel uneasy. It is, I suggest, this point that Governor Mario Cuomo and Representative Geraldine Ferraro, both Roman Catholics, have correctly made: A statesperson can support a widely based moral-religious policy, but she or he should not be required to implement a public policy based solely on the particular doctrines and laws of their own special group. Positive public policies of churches should represent a union or alliance of their own ethical concerns with the traditional goals of our democratic heritage.

This union with its secular context is important for the church to recall and to admit in its dealing with the world. We have a tendency, both the conservative and the liberal among us (though possibly for different reasons), to emphasize our spiritual separation from the world and our moral and religious criticism of the world. Thus has much of the humanist tradition censored us for being antihumanistic and anticultural. My point, therefore, is that the church should also support the world insofar as the social and cultural life that surrounds us supports personal values and creative social relations.

This support of the world's best values is also deeply a part of our faith. We know that humans are destined by their Creator to become children of God; that this means the fullest and freest development of their human powers of mind, soul, and body; and that this in turn is possible only in so far as men and women live in a society that fosters these developments, the nurture of persons, and fosters them justly and equally. The love for our neighbors—our most fundamental ethical requirement—means this fostering of a world, a social world, in which persons can become persons. It means just and equal social, economic, educational, and political opportunities. It means an order and a peace in which such just institutions are possible. At the deepest theological level, therefore, in our understanding of the creative power and infinite worth of each person, and in our requirement to care for all without favor, the Christian community is impelled into the world to remake that world in a new image.

None of us today sees the world as many did seventy-five years ago, as moving joyously toward perfection, as a committed host marching together toward a better world—although to listen to the political claims made all around us, this is the case! We are aware that many of the forces in the world that create public policy do not have the same aims to support, and certainly not the same means to suggest, as we do. Nevertheless, despite the world's vast ambiguity—and it is to us, after all, a "fallen" world—still there are forces there, and especially there are norms, ideals, and goals there, that parallel ours. In fact, far far back, our secular culture has in most cases learned these, its own goals, from us; and, in an equal number of situations in the modern period, it has been our secular antagonists that have had to remind the church of these, her own ideals. As Augustine said, the worldly city, too, strives for justice, order, and peace, as we do.

This congruence of the best aims of the secular world and the social implications of Christian love is quite remarkable. In fact, if one surveys important Christian ethics in our day, one finds it largely concerned with the same social issues with which authentic secular morals are busy; and, even more, one finds the norms or ideals of Christian ethics to represent largely worldly goals and values, namely, justice, equality, and peace. The issues in the last decades that have excited us as Christians have been precisely the major moral issues of public policy: civil rights, Vietnam, women's rights, poverty, and above all peace and nuclear disarmament and most recently the rescue of the earth. The relation of these to Christian ethics is clear enough; the fact that they are "secular" issues and that these values are "secular," and in that sense "natural" values, is equally clear. This is not true only of the church in a democratic and liberal culture. One notes that liberation theology south of us here represents a union of Christian self-understanding with a good number of secular social interpretations and social aims different from ours—too much, apparently, for Cardinal Ratzinger. It is ironic that a conservative church, thoroughly united from top to bottom with the theoretical and practical categories of Hellenistic culture, should look askance at its modern equivalents, which understand the church's role in public policy in the more relevant terms of modern social theory, democratic or socialist. In any case, this near identity in this broad sense of "natural law" and Christian obligation, of the health of the body politic with the concerns of Christian obedience, is noteworthy and healthy. If the church is in the world, its only responsible posture is at the same time consciously to represent in its constituted actions a parallel "responsibility" for the world, that is, for the world's good and so for the public policies (economic, political, military, and social) of the world.

I have suggested that this positive role of the church in supporting the humane aims of its cultural matrix, and in allying itself (both individually and institutionally) with secular and other forces implementing these aims, is a priestly role. It is this in several senses. First, it is a conserving role: conserving the ideals of justice, fairness, equality, individual rights, freedom, and responsible order that are our inheritance from the democratic tradition. These are part of the secular covenant in which we all share; and we should teach these traditional values of our secular inheritance as our values, too; we should defend them before their detractors in the world; and we should join politically with those who would defend and implement these values. But, more precisely, these constitutive elements of democracy represent, I believe, what one can call, somewhat paradoxically, the secular religious substance of our cultural life, those things in which we believe and which we value, what we as a society hold in common and so what binds us together, and those things for which — as many have shown not only in battle but also in protest — we would die. They are an ultimate concern. All cultures have such a religious substance; secular cultures, like ours and Marxist cultures, have a "secular" religious substance. Thus, in entering a culture, a particular religious tradition like Christianity makes uneasy but important union with that cultural religious substance. (An example of this is the very tricky, genuinely painful, union of Catholicism and Protestantism with the "secular religious substance" of mainland China.) The early church did this with Hellenism; we have done it with modernity: with its science, its views of persons and communities, and its democracy or socialism. It seems odd, but I am suggesting that priests, pastors, and the laity, therefore, become also and see themselves as "priests" of this secular religious substance: the values of peace, justice, equality, and freedom. These can alone rescue our common life in the world, can redeem it in a worldly way if it be redeemed — they are also of God, and thus they call for our priestly care.

But priests, in being priests, also call a tradition back to its origins and forward to its own fulfillment. Thus the church does not only support the going secular democratic self-understanding of our body politic and the allied secular efforts politically to enhance that tradition. It should seek to lure that self-understanding and those institutional structures to higher and nobler forms. Every social tradition represents a compromise of its ideals; it also represents a partial interpretation of them, an interpretation from the point of view — and in the interest — of the classes that established that social tradition and that articulated those ideals. Thus, modern democracy is never pure democracy at any point; it has always been tilted in favor of the propertied classes, the bourgeoisie, that helped to establish it. Even at their highest level, therefore, its articulated ideals need criticism, new formulation, wider and deeper application. Every tradition, Reinhold Niebuhr used to say, has in it indeterminate possibilities of higher forms: more just laws, more open economic situations, more creative peace. Thus, one "secular" role of the gospel, of its ideal of mutual and selfless love and its social norm of the Kingdom, is to criticize and lure long-established notions of justice, obligation, power, and equality into deeper interpretations and so onto higher levels. In our lifetime we have seen this dramatically illustrated in the new insights into what justice means racially and sexually, meanings of democratic justice undreamed of even fifty years ago. Thus does the priestly role of conserving the religious substance of public life shade into the prophetic role in relation to public life, and so let us now turn there.

PROPHETIC ROLE IN SOCIETY

The world is "fallen" as well as latent with glowing possibilities. This point, too, is deeply embedded in the foundations of our theology, as it is also daily verified by public experience. It affects, as it should, the character of the public policies and role of the churches.

Concretely this symbol of a fallen world means that the world's life, traditions, institutions, behavior, aims, and goals — yes, even its highest norms — reflect not only the image of God, the aim toward personhood, caring, and community but also the heartless indifference of the world, its avoidance of responsibility for the other, the concupiscence or greed of the world for plenty, for status and power and security; and the pride of the world in making its own life central and thus idealizing and divinizing that life in all its aspects. Thus are the world and its institutions and behavior ambiguous, *zweideutig:* filled with idealism, virtuous intentions, and noble aims but also corrupted, diverted from those aims into self-serving ones. It is thus characterized through and through by injustice, oppression, exploitation, and conflict. The world builds and rebuilds itself; it also destroys itself and then destroys itself again. In this process untold suffering, for guilty and innocent alike (for the children "to the third and fourth generations"), results.

Because this is so, the church finds itself involved in worldly affairs and policies. This manifest and universal evil — this oppression, conflict, destruction, and suffering — is in large part the result of sin. I do not mean that it is the punishment wrought on us by God's judgment for Eve's and Adam's sin, as the tradition insisted, although that is a somewhat skewed image of the truth. I mean that the indifference, concupiscence, pride, and self-love of the world — its condition of being in sin — represent the central causes of these our woes. It has been fashionable in modern life to blame our ills on ignorance, disorganization, faulty beliefs and ideals, organized religion. While all of these surely contribute to our social dilemmas, none is its root cause. What makes institutions oppressive and keeps them that way, what deeply endangers human good, is not our knowledge or lack of it, our instruments or lack of them, or even our bungling social structures; rather it is the driving self-interest with which they are reared, shaped, defended, and used. What threatens modern life is neither lack of theoretical knowledge, paucity of technology, nor faulty organization. We have knowledge, technology, and organization to spare. What threatens us mortally is the way we use or might use them—what we do with them. If we use our weapons, our scientific developments, and industrial power heedlessly and selfishly, we will blow ourselves up, dehumanize our common life, and despoil the environment. It is our sinful use of our creative cultural powers, of the image of God, that sours, distorts, and makes lethal our social structures and public policies alike. As that institution explicitly devoted to the conquest of sin and the mitigation of its effects, the church must be concerned with the public world, where the results of sins dominate every vista.

When a religious community seeks to tackle sin in the world's life, more often than not what it confronts there is not so much the secular order, strangely enough, and certainly not the secularity of that order, as it is a distorted form of itself, that is, of the religious. As I have asserted, sin is a religious phenomenon as well as a moral one: It is idolatry resulting in injustice, as Niebuhr put it. A religious phenomenon is, as its name implies, an aspect of "religion."

We have already pictured the baleful role of sin in social history. Who could doubt that greed for power, arrogance, insecurity of class, and self-loss create the roots of the slavery, the tyranny, the vast economic disparity, and the sexual domination that plague our communal life? Correspondingly, as sin makes social institutions radically unjust, it is the religious dimension of social existence that gives them their staying power and lethal effect. By this religious dimension I mean the common experience that a "way of life" that favors and defends one race, nation, class, or sex is made ultimate, declared holy, the source of civilized hope and legitimate faith, the peacemaker and the defender of rights for the world. Its rivals are accused of godlessness and therefore of spawning the world's share of evil. In such an unfortunate "natural process," this way of life is made absolute, given ultimate commitment and loyalty, made the center of trust and obedience. As a result, it claims military, political, and economic predominance and proceeds to achieve it. Correspondingly its rival makes the same ultimate claims, levels parallel accusations of imperialism and ideology, and proceeds to take what it can. Here two diverse but also strangely interrelated ultimate symbolisms, two cultural alternatives, clash; it is a struggle of cultural religious substances against one another, not at all unlike, even down to its details, the religious wars of the past or of, say, the present Middle East. The world's major conflicts, like the great tyrannies of the world and the most devastating revolutions, exhibit a religious dimension, a claim to ultimacy of power, wisdom, and virtue. What makes these conflicts infinitely cruel, fanatical, and devastating is this religious element. That element also provides the courage, self-sacrifice, and infinite drive essential to history's chaos.

This ambiguity of the religious in the world complicates life for the church in dealing with public policy; but it also provides her with her rights there. In a crucial public issue, for example, nuclear disarmament, one is dealing not only with technical and policy issues and not only with common legal and moral issues. At base this is also a religious issue, for what we are facing here is an ultimate commitment to national security, a nationalism with a religious dimension or tone to it, combined with a similar commitment to a capitalist ideology. Both nationalism and a social ideology can be, in fact are, secular religions, matters of ultimate concern, as Nazi Germany showed us. There the churches confronted (or should have confronted) not only technical, political, and moral problems; at the most fundamental level they faced an alien religiosity, Nazi paganism, as a dissident church in Poland and Russia has faced an absolutized Marxist ideology. This is not, mind you, only their problem; it can well be ours too. When the bishops' letters state a Christian position on nuclear war or on capitalism, they are countering the fledgling—and not so helpless either—idolatries surrounding the American way of life. It is important, as I have noted, for the church to give a reasoned critique of national policy based both on that nation's true self-interest and on a deep interpretation of our shared democratic and moral values. It is also important for the church—and only an institution adept at religion can do it—to uncover and critique the pervasive idolatries in our national life. As before in history, the church is called not only to support the humanistic values of the surrounding secular world but also, as prophetic, to counter its many and deadly idolatries.

There are times in history when union with their culture is no longer possible for the churches, although they may well not realize or want to realize this fact. I refer to times when the religious substance of the culture, its political, economic, and social institutions, and so also the patterns of social existence in daily life are antithetical in some deep, pervasive, and permanent way to the aims and standards of the churches for persons and community. Such times arise in a totalitarian society, in an oppressive colonial society, in a society oppressively exploited by both domestic and foreign powers. Here a demonic and idolatrous ideological base combines with an absolute political and economic structure to create a radical disjunction with the church's aims and life. Such an adversarial relationship is present obviously in several Central and South American countries, frequently though not always in communist nations, and, as we have noted, potentially present in the threat of a "Christian America." Since in such situations democratic procedures either do not exist or have been so disfigured as to be quite ineffective, a more direct adversarial role of the church in relation to public policy is called for, possibly including even revolutionary action, if that is politically relevant and possible.

Again, however, although such action represents a sharp break between church and culture, let us note the deep union on another level of democratic tradition (if not of its sentiments at a particular moment) with a Christian political ethic. To both, at least as I see them, the right of revolutionary action, in the name of liberation and against a crushing tyranny, remains a possibility, provided more peaceful means of the redress of ills and the improvement of conditions are fundamentally and permanently (in principle) absent. Thus, in liberating political action against a distorted "democracy" (and all forms of tyranny in our day also term themselves democratic), we illustrate ironically once again a certain union of the church with the democratic tradition—even more, so it seems to me, than with the Marxist tradition, which recognizes no right of continuing revolution.

GOD'S JUDGMENT ON ECCLESIAL SELF-ABSOLUTIZATION

When the church becomes radically critical of the social order, the situation becomes even more deeply complicated. The church is encountering (to its surprise) not only false religion in the world but also (to its chagrin) the false image of itself, or itself falsely construed. As history shows, an absolutized culture and an absolutized religious community feed on each other: They breed, encourage, and support each other in baffling interunion. An absolutized religion tends inexorably to absolutize its cultural base, as in Catholic Spain and now in Iran. Correspondingly, an absolute or totalitarian state, as the German churches showed, attracts to itself aspects of the church, both Protestant and Catholic, which in turn absolutize themselves and their union with the political. With the separation of the church and state in our Constitution, with the seeming insistence on that separation (against Catholicism) by evangelical Protestants, and with the appearance of Vatican II, the nightmare of religious theocracy combined with a nationalistic and capitalistic ideology seemed just that—only a bad dream. To our astonishment and dismay, however, the twentieth century has shown itself as the century not only of political but also of religious and clerical absolutism—and the fearsome union of the two. Totalitarian political movements and theocratic societies, both supposed to have disappeared from our history, have reappeared with increasing frequency. One must recognize, unfortunately, the bizarre reappearance of just this in our contemporary American life. I refer, of course, to the religious right and to its dreams of a "Christian America." Whether there are corresponding movements in Catholic circles, I leave to you; while certainly the aim at theocracy is not completely alien there, at present most of the bishops and almost all the clergy seem deeply to repudiate any return to this aim. But history is full of surprises. As anxiety about both our national security and our traditional values rises—and this may well happen—the demand to unite political power and spiritual values may well increase. Certainly some powerful voices both religious and secular will welcome it.

The real surprise is the Protestant religious right. Traditionally they are sectarian; officially they have formally defended the separation of church and state. Yet, in the right circumstances, churches, as well as other institutions, when they are deeply tempted, fall. It seems that at base every sect, or at least most, dreams secretly of becoming an established church, the spiritual ruler of its world. As we have noted, whatever their theological self-understanding, our churches are actually in culture, devoted to its benefits and opportunities—in other words, deeply committed to the religious substance of the American way of life. Thus, almost against their will and certainly against their largely Baptist theory, their religious devotion and their devotion to capitalistic America have steadily coalesced. Finally, aware of the threat to both, this union has now become explicit and has produced the "biblical demand" that America, God's chosen land, be returned to its founders and rightful rulers, the believing Christians who established it—a historical myth if there ever was one! As in a medieval, Counter-Reformation, or Protestant monarchy, the church in such a case is public policy and public policy is Christian. As a consequence, either religious or secular criticisms of the political or the religious aspects of such a unified society would be out of the question.

This is still a fledgling, and the forces of pluralism, not to mention the major churches and the Constitution, are still strong. Nevertheless, the level of anxiety in our immediate future will probably rise rather than fall. In periods of anxiety, moreover, religion waxes rather than wanes; and fanatical, absolutized, idolatrous religion, not prophetic, rational, and humane religion then appears in strength. We must keep this possibility in mind and guard against it as best we can. For Catholics and Jews to become allies of the political dreams of the evangelical right—whatever the temptations vis-à-vis Israel, abortion, or prayer in school—is to court self-destruction. Neither Jewish nor Catholic conservatives represent the kind of legitimate or rightful rulers of our "Christian" country that Jerry Falwell has in mind!

I have mentioned this because the relation of church or synagogue to public policy is more complex than we ordinarily conceive of it. Not only, to our surprise, must we support much of the secular world's forces and goals; not only must we criticize much of the world's purposes and methods. Also, surprisingly, our support and criticism represent conflicts about the religious, about ultimate values and obligations, conflicts concerning the religious substance of our secular culture. Moreover, when we enter, as we must, this secular-religious domain of public policy, we may well encounter, resist, and, we hope, defeat forms of the *ecclesia* that seek to dominate and rule the public realm for purposes other than those we support.

The theological lessons from all of this illumine some of the meanings of immanence and of transcendence. The relation of the church to the world begins with the immanence of God's power and purposes, through us and within our cultural life, and so entails the church's support of those creative forces. The relation of church to world moves dialectically to the church's critique of the distorted way society enacts these powers and purposes in the world, to the prophetic critique of the sin and suffering of historical life. Thus does the transcendent first appear in prophetic criticism of society, and thus does the church distance itself from the world in order to be true to itself. But the dialectic does not cease there in the opposition of church and world. For now we see, even if we do not wish to, that the church itself is — or has been — involved in the sins of domination, sovereignty, oppression, and conflict in the worldly world. Consequently, a further level of transcendence appears and must appear: the transcendence of God's judgment and grace over the church as well as the world, and so the call for a repentant as well as a faithful and obedient church, and faithful and obedient because it is repentant. In our day it is, ironically, Protestants more than Catholics who have forgotten this, but tomorrow it may be any of us. All of us must, to be faithful, be wary of ourselves as well as of the world as we seek to bring the world closer to the kingdom.

GUIDELINES FOR ECCLESIAL PRAXIS

In conclusion, let me suggest a few guidelines. The situation is far too dialectical and tricky for universal rules (following one of these might end us in the posture of Innocent III). Each situation must be assessed on its own. Here are some possibly helpful guiding principles.

1. The church must be clear on the bases, in its own tradition and in the secular order it inhabits, for its participation in public policy, for its claim for concern with justice, peace, equality, order, and freedom.
2. The culture is already "moral" about all of this, especially conservative, reactionary forces. We do not introduce that dimension but legitimately share in its concern.
3. The church must be aware of and sophisticated about the relation of its social ethic to the culture's ideals — where they agree and where those of the church differ from and even transcend those of the world, for example, deterrence and disarmament.
4. The church must be aware of and guard against the ambiguity of both institutions: worldly and ecclesiastical.
5. The church must recognize that every community — like every individual — needs a conscience, a conscience both supportive and critical. It is clear that the state will not provide this, that only private institutions in the community will. Private religious institutions, that is, churches and synagogues, thus especially have this responsibility.
6. The church must recall that a community — again like an individual — needs courage, confidence, norms, compassion, faith, and hope to live effectively. These do not appear naturally, and if they do appear at all, they can quickly become demonic. As well as being a conscience, the church must be a spiritual source or resource of this common spiritual strength.

PART FOUR

Christian Symbols
of the Faces of Evil

CHAPTER 12

THEODICY AND
PLURALITY

This chapter concerns the effects, as I view them, of the plurality of religions on theodicy. Let us begin with the first, the plurality of religions.

THE PROBLEM OF PLURALITY

Clearly I mean here more than mere plurality; the churches, not to mention the Hebrew Scriptures, have always been conscious of the presence of other religions. What I refer to, therefore, is a new attitude toward these religions, especially in their relation to Christianity. I have, for better or worse, called this new attitude one of rough parity, the recognition of some sort of parity with the others in dialogue, the elimination of our assumption of unquestioned or a priori superiority of our religion, the recognition that each has something to hear and to learn from the other, that we listen as well as speak. Clearly this attitude is the presupposition of dialogue; without it dialogue is a disguise, a mask, for old-style techniques of conversion. To those who do not share this attitude, this chapter is more or less irrelevant; to those who do or suspect they do—and there are many in the churches—it is this new attitude that I name *plurality*. It is in this form, as a sense of rough parity among religions, that plurality poses considerable issues both for theology and theodicy.

It is relevant in understanding the problem of plurality, of this new attitude among religions, to seek to understand its causes. (Chapter 2 explores this in detail.) It is indeed new, as recent as the last decade or two, not only post–World War II but post–Vatican II. There are a number of important theological causes that have been around and been effective for some time: (1) the new sense of the historical relativity of doctrinal propositions and so of the perspectival character of the doctrines and creeds of particular churches (this sense made possible the ecumenical movement among Protestants and Vatican II); (2) the new emphasis on love and tolerance, rather than purity of faith or defense of the faith as the main virtue of the Christian (as reflected, for instance, in our new attitude toward the Crusades); and (3) the new emphasis (as found in Kierkegaard) on hidden inwardness rather than visible externals in religion. Thus, Catholics and Protestants could no longer see each other as enemies or even aliens; thus, they began to recognize Jews as comembers of God's covenants; and gradually all this spilled over even into other religious traditions. Could I see myself as saved by the infinity of divine grace and not by my works of piety, correct doctrine, ethical virtue, or especially church membership and not see my Buddhist neighbor in the same way? One marks these shifts in the great theologians of the early twentieth century: Karl Barth (note his universalism), H. Emil Brunner, Paul Tillich, the Niebuhrs—all agreed that the work of saving grace far transcends the bounds of the visible *ecclesia.* Karl Rahner put this elegantly, if for many undiplomatically, when he recognized the presence of saving grace in other religions and thus termed their faithful adherents anonymous Christians, sharers without knowing it in the universal benefits of Christ. This is the "liberal" position; it is often called inclusivism, and it has been characteristic of the tradition of liberal Protestantism since the Enlightenment (for example, Schleiermacher), of many liberal Catholics in the nineteenth and twentieth centuries, and of much of Roman Catholic teaching since Vatican II.

Rough parity goes beyond this liberal position, however: It recognizes, or seeks to recognize, the value and validity in its own right of the other's religious tradition. Other religions are not regarded as underdeveloped forms of our religion. Rough parity is loath to claim a definitive, final, and absolute validity and efficacy for our own; our religion, even our revelation, does not define what is true and of value in theirs. Thus, again, is dialogue possible when both listen as well as speak. If then we ask for the causes of this further movement toward parity, they are not, I think, theological but social and cultural in character. The theological interpretation beyond this is only now forming itself; it is not, therefore, a cause of the further movement.

Since 1945 the absolute dominance by the West of the entire rest of the world has dramatically ceased. Recall that before 1945 almost the entire globe was ruled by European powers. Their military and political rule was accompanied by a vast sense of cultural, moral, and religious superiority.

In the West's eyes the United States inherited that power; but with the loss of the colonial empires, that inheritance itself and the power that went with it have vastly shrunk. Now other centers of power (such as the Eastern Bloc, the Third World), other cultural forms (Japan, China, for instance), other vibrant and potent religious forces (Islam, for example), appear on our scene. Many of them have even entered our own space in mission movements of their own, and it is our children, not theirs, who are converted to non-Western forms of religion. All this represents an entirely new set of relations. It dazzles us, American and European alike, and it makes us anxious. These cultures (Japan, China, India, and the like), moreover, are determined to be modernized but not Westernized. They are adopting, as we did, modern science, technology, and industrialism, but in their own way, not as an underdeveloped form of us but as maturing cultures with their own integrity. Neither we nor they fully recognize this new set of relations yet. But parity is on its way, and the dream of a universal Western culture is now as utopian as that of triumphalist Christianity was.

This parity has for a number of reasons appeared first among the religions, as a new sense of religious parity. It will sometime soon make its appearance in the culture as a whole, and even in the academy, when the Western consciousness and self-consciousness ceases to regard itself as universal and recognizes itself as one particular and limited form of human and cultural consciousness. At present, our universities remain, if I may so put it, the Vatican, the Holy See, of Western cultural dominance, the central proponents of the universal relevance and validity of the Western scientific consciousness. This consciousness studies everything, reinterprets everything, and relativizes everything — except, of course, itself. Its denouement, as *the* universal consciousness, when cultural colonialism finally expires, will, however, come soon enough.

So much, then, for plurality as parity, in both religious and cultural matters. Its benefits are evident: tolerance, mutual understanding, the beginnings of mutual trust, creative and fruitful interchange, and a possible basis of one world community in principle if not in immediate actuality. Unity here (in religion and culture) is possible only if first of all the brute facts of diversity and then of parity among those elements that are diverse are openly recognized and then creatively engaged. An enforced unity, in politics or religion, where one power rules, where one culture remains dominant, and so where no authentic diversity and no equality are recognized, represents no real community and thus no viable unity. We in the West have tried this in the world as a whole. This colonial mode of unity had its own inevitable consequences — namely, angry and violent reactions, seen in the excessive violence and brutality of the Boxer Rebellion, of Shinto Japan, Maoist China, and Khomeini's Iran. But parity and its child tolerance do not come free; they present their own bill, the abyss of relativity. In religion this means a new relativity of special revelation and of covenant, scriptural and ecclesiastical authority, Torah, and Christ. In culture it means the relativity of Western cognitive methods, individual and political values, and the Western sense of meaning in history. At this juncture the question is unavoidable: How is it possible to ground, establish, and preserve these veritable pillars of our religious existence and of our common life, if all religions and all cultures are enjoying parity?

THEODICY AND RELATIVISM

Now let us juxtapose this new situation for theology and philosophy with theodicy. Theodicy has been defined—and this is good enough to get us started—as the rational effort to defend God's omnipotence and goodness in the face of evil. I need not remind you that this effort—not difficult for the upper classes in the eighteenth and early nineteenth centuries—has had a rough time in our twentieth century. Since the First World War, evil has increased seemingly exponentially; it appeared almost impossible to justify God, perhaps even to believe in God, in the face of such depths of evil; and most certainly a "rational" or "natural" basis for theodicy, or even for theology, seemed futile. From 1914 through 1945, evil ceased to be an intellectual puzzle for the serene and became an overwhelming power over us, a power that we alone could neither conquer nor comprehend. The reason that was capable of adjudicating objectively between evil and God, paring the latter down to be "coherent" with the former, was itself submerged by historical evil. Thus, in subsequent theology evil appears as an existential problem in our personal and our sociohistorical existence rather than as a theoretical problem in our system of understanding. The starting point is not a serene overview of all things but the experience of outer and inner helplessness in the face of fate, sin, and death—and the desperate need for God. Here then begin the powerful dialectical theodicies of revelation, interpretations of evil on the basis of revelation and grace, interpretations in which human helplessness and need are rescued by divine power and divine love. Here it is we and our being, not God and God's being, that are justified and made whole; and instead of being coherently included in a rational system, evil is conquered by divine grace and tempered by faith in God's providence (power) and God's ultimate promise (goodness).

Shortly on the heels of the dialectical or *Krisis* theologies of revelation, and joined in the 1960s by many Catholic theologians, came another form of Christian theodicy: political or liberation theology. Again, God's power and goodness are related to evil in terms of victory over evil rather than in terms of a rational coherence that incorporates evil. Only this time it is the promise of God's future victory in history over oppressive institutions and the subsequent establishment of the reign of God that move center stage. The answer to the question of evil is neither a rational understanding of how evil fits into God's world nor the inward experience of judgment and of justifying and sanctifying grace; it is rather the triumph of God's liberating gospel over the inherited evils of social history. Here theodicy depends not so much on reason's systematic talents, nor even on the commitments of faith, as it does on hope in God's promises and on liberating political action by the religious community, now at last truly understanding its real task. While, therefore, the interpretation of Scripture and church tradition is different from that of the Protestant and Catholic predecessors of liberationist theologies, still the bases of liberationist theologies—except as some of them find their deepest roots in Marxism—remain that of the authority of word and the calling of *ecclesia*. Both of these twentieth-century forms of theology have been tremendously creative. Both, however, encounter in plurality a deep, even an essential, challenge.

Pluralism challenges theodicy on several different levels, corresponding to the different forms of theodicy we have mentioned. The classical modern forms were, of course, philosophical or metaphysical. From Leibniz through Hegel to Whitehead, F. R. Tennant, and Teilhard de Chardin, these theodicies depended on a rational scientific and philosophical base, that is, on the objectivity and universality of reason. In these cases reason is speculative reason, the construction of a metaphysical system; in others it might be transcendental reason, the uncoverer of reason's universal principles of inquiry and thought. In either case, from this rational base then, in such philosophical theologies the deity of God, now philosophically defined, could be metaphysically or transcendentally established and coherently related not only to experience as a whole but especially to the evil so evident in experience. Each one is, therefore, both a "natural theology" and a rational theodicy.

From the high vantage point of Enlightenment and modern reason, of course, the dogmatic traditions of the churches seemed parochial. While religion in this view is subjective and local, reason is universal—or certainly that seemed evident to the modern universities where this sort of work was done. But from the contemporary perspective of the plurality of cultures, these rational efforts too seem local, important manifestations of the Western viewpoint but confined in their direct relevance—that is, their "self-evident" validity—to the Western culture that had bred them. Are the arguments, warrants, and criteria of Western reason persuasive in Islam, in the Indian, Chinese, or Japanese cultural matrices, in the Marxist countries? Or do these intellectual edifices, as R. G. Collingwood said, reveal more about the presuppositions of Western culture than they do about the rationality or *logos* of universal being itself?

Distant harbingers of these questions had surfaced shortly after World War I, when the possibility of metaphysics as an objective and universal form of discourse about reality was radically questioned by positivism, empiricism, and existentialism. These critical movements (joined recently by deconstruction) have long been scornful of the pretensions of speculative thought, in vain seeking a universal standpoint, a universal set of principles, and really only repeating in systematic form our own Western assumptions. Ironically these critical movements themselves, once radical pluralism appears on the scene, reveal themselves, despite their utter lack of universal speculative intention, to represent the ghost, if not the flesh and blood, of Western rationalism. The deepest challenge, however, lies further on: Philosophy—as all human thinking—is grounded in, represents, and elaborates the presuppositions, perspectives, and values of a particular culture. If, therefore, in a genuinely plural world the Western consciousness, identifying reason with scientific reason, claims universality of relevance and validity, it can do so only by claiming an unwarranted superiority over the viewpoints of other cultures. Like the metaphysics on which it is founded, philosophical theodicy is faced in a plural situation with the threat of relativity and so of irrelevance. At the least it is now faced with the following question: If reason is inescapably cultural, and so in that sense relative, how is it possible that a culturally relative ontology can still have validity?

Correspondingly, the theodicies based primarily on revelation—as the Protestant dialectical theologies, most liberationist theologies, and the great Catholic syntheses of Lonergan and Rahner were—are also relativized. Insofar as this revelational authority was established on the covenant events founding the *ecclesia* and on the accounts of those events in Scripture, clearly a new sense, that there are other religious traditions that enjoy parity with this one, strikes at the heart of the absolute authority on which these theologies were founded. In classical theology it is, of course, through revelation that God is both clearly known and authoritatively defined; it is through revelation that human nature and its historical career are interpreted and understood; and thus—as in such classical theological theodicies as those of Augustine and of Calvin—it is on the word in Scripture and in church that the interpretation of God's relation to evil is based. Perhaps at the very start (as in Barth), perhaps somewhere along the way (as in Tillich, Rahner, and Schillebeeckx), ordinary experience and reason are regarded as insufficient, even misleading; at that point what is known about humanity, history, and God in and through Christ and the word becomes essential. Although clearly each of these forms of theology is liberal enough to regard the small words of Scripture and the precise formulations of doctrine as historically relative and so perspectival, nevertheless in all of them the revelation, the Word to which these human words point, is absolute, final, unique, and therefore universal in validity and relevance. Again, a theologically based theodicy (and I have sought myself to propose one[1]) is challenged at the very center of its authority by the recognition of parity with other modes of revelation or—as in Buddhism and most of Hinduism—other modes of religious consciousness in which ultimate reality is encountered and by which it is known. Again, at the least, such theologies are faced with the question, Is it possible to have a true revelation that nevertheless remains in this sense relative, a valid perspective and yet only one perspective on experience and God?

The moment a radical pluralism is recognized, there arises both for philosophical and theological theodicies a serious problem of authority. The usable, ordinary, and heretofore established starting points—universal reason or an absolute revelation—now elude us; we have in their place a plurality of cultural reasons and a plurality of ultimate revelations, each of which at some point certainly qualifies and probably cancels out the validity of the others. If we seek to understand reality by means of an established

---

[1] Langdon Gilkey, *Reaping the Whirlwind: A Christian Interpretation of History* (New York: Seabury Press, 1976).

religious tradition, we find we are looking at reality, ourselves, and evil from only one perspective, and we wonder if this one can, therefore, tell us of God and God's work in history or only of the ways our culture has thought about these sorts of issues. If we seek the universality of thought, we seem embroiled in only one form or another of the Western consciousness and self-consciousness, a quite particular and limited way of experiencing and knowing, and now a way subject to important challenge from other cultural viewpoints. The problem of a firm starting point for theodicy is, of course, a symptom of a much deeper issue — namely, a loss of confidence in both reason and revelation, the onslaught of relativism, the sense of the quite possible futility of either thinking or believing.

Where then can we start? A theodicy is a complex and often high edifice: To spell out the relations of actuality as experienced to the divine, to establish the nature and modes of activity of the divine, and thence the relations of the divine so defined to personal and historical evil is a massive constructive task. As in every large construct, a firm base must be present, an authority on which all that is said to be known is truly known. Without such an epistemological base for the validity of theory (whether that base is empirical science, speculative reason, or revelation), there is, apparently, no dependable theory, no warrantable claim for presenting a reliable description of what is real. How can we speak of God's nature and activity, of human and historical being, of the rationality or the conquest of evil if everywhere we seek to stand is itself sinking in relativism? Do we even know God any more? Can we speak still of all of history or all of evil? Is there anywhere on any grounds a creditable basis for ultimate harmony or hope? These are some of the questions plurality raises for theodicy.

The questions, however, do not stop here. The issue of authority, of the authority for a metaphysical viewpoint or a theological system, is not the only issue here raised, as if, when we got that straight, we could go on as before and construct a theodicy. On the contrary, each of the crucial notions of any coherent theodicy — God, nature, human nature, evil, history, and so on — represents a concept within a particular religious or cultural tradition and not within all such traditions. God in any reputable revelational theology is a recognizable "Semitic" and thereby "Western" notion; in the same way, any Western philosophical conception of God represents a coherent notion within the European philosophical tradition. Such concepts have of course analogous similarities with concepts in Hinduism, Sikhism, and in some forms of Mahayana Buddhism, and of course especially in Islam; but these are by no means identical notions, as if each of them recognized "God" as we speak of God. Moreover, when one moves further into Confucianism, Shintoism, native American religion, and especially Theravada (or Zen) Buddhism, the relevance of "God" — unless we assume *ab initio* that God is necessarily the referent of their religious speech — recedes radically. But to assume God as the referent of their speech is to adopt as valid the Christian view of reality in seeking to understand the relation of Christianity to other religions, which is hardly to recognize the new situation of parity. Correspondingly, the Hebrew, Christian, and Western assumptions that nature and history are real and of value, that they set the frame for our single life, that there is only one "life" after death are by no means universal. Nor is the associated presumption that evil can only be justified either here and now in this life or in the next life (or in both). On the contrary, these are assumptions peculiar to only one cultural tradition.

Where, for example, transmigration provides the largest framework for understanding existence and evil, the entire question of theodicy assumes a quite different form, as do the questions of the value of individual historical existence, the relation to nature, and the ultimate character of our obligation. For example, *suttee* in our framework represents a cruel and indefensibly immoral act, almost murder, possibly enforced suicide, a monstrous action against the dignity and integrity of a woman's existence. In the framework of transmigration, where this "soul" can now move into a higher form of existence, it represents a difficult, certainly challenging and "testing" but nevertheless justifiable, even prudent, act of loyalty and virtue. My point is that the assumed conceptual ingredients to any theodicy (God, linear time, nature, humans, history, the end), each in its recognizably Christian or Western form, are by no means assumed in the discussion. Each in that form is essentially Western when compared with analogous notions in other religions or analogous metaphysical principles in the philosophies of other cultures. Thus, since the particular question of theodicy (the justification of God) does not arise elsewhere, the relevance of our answers to it are surely questionable. Each religion and culture is forced to deal with the question of meaning in the face of evil, to be sure. But each one defines both evil and meaning differently enough so that it is not easy to find any relevant set of universal notions with which to begin.

We are dealing here with the deepest levels of plurality. A plurality of choices of breakfast cereal is one thing. A plurality of ultimate grounds for rationality and meaning, for understanding the self, the community, and the divine, not to mention nature and history, represents something quite different. At this deep level plurality raises the specter — at which we have here only peeked — of having nowhere firm to stand and to begin and so of not being able to know, to think, and thus to understand or to believe anything. Without the capacity to know, to understand, or to believe, there is no possibility of serious and intentional action. This is not a trivial matter.

In our cultural tradition certain forms of relativism have been recognized. For example, since the Enlightenment the relativity of religions has been widely assumed. In its place, however, an absolute and so universal culture, modern scientific and so rational culture, "secular" culture, was held to provide a firm place with which thinking and understanding could start. The relativity of culture, too, has been acknowledged, but from the vantage point of an absolute revelation and the firm framework for nature, history, and self that such a theism provided. Now, my point is that as both of these examples, of what one must call Western forms of absolutism, extend their claims of universality and relevance into the non-Western world, they seem inescapably to exude the stale whiff of colonialism, of a remaining spiritual — if no longer a military and political — dominance and superiority. We are aware that we have now moved in principle, if not yet in fundamental consciousness, out of the once Euro-centered world into a new global, a post-Copernican, situation. Is such a situation intellectually, religiously, morally, viable? Or is there for us — as there was for mariners before Columbus — only the abyss of relativism to threaten us on this new sea? Is there any place where we can stop short of that abyss?

THE INTOLERABLE AND THE ABSOLUTE'S RETURN

Successful arguments have been mounted against an all-consuming relativism. We remember Augustine (when I doubt, I at least know I doubt) with gratitude and know that in principle relativism is always conquerable and that as a consequence we can begin again. In modern culture the ravages of skepticism have been overcome by confidence in empirical science: We may begin with doubt about every certainty, but before the day is out at least we will have falsified in experiment an improbable idea and established the probability of its as yet unfalsified alternative. But science cannot out of itself provide the rational grounding for the presuppositions essential for its empirical methods; nor can scientific theories give us any clue as to how to use the knowledge those theories embody; nor can even more extensive theories help us with our understanding of the meaning of all this knowing and doing amid the waxing presence of evil and so of meaninglessness. Relativity at these points — which is where modern relativity arises — can, as Alfred North Whitehead argued, undermine the careful but superficial rationality of our culture's career. Where then in our most important experience does the perilous slide toward relativism stop?

I would suggest that for all of us, there comes a point in life where relativism does in fact stop; and this point is, ironically, one also conditioned by the fact of plurality. Plurality not only ushers us into the experience of parity and tolerance, recognition of the Other, and with that the dizziness of relativism. Plurality also confronts us with the appearance of the intolerable. By "the intolerable" I mean some reality in our contemporary situation that should not and therefore cannot be accepted, and thus a reality that must be resisted. It can be an attitude, a viewpoint, an ideology, or a set of religious beliefs that, when embodied in persons or communities, we find so unequivocally destructive that it calls for, whether we will or no, our resistance. We may in fact not find in ourselves the inner courage or the strength to resist. But in that case we have not escaped the problem; rather we find we have lost ourselves, we have disappeared, our integrity and so our humanity have fled the scene.

The intolerable in that sense has also been as much a feature of twentieth-century existence as relativism has. The most vivid case of its appearance was, of course, Nazism in all its features but particularly in its culmination in the Holocaust. It called forth classic examples of resistance. But there have been other examples: against the Japanese empire in China, against Stalinism, against the excesses of Maoism in the cultural revolution, and in the United States against segregation and the Vietnam war. There is no sign that the problem of the intolerable is declining in intensity in our day. In my own country the recent appearance of a fundamentalist religious right with new dreams of theocracy and old dreams of economic autocracy and nationalist imperialism calls for the most indomitable resistance. Correspondingly, the need for liberating political action and for the social and theological viewpoints to undergird it continues across the globe. Oppression — military, imperialistic, political, economic, and social — still ravages our world. Wherever it appears, it confronts us as intolerable and so calls forth resistance. The relevance of this not only to the problem of relativism but to theodicy is clear.

The intolerable is a searching, disturbing, as well as interesting category, as each of us finds when we face an unwanted example of it in actual existence. It measures us rather than the reverse; for we lose our humanity, certainly our authentic humanity, if we turn away from it and try to hide ourselves in some unseen corner. In this it is, ironically, like its apparent opposite, the recognition of parity, which is also a child of plurality. As we are hardly authentically human if we refuse to acknowledge and accept the diverse other in tolerance and respect, so in this case, too, we are hardly human if we do not resist what is an outrage against some neighbor's humanity. Apparently our humanity can be lost at either end of these opposite directions: a fanatical repudiation or a superior nonrecognition of the other, at one end, and a timorous retreat from injustice, at the other. The intolerable can therefore hardly be taken as a trivial or superficial category. It erupts in history and disrupts it, and it measures us whether we will or not.

What is for the purpose of my argument most significant about resistance to the intolerable, however, is that it brings us surging out of relativism. In resisting with our life, we now stand somewhere, namely, against this that is intolerable; and we stand firm and cannot be moved. Nothing can budge us, nothing. If there is an actual and so useful definition of the ultimate or the absolute, this one is it, I should think. What is more, we stand somewhere. Our resistance is not merely negative, against; it is also positive, for something. Moreover, what we are for is neither arbitrary nor notional, a matter of taste, a subjective preference. It is a declaration of what is, of what is the case about the world. To stand for something in moral and political life is to affirm something to be true about human existence, society, and history — even if we never get to speaking of God. A particular "world" is thus entailed in resistance, be it the Enlightenment world of Sakharov, the Jewish world of Schransky, the Christian world of Martin Luther King, Jr., and Dietrich Bonhoeffer. As the great Barmen Confession made clear, a consistent and unwavering resistance to Hitler necessitated a consistent and unwavering commitment to the one Lord. To resist the intolerable is to become human; that humanity is also made possible and undergirded by an absolute commitment to a definite world. Paradoxically a movement toward the absolute has returned when action is taken against oppressive evil, as the descent toward the relative first appears when the refusal to be intolerant is made and the other is accepted in his or her diversity. Perhaps these two apparent opposites have more in common than we thought.

PARADOX OF A RELATIVE-ABSOLUTE

Resistance against oppressive evil implies, as noted, an absolute commitment to a quite particular world, in short a definite "faith." Nevertheless, it is clear that a fully uncritical adherence to that cause or that faith will only repeat in ourselves the very intolerant, totalitarian, and oppressive evil we seek to resist and counter. No gain is made if one absolutistic commitment challenges another; whoever wins then merely continues the oppression we originally sought to resist. There can be a creative resolution only if the absolute commitment, if that stubborn loyalty that will not budge and will persevere, is itself tempered by self-criticism, by recognition of error and partiality in ourselves, and recognition of the possible value even in the opponent; only thus can a reconciliation beyond the resistance become possible. A creative and re-creative community is possible only if commitment to our cause is paradoxically qualified by our recognition of its ultimate relativity, if loyal devotion to our vision of the ideal is balanced by our realization that even our vision remains incomplete and must therefore be transcended by a still higher one. Only, in other words, if faith and obedience are qualified by the repentant consciousness of our own shortcomings and partiality can there be real conquest of evil—real theodicy. This was surely the secret of the remarkably creative lives and deaths of both Mohandas Gandhi and Martin Luther King, Jr. In them the absolute of utter commitment was balanced by the recognition of their own fallibility and the potential value of even the antagonist. Thus, in the end, evil was not only resisted but in part overcome.

Another example of this strange, almost contradictory, phenomenon of an absolute commitment, a faith, mated to the relative appears with the very central experience of religious plurality, namely, in the experience of dialogue. Dialogue seems to enact a paradox that we have found it difficult to think. Here a strong faith and commitment—and sense of participation both in truth and grace—strangely unites itself with an acceptance and recognition of the other that grants the other parity. In that acceptance, moreover, both truth and grace (effectiveness) are recognized as present in the tradition of the other as well as in our own—and that is a strange, paradoxical recognition.

I recall long talks about our faiths and about our being theologians within them that I was privileged to have with my elder Buddhist colleague at Kyoto, Professor Takeuchi. One afternoon, walking in a Zen temple garden, we talked about our talking, about dialogue. I murmured a kind of apology that I always spoke from a Christian position. "Do not for one moment consider in our conversations ceasing to speak as a Christian," he said. "Do you wish me to cease to speak as a Buddhist? Then we could no longer teach each other anything—and, above all, our conversation together would become a bore, like those secular philosophers in Tokyo who stand outside every position and so stand nowhere at all." And he concluded with the paradox, "Remain what you are, and then and only then can we converse."

I realized with this that dialogue itself required the same balance of the absolute and relative to which I have alluded. If we are to converse with one another creatively, we cannot immediately resign our own viewpoint and seek to stand somewhere else; somewhat stubbornly we must stand where we are and represent our own faith as strongly as we can. Nevertheless, if we are to converse, if there is to be dialogue, and that implies listening and learning as well as proclaiming and teaching, then in some strange way that stance must recognize the truth and grace also in the other and must recognize its own relativity, as itself a perspective on the truth and not yet its wholeness. Again, we embody a relative absoluteness. To *exist* in this paradox is strangely not so difficult as to *think* it out; it is easier creatively to carry on dialogue than it is to theologize on its basis. Let me say that I am only beginning to reflect on the strange consequences of this mode of existing, what it means or might mean theologically to exist as loyal and centered and yet open to the other.

To me this strange combination of the absolute and the relative well befits the way Christian existence should appear in history. Those who stand for nothing can hardly do the Lord's work; but neither have "saints" done that work who, accompanying their message of grace with threats of the Spirit not to mention those of the sword, have sought to eradicate in the name of the Lord every other mode of belief or worship. It seems evident that if both oppressive injustice and destructive conflicts are to be avoided or at least minimized—and that reduction represents an actual theodicy—an absolute resistance against the evil of oppression must be complemented by a self-critical and repentant relativism that eschews endless and reiterated conflict. The world of political and cultural communities and religions will remain stubbornly plural. In this situation only a relativized commitment to the absolute, or a relativity balanced by firm fidelity and obedience, can redeem our troubled times. It represents, so it seems to me, the paradigmatic model of creative faith for our pluralistic age.

What this pluralism as parity means for theology, however, is a question that fascinates, frustrates, and lures a number of us who seek to do theology. We know neither how to abandon this problem nor how to deal successfully with it. In our time it is simply there and must be puzzled out. Plurality cannot be understood by finding a position—either religiously or philo-sophically—above or beyond all faiths and viewing them all from above, as if we had already entered eternity. Rather progress can be made, as in dialogue, only by a relative absoluteness, only by doing theology on the basis of our own sources, authoritative tradition, and mode of current ex-perience but reinterpreted so as to make room for the other. This is the way ahead, but we have only just begun to move forward, and not much more can at present be said.

CHAPTER 13

HUMAN EXISTENCE: SELFISHNESS AND ALTRUISM

My subject is the strange presence of an almost universal selfishness in human behavior, both individual and social, yet also the longing for the ideal, the altruistic, the claim of self-giving love. Both of these, selfishness and altruism, are universal characteristics of human existence; wherever one of them is denied, it persistently reappears. The researcher and author outlining the inherited necessity of our selfishness and deception will conclude with wise and apparently sincere words about the creative use of this new knowledge to resolve the problems that selfishness has created. As has been universally remarked, human beings are ambiguous, good and evil, cynical and hopeful; this baffling mixture is undeniable, and there are as many questions arising from this puzzle as there are explanations of it. Is selfishness necessary, quite inescapable, and so unredeemable? Is altruism unnatural and so impossible? Is our self-destruction therefore a doomed fate, now certain because we have through our knowledge the power to achieve it? Are there then any grounds for renewal, for cooperation, for hope? It is interesting that both theology (traditional and contemporary) and present biology address this issue. I shall here present one interpretation of the theological answer; in so doing I will begin with and concentrate on the traditional symbol of original sin and make running comments on its surprisingly close kin, the selfishness gene of current biology.[1] I shall conclude with the grounds for limited hope offered in both traditions.

---

[1] Richard D. Alexander, *The Biology of Moral Systems* (New York: de Gruyter, 1987), and Richard Dawkins, *The Selfish Gene* (Oxford: Oxford University Press, 1978). Both authors enunciate as quite natural and authentic a very "high" liberal, in fact altruistic, set of moral

The universal fact and overpowering presence of evil are undeniable, recognized by every culture, except perhaps by the articulate classes of the eighteenth- and nineteenth-century West. The awareness of pervasive evil and suffering appears as the direct conclusion of important primary experience: the experience of universal confusion and conflict in all social life, of unwisdom and deception in public and private policy, of rampant exploitation, corruption, and cruelty in every institution and sector of our existence, ending in sexism, racism, persecution, and war. These latter are the objective symptoms of a heedless and driving selfishness that human reflection of all sorts has uncovered as one of the major characteristics of our personal as well as our social existence. Further, there is, again universally, the nagging sense of responsibility, group and personal responsibility, for this universal situation. We are not just its victims but in some puzzling way its willing perpetuators as well: "in each the work of all, and in all the work of each," as Schleiermacher put it felicitously.[2]

As a consequence, many ancient religions have spoken of the rule of the demonic powers over our history: Hinduism of the dominance of ignorance and *maya;* Buddhism of the universal force of desire or attachment; Hellenistic religion and philosophy of the sovereignty of the flesh over the spirit; and Christianity of the consequences of original sin—all of these infecting our being to its depths and leading to conflict and death, on the one hand, and suffering and despair, on the other. These traditional explanations may seem bizarre to an advanced scientific civilization; but the problem each sought to clarify is real and destructive enough, as the biologists who offer the explanation of the selfish gene recognize.[3] Until 1914 the optimism of modern culture found these religious traditions excessively gloomy and thus untrue, the results of the ignorance and anxiety of pre-scientific eras. The unfolding twentieth century, however, has experienced evil, personal and social, as deeply as any age before it has; and, more than any other epoch, it is also aware of the ultimate destruction threatening at the end of a history thus riven with aggression, injustice, deception, and mortal conflict.

---

sentiments concerning present-day world problems, and both seem sincerely to recommend rational science as a means for resolving these problems (Dawkins, *Selfish Gene,* 2-3, 118, 126, 150, 213-15; Alexander, *Biology,* 21, 40, 126-29, 186, 192-94, 202-4, 221, 254-56). All this is despite the fact that for the biological theory of both, morality, consciousness, and reason alike arose, as we shall see, to protect and preserve through deception and the manipulation of rivals the gene and its "survival machine," the individual organism.

[2] Friedrich Schleiermacher, *The Christian Faith,* trans. and ed. H. R. Mackintosh and J. S. Stewart (Philadelphia: Fortress Press, 1976), 288.

[3] Both Alexander and Dawkins seemed oddly unaware of this long tradition of religious or theological reflection on the Fall and its results, namely, the overwhelming presence of selfishness and consequent conflict in all of human history. They consulted mostly post-Enlightenment philosophers and their own untutored sense of theologians as idealistic and moralistic. Although, as I shall indicate, the tradition of Christian theology and current biology are by no means identical, the two do share surely as many formal and material similarities as differences.

THE CHRISTIAN SYMBOL OF ORIGINAL SIN

Let us now turn directly to the concept or symbol of original sin to see what it says about this universal and oppressive selfishness that harasses our life and unsettles our history. There are a number of important themes present in this symbol.

RELATION OF DIVINE AND HUMAN

Original sin is, first, a religious symbol, centering therefore on the relation of humans to God, their source and end. It is this relation that determines the good or ill, the creativity or destruction of human life or behavior. The fundamental or "created" nature of human being is, then, good, replete with trust in God and the possibility of love for the neighbor. The Fall, therefore, represents a break in that fundamental relationship to God, with the consequences of the loss of the goodness of our nature, a warping or estrangement of our humanity, a turn to selfishness and away from love, radical disorder in all human affairs, and in the end (in the traditional interpretation) disease and death. In this situation we find ourselves helpless to rescue ourselves, in bondage, as Paul puts it, to an alien force, unable to return by our own resources of will or mind to our original goodness. Freedom from these ills can come only religiously, with the return in faith and obedience to God, resulting in a new possibility of love or altruism to the neighbor. Without such return, life is left, however advanced in civilization it may be, characterized by self-love, injustice, suffering, and ultimately death.[4]

HUMAN RESPONSIBILITY FOR ESTRANGEMENT

Clearly the fundamental break (in the relation to God) is a spiritual and not a fleshly matter, although common Western folklore mistakenly thinks that original sin is sexual. On the contrary, it has been called in the tradition

---

[4] Here we see the deepest similarity between this theological account of selfishness and evil and the biological account: In each there is a situation, and with it a force or power "binding us," often against our conscious wills, to a selfish course of action that we explicitly, though hardly wholeheartedly, deplore. In the biological case it is the so-called selfish gene that rules us; in the theological case, it is the break in the relationship to God, the Fall, that has distorted all our powers and thus our ability to renew and transform ourselves. In both, therefore, help must come from outside: in the one from objective reason, apparently unaffected by the machinations of the gene, and in the other from the grace of God. Which one of these sources of rescue is more incredible represents a real debate in the twentieth century! In Dawkins the selfish gene "creates" and so fashions its survival machine for the sole purpose of its own survival, and "programs" the machine to preserve the gene's existence over time. Thus, it is the gene and its "will to survive" that is, as Alexander puts it, the "ultimate cause" of what are really surface or proximate symptoms or effects of that cause: desires, emotions, intentions, altruism, individual self-interest (see Dawkins, *Selfish Gene,* chaps. 2, 3, 4; Alexander, *Biology,* esp. pp. 20, 25–26, 36–40, 64).

pride, unbelief, disobedience—all pointing to the movement at the center of the self from dependence on and love for God to dependence on and love for the self. Thus, it represents an elevation of the self to the divine center of life, even to divine status: idolatry and the demonic. Since the relation of the self to God is the center of human existence, this break affects and distorts all aspects of human life: its desires, its fundamental love (from God and neighbor to self), its will, and even its reason—none are as they were (good), but now all are tainted, ambiguous, destructive as well as creative and destructive even in their remaining creativity. Since all our powers are affected, all sorts and conditions of humans are affected alike: good and bad, righteous and unrighteous, powerful and weak, intelligent and not so intelligent.

INHERITED CONSEQUENCES OF ESTRANGEMENT

In the traditional form of this symbol, we each inherit the consequences of this break, the defiant act of Adam and Eve. That inheritance is experienced as a condition in which we find ourselves, "are born into," a condition of inordinate desire (selfishness), ignorance of what we ought to do and be, unwillingness and even inability to do what we know we ought, the total absence of God, and hardship, disease, and death. Again let us note that all of this is in fact experienced directly. Nevertheless, we also experience directly our own responsibility for our participation in this inheritance; we also will it, enjoy it, and further it; we freely and naturally blame others as well as (occasionally) ourselves. We know we, too, are involved in the world's evil, and yet continually we deceive ourselves that this is not so but that, on the contrary, we are righteous and the other is to blame. Each foreign office shows this over and over again. Through our estrangement, which is also our responsibility, we have lost not only God but ourselves and our neighbor as well; true self-identity and true community, as well as true religion, are thus ambiguous, ever dissipating and infinitely elusive.

ESTRANGEMENT'S LURE

The direct experience of responsibility, with its intimation that freedom or decision are somehow involved in estrangement, means that the problem is not our finitude, the fact that we are particular individual and mortal creatures. These latter are part of our fundamental "nature" and, insofar as we are at all, are necessary aspects of our existence. We are responsible to use and deal with our finitude as such. Thus, the story has emphasized that we are tempted or lured but not forced into estrangement or sin. Since Søren Kierkegaard, it has been generally agreed that anxiety thus tempts us to secure ourselves at all costs and by a kind of infinite self-elevation. Because we are finite and contingent, mortal and dependent, and yet spirit or consciousness with infinite possibilities, we are anxious—about our security and about fulfilling our possibilities. In this situation we "fall" into a false security of self and a false fulfillment.

THE GOOD'S CLAIM ON HUMAN EXISTENCE

Despite this bondage to selfishness and destruction, we also experience ourselves as claimed by the good, by an altruism that balances and heals our selfishness (*agape*—in the New Testament, a love for the neighbor, the helpless, even for the enemy, in short for the unworthy). In other terms, we are claimed by a morality that transcends the usual morality based on competition, security, and love for the self and its group.[5] This continual moral pressure, nagging, inspiring, condemning—conscience—represents, in the terms of the story of the Fall, the presence of our fundamental nature or structure in and on our existence, our created goodness, a structure characterized by trust in and dependence on God and consequent love for the neighbor. We know this is our obligation and represents our true selves, who we really are and wish to be. We know this through awareness of ourselves as moral persons not through objective scientific inquiry, and most scientists write as if they too shared this moral self-knowledge.[6] Finally, this

---

[5] Note the striking similarity here to the theory of the selfish gene; all aspects of the "survival mechanism" (individuals) are affected, even dominated, by the gene's irresistible drive to its own perpetuation: the individual's will, its desires and instincts, its consciousness, its rationality, its morality, and its behavior. In Alexander's *Biology*, for example, consciousness and reason originate in order to preserve the gene and thus as mechanisms for competing with rivals (76–78, 100–3, 107–15). Morality, particularly conscience, arises solely (1) for reciprocal cooperation that directly or indirectly aids survival and (2) in order to deceive others (that one is more rational and moral than one actually is) into being altruistic toward oneself (102–3, 116, 118–25). Helpful as this is in interpreting the deep ambiguity of both moral conscience and objective reason, this theory from biology quite fails to explain how and from where the high moral conscience and objective reason of the two biological authors derive and how that moral conscience and objective reason are related, if they are at all, to the immensely selfish and deceptive morality and reason described in the theory itself. One almost envisions here two separate species: one, the ordinary organisms of nature and ordinary humans of history driven to unmitigated selfishness and deception, and the other, rational and moral scientists, interested in truth and serving others. There is a whiff here not only of metaphysical dualism but even of sociological dualism.

[6] Despite their insistence on the sovereign power of the selfish gene over all of human existence, both biologists, as we noted, also witness to (perhaps unconsciously) this claim of a higher morality. This has revealed itself not in their biological theory, where everything from conscience to rationality is governed by manipulative self-interest, but in their own splendid moral sentiments, judgments, and hopes for the future. These latter are clearly altruistic, universal, just, nondominating, pacifist, rational, clearly transcendent to the nationalistic, class-conscious, sexist, and racist "morals" of ordinary social life. This higher level of morality (although they never called it that) was not for them "nature"; it was even "against the genetic inheritance." Consequently, it has to be taught to our children (Dawkins, *Selfish Gene*, 150, 214–15); and it results from, at least it is incarnate in, science, its knowledge, and its objectivity of attitude. One wonders when this transselfish element in the human makeup first appeared—with Galileo or Newton, possibly Darwin? If a genuine conscience and a really objective reason were there in history before, say, in archaic cultures as well as in our own modern culture, surely it forces a reconsideration of the status and possibilities of moral systems in the main body of the theory. Since the appearance of these higher levels of the human self was quite unexplained, even unarticulated, in these volumes, it remains incoherent with, or at least

ever-present claim of the good on us by our essential nature results in the
continual need for self-deception. Actually we are driven by self-love, and
all our acts reveal it; but we cannot accept that this is what we are. Hence
we need to deceive ourselves that we are as righteous as we claim to be.
Propaganda, individual or corporate, is not in order to deceive the other —
although that is a bonus — it is to deceive ourselves, placate our conscience,
that we are virtuous in pursuing the self-interest that our actions embody.[7]

THE DISTINCTION BETWEEN SIN AND SINS

It is perhaps clarifying to point out that the symbol of original sin represents
what we may call a double-level explanation or interpretation of human
behavior. In the deeper level of estrangement or sin we find ourselves
dominated by inordinate self-love, making ourselves the center of the
universe, and by concupiscence, the desire infinitely to possess others and
the world. This dominating tendency, this false love, as Augustine termed
it, lies back of our conscious desires, attitudes, goals, judgments, and reason-
ings and thus even behind decisions and actions, perverting them, pushing
them into a hostility they did not intend, and corrupting them in ways we
did not at all envision.

Thus, the tradition has distinguished sin from sins, the acts we do that run
counter to moral rules. The first, *sin,* is characteristic of all of us at a level
below conscious awareness and even intention; the second, *sins,* represents
the conscious decisions and actions we make on the surface of life. All are
sinners in the sense of inordinate self-love; not all are sinners in the moral
and social sense of committing crimes or enjoying recognized vices. As the
social crises of historical life show, sin includes the respectable and un-
respectable, the pious and impious, the elegant and the boorish, the brilliant
academic and the unlearned oaf: ecclesiastics, scholars, scientists, and brilliant
professionals share in the deep problems of inordinate self-love, ruthless
competition with the neighbor, and scorn for the other. The sins of the
mighty, the rich, the brilliant, and the pious have, because of their power,
more lethal effect; their power spreads the destructive consequences of their
selfishness, cruelty, and indifference more widely.

Similar double-level interpretations have been common in our day,
although not all are as profound as this one. Marx and Freud are the prime
examples. For each an underlying unconscious factor (class consciousness
and neurosis, respectively) warps conscious rationality and morals alike on

---

disjoined from, the more realistic and cynical biological theory, a kind of unformulated dualism
of evolutionary nature set over against rational science (the object of the scientific inquirer over
against the inquiring subject, the scientist) — a sort of up-to-date Cartesianism (see esp.
Dawkins, *Selfish Gene,* 157).

    [7] Again, this is recognized though not articulated in every science book, where a high,
usually liberal-moral stance and an optimism about what science must do in the future
permeates all the writing.

the surface; and for each the self deceives itself — via rational argument, morality, and religion — that its inordinate self-love is actually rationally and morally justified.[8] Another two-level interpretation has appeared in current biology when, for example, Alexander distinguishes the "ultimate cause" of behavior of which we are unconscious from the "proximate causes" on the level of conscious decisions.[9] Each seeks — through Marxist dialectic, therapy, biological knowledge, or religious disclosure — to pierce the ignorance and deception of this false surface and to uncover these hidden factors in the depths and so begin the process of renewal. This is, of course, precisely the role of religious symbols, of proclamation, sacrament, and worship in the Christian community.

GOD'S REDEMPTIVE ACTIVITY

The situation of bondage, conflict and death, and longing for a lost or elusive good are not the last word. On the contrary, according to the entire Christian tradition, there has been and is present to us the redemptive activity of God reestablishing in us all, on a new basis, the lost or distorted relation to God, the unattainable cooperation and love within human relations, and the purpose and meaning, as well as the courage, of the life of the self. Instead of fate, sin, and death — the three enemies traditionally resulting from the Fall — there have come through new faith and courage the promise of hope, love, and eternal life. This promise and hope represent the substance of the Christian gospel, its witness or message, centered on the covenant with the Jews and the incarnate life, death, and resurrection of Jesus Christ but held to represent, manifest, and define a universal redemptive work of God among all the races and nations of humankind.

---

[8] Both Alexander and Dawkins develop a complex and interesting theory of deception, the pervasive deception practiced by animal and human species, even in the latter's supposedly rational and moral practices. For both authors reason and moral sense are essentially deceptive; that is, they arise as mechanisms designed to deceive others into believing the deceiver is more altruistic than he or she is, thus luring their victims into becoming themselves altruistic and so vulnerable to the deceiver's self-interest and competitive aggression (Alexander, *Biology*, 100–3, 110–25, 177–78). The reader cannot help but wonder why, if this theory is valid, the moral sentiments expressed by these scientific authors, however persuasively argued, and their scientific conclusions, however empirically verified, should not themselves be products of this intricate, infinitely devious, and yet quite ruthless process of deception, designed or programmed to deceive the reader into altruistic political acts (pacifistic ones) helpful to the interests of the biological community and their genes. One can only assume that somehow to these authors these moral sentiments and rational arguments represent a sort of morality and rationality different from those described in the theory, and so again we encounter a sharp dualism. For an alternative theological theory of deception as described further on in this text, see Reinhold Niebuhr, *The Nature and Destiny of Man*, vol. 1, *Human Nature* (New York: Charles Scribner's Sons, 1941), chaps. 7 and 8.

[9] Alexander, *Biology*, 14–19.

DIFFICULTIES IN CONCEPTUALIZING
THE SYMBOL

The above themes have characterized the interpretations of the symbol of original sin since with Augustine (335–428 A.D.) it became a subject for reflection. As we have noted, most of these themes were directly experienced: the "given" character of evil in us and around us; its presence in us all, good and bad; our strange responsibility for it; its bondage; the call of the good despite this situation, and so on. Still, it has proved a difficult matter about which to speak clearly, as is also the case with its kin theory from biology, the theory of the selfish gene.

THE DUAL EXPERIENCE OF EVIL

The first cause of linguistic difficulty is the dual nature of the experience of evil and so of the symbol that expresses it. The evil (selfishness) around us and in us is experienced as a condition or situation into which we come; it appears with us as a state already there from the beginning, apparently in no way created by us as individuals. Such are the deep corruptions and conflicts of social history (we all inherit a mess); such are the enmities and abuses of communal and family life (as therapy teaches); such are the instincts of self-love and desire resident in us, as biology and personal experience both inform us. As is so clearly stated in the theory of the selfish gene, this situation is given to us, in a sense therefore necessary, and this destructive selfishness is on reflection seen to be universal, that is, everywhere and in everyone. Evil thus seems like one of the fundamental conditions of our nature, like our characteristic powers, dependencies, and limits, our finitude itself, to be necessary, inescapable, a part of our ontological structure.[10] Hence much of the language and the metaphors of original sin (like those of the genetic inheritance) express this aspect of universal givenness, of an inalterable state of our being: inheritance, transmission, born into. Is not evil a necessity of our present being, deriving from our genetic makeup, our embodiment in the flesh, our ineradicable ignorance, our particularity, our unavoidable attachments? So most if not all of the great theories of evil have concluded.

Yet we do have distinct experience of responsibility and, with that, freedom. We are beings who constitute ourselves, in thinking, willing, action. We are not until we choose ourselves; we enact ourselves in freedom.

---

[10] This is, of course, the main implication of the genetic explanation of evil. Since we as organic beings bear a selfish gene that created us for the sole purpose of preserving itself, we are blindly programmed, determined to enact these purposes in all we do. Except for the sudden and arbitrary advent of rationality, science, and the morality scientists represent, this represents an unalterable and sovereign condition for all we are and do, the ultimate cause of everything else on the surface of life. Clearly there is and can be little hint of responsibility on our part for this fundamental bent of our nature.

A scientist chooses and wills to become a scientist in freedom. Thus is autonomy central to our humanness, and thus are we responsible for what we think, judge, will, and do. So direct is this intuition of autonomous responsibility that common discourse never questions that people, especially others(!), can legitimately be blamed for their misdeeds and lauded for their creative acts. This pervasive and primordial experience of freedom and responsibility is assumed by most religions and by all science; it is in fact an essential condition of both, science as much as religion.[11]

Original sin, therefore, is not only a given condition of which we are the unwilling victims; it is also experienced as a condition in which we willingly participate. It is, as Augustine said, something my own freedom does, not something done to me; I will it and will it willingly. It is, therefore, my own freedom, my deepest love, that is bound,[12] and, most surprisingly, my reason itself: and, for that I am responsible; and because of that I can be renewed. Thus, throughout the traditional concept of original sin, there are words and metaphors connoting responsibility, on the one hand, and culpability, on the other; the first sin was an act, an act of rebellion, disobedience, guilt. Thus, the original cause, if we may so term it, is not an aspect of our structure, of our created nature, but a fall from that structure, an event distorting it. The Fall is, therefore, also an act of freedom and not a necessity; it is a part of history and not our created and so inescapable nature. Hence we can be rescued from it and renewed. This emphasis on freedom and responsibility differentiates the Jewish and Christian interpretations of evil from many other religious interpretations (Hinduism and Buddhism especially) and also (except for the introduction of the scientist's own rationality and rational morality) from the theory of the selfish gene.

The Two-Level Interpretation

This dual nature of the experience of bondage—at once as a necessity and as a responsibility—is further complicated by a second factor: the two-level character of this interpretation. It is not difficult to speak of conscious volitions and actions; nor do we have difficulty with apparently necessitating causes uncovered in ordinary experience. But this is neither one. It is a factor below the levels both of decisions and ordinary causes, experienced paradoxically as characterized by both of these modes of awareness and speech.

---

[11] Although no scientific inquiry can uncover this freedom—it being a characteristic of the active inquiring subject and not of the passive object of inquiry—it appears in all scientific writings: in the effort to persuade and in the logical and empirical justification of the theory, both appealing to an autonomous rational judgment. In biology it appears in the responsible and even altruistic moral stance suffusing every biology book that touches on the problems of our current world: "We must use our new knowledge to make the right choices if we are not heedlessly to destroy life on this planet." Such sentences are pervaded with the awareness and so the certainty of our own freedom in and even over the impinging future.

[12] Augustine, *The Confessions* 7.

Thus, our words here are all analogies of responsible decision and action (rebellion, disobedience, and so on) taken from the areas of conscious personal experience, and analogies of determination and "being caused" from another area of experience. The same difficulty haunts biological explanation that must speak on two or even more levels, and so speak analogically, not only of unconscious purposes within an animal and organic life but even more of the traits, intentions, and behavior of the gene itself, the "ultimate cause" of the behavior patterns in all organic existence.

Excursus 1
Problems with the Language of Biology

Problems of language abound in the biological accounts of this genetic inheritance. That is to say, analogical language is quite unavoidable and appears on several different, quite undiscriminated levels. First, biology universally uses purpose (in order to) language (such and such is developed for this or that function) and must translate that into the nonpurposive language of the mechanics of natural selection. Further, biology shifts the dimension or level of conscious purposes in human existence to unconscious yet purposive behavior in animal, plant, and organic life generally. These represent the only levels of analogy of which Dawkins and Alexander seem to be aware.[13] But most interesting is the shift from the conscious-unconscious "purposes" of the phenotype ("survival machine") to the vastly different level of the gene, an immense shift[14]. The gene is not an organism but the maker of organisms; it has surely a very different sort of drive than an organism does (if it can be said to have a drive at all), an internal élan pressing it toward its own preservation or fulfillment. Yet such language is continually used by both authors. They deny, of course, that in the gene these are conscious purposes as they are with us;[15] but that is hardly the point. The question is whether this language has any referent at all, and of what sort it is—the questions that arise with any sort of analogy. Without something akin to what Aristotle called an *enteleche* or Bergson's élan, a "will to survive," and so forth, clearly present in the case of organisms and animals, it is hard to know what all this speech means, a problem uncomfortably ever-present in theology!

The use of purposive language for the gene is universal throughout both volumes, although Dawkins's usage is, so to speak, fruitier: "The gene is the most fundamental unit of self-interest"; "its business is . . ."; "its task is . . ."; "what it is trying to do is . . ."; "it manipulates for its own ends"; "the true purpose of the gene is to survive"; "Genes are responsible for their survival in the future"; "for its own selfish ends"; "they [genes] are programming for their lives," and on and on. The point is not whether or not these so-called purposes are, like ours, conscious[16]. The point is whether the referents of this purposive language (the genes) have any intent of any sort (as an organism or an animal surely does), and so whether there is any sense of any sort to all these analogies. Is there any drive, élan, or intent in the gene that can be the referent of the analogy of "selfishness" as there is in the life of the organism

[13] For instance, Dawkins, *Selfish Gene*, 50–53, 132, 149, 156–57.
[14] Dawkins, *Selfish Gene*, 50; Alexander, *Biology*, 14–19, 34–40.
[15] Alexander, *Biology*, 19; Dawkins, *Selfish Gene*, 24–26, 50–54, 117, 132.
[16] Dawkins, *Selfish Gene*, 12, 39, 40, 95, 36, 47, 24, 46, 67, 25.

or animal or as Aristotle believed there was when he spoke of the *enteleche* or *formal cause* of development in what he called vegetable and animal nature? Without this analogical referent of some sort, it is hard to know if we are talking about anything at all in this kind of discourse about genes.

In any case, as a result of these three distinct levels of analogy and their mingling without discrimination, the analogical linguistic confusion is immense. For example, analogies such as mechanism, programming, blindly determined, on the one hand, and choices and decisions, on the other hand, appear on the same page and in profuse reference to the same entities[17].

The traditional form of the doctrine of original sin reflected both of these aspects of the symbol: its character as a free act, on the one hand, and as an almost necessitating inheritance, on the other. Eve and Adam, so the tradition went, having been created good, were tempted. They then quite freely acted in conscious and willed disobedience to the command of God. This initial act of prideful rebellion was the original sin in the sense of initiating event or cause. As a consequence and punishment of this first act, the descendants of this first pair have, so the dogma runs, inherited as a sort of virus transmitted via sexuality (a metaphor if there ever was one!), the bane of concupiscence (*cupiditas*), the inordinate desire that beclouds the mind, perverts the will, disorders the emotions, and brings on disease and ultimately death. Because of this inheritance, sin (original sin now as transmission) rules our entire present existence and proliferates in all the wide variety of selfish acts and vices in ordinary life, much as the inherited gene is responsible for our common and universal selfishness on the level of ordinary experience. As is evident, the two sides of the experience of human evil—its given character and its voluntary character—are here sundered into the voluntary act of the first pair and the involuntary inheritance of concupiscence that engulfs all of us. This story of the source of all of our present ills was believed to be true by generations of Western people, partly because it commanded the immense authority of Holy Scripture and partly because, as I have argued, it fitted so well the direct experiences of responsibility combined with submersion in a sea of ills beyond our control. So much for the traditional form.

In modern times this literal, historical form of the doctrine has had a very rough time, much as the original form of the six-day creation story has. Astronomy, physical cosmology, geology, and of course evolutionary biology, not to mention the development of a new understanding of human prehistory, have presented us with a picture of the distant past entirely different from this simple picture of a very recent creation believed and affirmed by almost everyone before the eighteenth century. The result is that the narrative of Adam and Eve in the garden has become, as a literal, historical account, quite incredible to all of us who respect the results of modern scientific and historical inquiry. Also, and of vast importance, the new view

---

[17] Dawkins, *Selfish Gene,* 132.

of nature, especially the prehuman nature, meant that few theologians could ascribe disease and death to sin; they are seen now as aspects of our finitude, not as results of the Fall. Whatever truth this narrative may have, therefore, it is not that of a truth referent to a historical event of the distant past; and whatever the cause of our ills, waywardness, and death, it is not such a single historical event and its consequences, even such a unique event as the rebellion of the first pair. This is, of course, where most of the current Christian churches and the Jewish community separate themselves dramatically from the fundamentalist wing of the first and the ultraorthodox wing of the second.

One should add that part of the unacceptability of this dogma was also that it ran counter to the deepest sentiments about human life and its possibilities widely held during the eighteenth and nineteenth centuries. To them this picture of humanity in some sort of self-inflicted bondage to selfishness and conflict seemed far too gloomy to be valid: in fact, it seemed to contradict their direct experience of a growing human goodness. It was thus held to be excessively pessimistic, "untrue to ourselves," as Albrecht Ritschl said in the 1870s. This old dogma appeared to be incognizant of the immense new possibilities for resolving our dilemmas and bettering human life that science, technology, industrialism, and democracy had now brought into view. In an age optimistic about human rationality, human virtue, and the perfectible future, this dogma seemed not only incredible scientifically but in its pessimism to reflect a pre-scientific, predemocratic, and anxious, despairing age, a concept hardly appropriate to the obvious progressive advance of modern Western civilization.

It scarcely needs to be said that in the twentieth century, both on the European continent and in America, this optimistic assessment of the modern prospect, of history as a steady progress toward knowledge, technology, and virtue, has seemed to be fully as illusory a myth as the narrative of Adam and Eve in the garden was. Thus, since 1918, theology has turned with renewed interest to the biblical story of the Fall and the traditional doctrine of original sin. These have been found to be profoundly illuminating about the human situation, disclosing factors hidden to our ordinary common, secular understanding and yet crucial to our self-understanding. Almost without exception, however, these same theologians have also been modern in the sense that they have accepted as valid the major results of empirical science, including the geological and biological accounts of our earth's and our own prehistory. As a consequence, the doctrine of original sin—like that of the creation—has ceased to provide a literal, historical account of past events, of a historical act of Adam and its consequences; it has been fashioned into a symbol disclosive or revelatory of our situation. Adam here becomes a symbol of our own existence in its contingency and dependence, its freedom and possibilities, its temptation and consequent pride and anxiety, its quest for meaning and security on our own, and the denouement of self-centeredness, injustice to the other, and self-destruction that follows inexorably from that autonomous quest. The symbol of original sin does not explain our predicament by assigning to it a cause; it discloses that predicament by uncovering its hidden but destructive features and by revealing unsuspected new possibilities for renewal despite our apparent bondage.

CONTEMPORARY MEANING OF
THE SYMBOL

The doctrine of original sin is, we have said, a symbol disclosive of our situation. What then does it disclose? What hope does that disclosure hold for us all? I have outlined some of the major themes of that symbol: the centrality of the relation to God, the spiritual character of the break, the dialectic of destined situation and freedom, the role of contingency and anxiety in the temptation to sin, the claim of the good, of our created nature, upon us, and the promise of grace, of renewal. Let us continue this analysis by outlining further themes latent in this symbol, aspects of our personal and social reality disclosed or revealed to us in and through this symbol.

Ambiguity of Human Existence

Human existence is here understood to be fundamentally ambiguous, strangely paradoxical. Made in the image of God, as an embodied spiritual, personal creature, self-constituting, intelligent, moral, and amazingly ingenious, imaginative, and inventive (and, above all, capable of love), human being is almost infinitely creative of family and community, culture, art, literature, science, and technology, of civilization in all its facets. This "goodness" is elegantly manifest in biological treatises—namely, in the rational inquiries and their conclusions, in the speculative brilliance, the moral sentiments, and the political hopes—even amid obvious dangers— evident in both of the scientific authors I have mentioned here, Alexander and Dawkins. Yet, as estranged and alienated from this original or created state, humans (other humans?) are also almost infinitely destructive: aggressive, domineering, oppressive, and cruel, as no other living organism is. These two go together: We are destructive as well as creative. Even more, it is precisely through our creativity and human uniqueness, our spirit, mind, and intelligence, that we become anxious and through anxiety that we fall into aggression and self-destruction. Thus, paradoxically, we are destructive in our creativity; the two unite in baffling mixture.

Our most lethal faults appear as distortions of our most creative powers: our religious capacities, moral striving (as ideology shows), and, especially evident today, our scientific brilliance and technical gifts. The intellectual and spiritual creativity of humans sets them apart from all the rest of nature;[18] but the warping of just this spiritual creativity threatens our future,

---

[18] This uniqueness is recognized by both biologists: Dawkins, *Selfish Gene*, 3, 63, 203, 214–15; Alexander, *Biology*, 40, 77, 116, 201–2, 252–56.

as the ultimate danger facing us through our most brilliant scientific and technological advances shows. Most biological accounts see the source of our problems as arising from our genetic inheritance, as an inherent given; and they see the resolution of these problems as appearing through a transcendent, almost supernatural power of objective reason resident in science and in the rational and moral teachings of higher cultures: the *memes*. This view is, so the historical evidence seems to say, overly optimistic as well as dualistic. Our deepest problems arise, as they always have, at both levels, that of mind and spirit as well as that of genetic inheritance. The manipulative and deceptive tendencies of consciousness and morality, according to the biological accounts, affect the scientific minds that do science as they affect the religious and moral spirits of every higher culture. Only a view that sees us as a good thing spoiled, a good nature distorted, can understand these clear, if paradoxical, facts of historical experience.

INFINITE POSSESSIVE DESIRE

Estrangement is not only pride, making the self and its group the center of the world; it is also, as the tradition has emphasized, concupiscence, the desire to possess and enjoy the entire world, an infinite possessive desire. Traditionally this was regarded as centered in sexual desire, in lust; hence, the permissive, post-Freudian twentieth century tended to ignore this side of sin. Concupiscence, however, stubbornly reveals itself in all aspects of our being: in our infinite desire for material things, for consumer goods, for ever more amounts of money, power, men, women. We and our entire consumer culture are driven to imbibe the whole world, to "jam it into our craw," as Tillich put it, to possess and to possess infinitely. Only a spirit destined in its nature for infinity could desire an infinity of possessions, and it is this unlimited desire that drives our industrial machine to grasp and process for consumption the resources and life of the entire globe. As is clear, this infinite possessive drive destroys relations with others, the natural world around it, and ultimately itself; it leads inexorably to the loss of self, the loss of the other, and the loss of world. It is the infinite dimension as well as the spiritual and rational dimension of selfishness and desire, in short the human dimension, that the biological accounts cannot seem to comprehend.

SELF-DEIFICATION

Sin or estrangement means centering the world around the self or (usually) its group, making the self and its own into God. Anxious about its life in a precarious world, the self seeks to secure itself and the meaning of its life; but, as spirit, it can see, imagine, and invent an infinity of anxieties that goad it into pursuing this security with infinite energy and rational ingenuity, as every foreign office and corporation manifest. As the biologists recognize, this is generally a group activity, since few individual selves can hope to secure themselves by themselves. Through the group's power and glory, the self is enabled to secure its own life and its prospects for the future. Patriotism unites self-interest through the group with self-giving to the group to create an irresistible fury and energy. This infinite drive for security and dominance leads, of course, to injustice to the other: to conflict, conquest, slavery, and exploitation. Whether on the level of tribe or nation, of family, class, race, sex, this pattern of domination, subordination, and even extinction of the other has characterized human history since the beginning. At each "higher" level of civilization, this same infinite drive to mastery has remained. Over and over, as theologians as well as biologists recognize, this drive has subordinated to itself both morality and religion and used both for its own ends. What seemingly the biologists have failed to recognize (although their theory of deception might suggest it) is that the science and technology developed by the best minds have also been tainted and used to the same effect. When the self or its group loves itself inordinately, worships itself instead of God, the first result is injustice to the neighbor as the second result is the destruction of both self and world.

CULTURAL TRANSMISSION OF EVIL

The traditional doctrine, recognizing the given, inherited character of sin, spoke of the transmission of sin as concupiscence through the sexual act of conception. As noted, this theory has horrified most twentieth-century theology (as it did the Reformers) and has been largely ignored. Nevertheless, some mode of transmission is real enough. Partly selfishness comes to us, of course, through the pressure of the selfish gene, although both biologists refuse to term this influence necessitating or determining. It also comes to us, as the cultural evolutionists tell us, through cultural as well as genetic transmission; through miming our elders, apprenticing to them, and being taught by them, we become who we are, namely, participating members of our culture and tradition. From each passing generation, the new members of a culture have received and appropriated the institutions of their society, its social roles, rules, and customs, its expectancies and standards, its moral norms and ideals, and its camouflaged hostile attitudes, competitive habits, prejudices, anxieties, and hatreds, its modes of deception and manipulation of the other. Cultural evolution emphasizes how the positive learning, techniques, mores, and rites of a society are passed on. What they have not emphasized, however, is how the unjust institutions with their habits and demands (for example, patriarchalism), how patterns of competitiveness and self-love, group pride, and scorn of the other, how these, too, are passed on or inherited. These deeply ingrained forms of self-concern shape us as thoroughly as do the positive cooperative and creative sides of culture. This transmission of evil (the Kingdom of Evil, as Walter Rauschenbusch called it) is both objective, resident in the cultural and institutional patterns of bias that we inherit, and subjective, internal, latent in the inordinate self-love running through every social group and through each social institution. This inherited taint characterizes both religion and science;

both are thus not only part of the answer to our ills but also part of the problem. Culture in all its facets is both creative and fallen.

AMBIGUITY OF MORALITY

Morality is a subject of concern to both theology and current biology. From the perspective of Christian theology, morality, like intelligence and custom, science and law, is essentially ambiguous. As we noted, the moral—the concern with right and wrong, with care for the other as well as the self, with, that is, altruism (love)—is an essential ingredient of the created nature of the human, made in the divine image and thus essentially characterized by love for God and neighbor. Faith in God, love of neighbor, and hope for the future are thus essential aspects of the structure of the human. With the Fall as I have described it, however, we find ourselves estranged from God, from ourselves, and from others; we are dominated by self-concern, inordinate and indefinite self-love in place of love of God and the neighbor as the self. This domination by *amor sui* or *cupiditas* also characterizes our society, as it does all societies. The kingdoms of the world, said Augustine, are energized and united by self-love rather than by the love of God; hence even their virtues are magnificent vices.[19] Society, as well as the individual, is fallen into ambiguity, and the moral sense as well as reason is clouded by ignorance and tainted by self-concern and self-deception. Thus, as the biologists rightly said, moral systems represent the codification, as legal systems do, of the rules of indirect reciprocity that serve, via cooperation, the self-interest of each individual. This has been put long ago, and in more credible form, by Augustine: Each society, he said, strives for peace and order, but, the ruling elite being self-interested, what results is only an uneasy peace, in effect a latent war. Moral systems, therefore, while necessary for social cohesion, articulate also the biases, prejudices, and self-concern of the dominant groups of their society. Genuine morality, therefore, represents more frequently a challenge to resident moral systems than it does their approbation. Such higher morality is as rare as it is precious.

What the biologists apparently do not comprehend in their discussion of morality is the ground or source of their own moral stance as of their own evident trust in the objectivity of scientific reason. In the case of both authors, their own moral goals and their rational thinking as scientists clearly transcend mere selfishness, the selfishness that, according to their biological theory, originates and dominates consciousness, reason, and moral conscience alike. Thus, they provide no reasons that we should trust their reason and their moral goals as objective, genuinely disinterested (altruistic), and,

---

[19] Augustine, *The City of God.* Why neither biologist referred to this Augustinian and Reformation tradition of interpretation as similar to their own theory of selfishness, especially as the basis of custom and common morality, I do not know. This theological tradition emphasizing original sin and its universal effects in group life (see especially Reinhold Niebuhr) represents their best, if not their only, ally, even better than Hobbes, Marx, and possibly Freud.

above all, nondeceptive and nonmanipulative. Unless they are deceiving us, they write as if they intended us so to trust them and to take them at their word as morally serious. Clearly both represent as authors liberal citizens deeply concerned with distorted communication, with the goal of a universal, nondiscriminatory social system, and with inspiring an international order that transcends mere group self-interest, exactly the reverse of the deceptive, manipulative, self-serving "morality" (and reason!) that was portrayed by their theory.

Excursus 2
Problems with Biological Explanations
of Morality

Both Alexander and Dawkins describe, analyze, and explain "morality"—that is, the distinction between right and wrong, moral rules and norms, and especially "conscience." All of these are interpreted as developments "designed" to serve the "selfish" purposes of the genes, which (who?) have "made" or "created" all the attributes and powers of organisms. Since (1) most genes will survive and perpetuate only in organisms that in turn survive and propagate successfully, and (2) since individual organisms survive and reproduce best in groups that cooperate (direct and indirect reciprocity), it is essential for gene survival that phenotypes live in groups, care for one another (parental, sibling, and kin care), and cooperate socially; hence the appearance of moral sentiments and the need for moral rules. Like laws, they are rules of association for the survival of the group and developed, therefore, largely to express and to defend the interests of the group against rival groups (or, translated, these genes that program their organisms for cooperative group life will in fact be perpetuated and spread). Thus, what is regarded "morally" as altruism on the part of an individual is, from a biological standpoint, an act genetically "selfish," for on occasion the real interest of the gene may be served by the sacrifice of its particular bearer (the other copies of that gene thus having a better chance to survive). Like consciousness, therefore, morality is (1) a reflection of fundamental self-interest on the part of the gene and (2) a reflection of the survival drives of a given cooperative group in the competition of life. As a consequence, there arise parental love, cooperative morality, and even altruism within a given group.[20] Morality is thus ultimately self-interested, at least on the part of its prime or ultimate instigator, the gene; and, therefore, altruism, while perhaps descriptive of the individual, is seen biologically as a function of genetic self-interest. As we have noted, this account of morality as a function of self-interest—and of moral idealism as a mode of propaganda or corporate deception—does not explain at all the clear and "high" moral sense of the authors themselves, which systematically if not explicitly defies this genetic and group self-love and seeks, as an authentic obligation, a just, fair, universal society based on science and so not on deception.

There are three elements in this discussion that many such commentators from the sciences seem to overlook. (1) The problem of morality centers as much on the moral defiance of the moral customs of groups as it does on the subservience of moral conscience to the interests of the group. The morality of the authors illustrates this point.

---

[20] Alexander, *Biology*, 1–3, 37, 72, 77–103, 115–16, 163–64, 177, 182–84; Dawkins, *Selfish Gene*, 7–8, 97–103, 137–38, 179–202.

(2) An interpretation of human being, or human morality, as a whole transcends any given science into philosophy. Specifically it transcends looking at groups as objects (where we can see clearly the group self-interest evident in their ordinary or customary morality). The reason is that a view of morality as a whole must include the moral conscience of the inquirer, the biologist and the anthropologist, for their moral judgments generally (although not always) transcend the moral rules of society generally. Morality seen from the inside of the subject, like consciousness seen from the inside as rationality, has a self-transcending, authentic, and responsible character. In the great historical instances, such moral integrity has challenged and upset the morality of the society; and these historical instances represent the highest, if not the most common, types of the moral: Socrates is, of course, the great example of this, as are the Hebrew prophets and Jesus and as are in our own day Gandhi and Martin Luther King, Jr. (3) Finally, however, the really transcending rational and moral consciousness, evident in all historical life and very clear in Alexander and Dawkins, is itself not as pure as its admirers believe and frequently as its bearers themselves believe about themselves. Even high morality (even among liberals) itself illustrates in part the human condition of bondage to self-interest described in this text as well as in their pages. "Thus, even the saints know that they are sinners." This point was quite absent from these biological accounts of the moral answers to our current problems, accounts that seemed to regard their own resolutions based on scientific rationality and their own higher morality as exceptions to the problems of genetic selfishness. Thus, in sum, strictly biological accounts of morality remain incomplete because they do not discuss, articulate, or explain the higher morality of the scientific authors and because, as a consequence, they have then no possible reason or ground for seeing the ambiguity of even that higher morality.

As noted, however, the main problem of scientific accounts of human nature as a whole is that they seek to interpret the whole of experience from the vantage point of an abstracted portion of it, whether a perspective that is economic, chemical, physiological, biological, neurological, psychological, political, or theological. What is needed, as well as being unavoidable, is the mediation of philosophy to raise or generalize the abstractions of the special sciences to enable them to include (1) the rational and moral subject as well as the object of inquiry, (2) the whole width of experience, personal, social, and historical, as well as empirical-scientific, and (3) thus to develop categories that can deal with the whole width and strange depth of experience. Without this mediation, reflection is left with the alternative either of reductionism of the whole to an abstract area within the whole (for instance, to physics) or of an incoherent dualism in which the personal and rational subject is arbitrarily introduced into a theory developed from objects alone, as in both of these cases. In either alternative, since the discussion purports to be about the whole of human experience and to present a theory about human nature as a whole, it must include the subject, intellectual and moral, as well as the objects of inquiry.

One result is that the conclusions of such a discussion and the theories that result, including as they do much more than the restricted area of a special science, do not bear the authority of that special science. The conclusions from the special sciences surely bring with them very great authority when they enter such a general discussion about human being; but there they must join other perspectives — for example, interpretations from other physical sciences, from psychology, social science, anthropology, religion, morals, and law, which also deserve a hearing. In relation to the whole, each remains an abstraction, a limited field. The conclusions from such a special field, stretched (by metaphor and analogy) to take in all of experience, remain at best speculative and are subject to the criteria appropriate for philosophy — namely, coherence with other forms of knowledge and adequacy to the entire width of experience. This is as true for theology as it is for the special sciences. Biological theory can, as these volumes show, certainly contribute greatly to the understanding of human nature. But in the unprepared form of dualism, also illustrated here, such theory does not bear the authority of biological science and awaits the synthesis of its findings with those of other perspectives on the mystery of human being. Such a synthesis is the enterprise of philosophy, the sort of faculty club of the disciplines, where they can talk together and reach a common understanding, or at least a shared discourse.

Each special perspective tends to see itself as providing the key that will unlock that mystery. Theology certainly made this claim successfully for many generations. So have economic theory (in Marxism) and psychology (in psychoanalytic theory and behaviorism); and now we see it with evolutionary biology. As this history shows, such claims are not antithetical at all to the creative advance of understanding; in fact, it is such enlargement of special perspectives into comprehension of the whole that most effectively furthers self-understanding. These claims by each discipline, however, also illustrate the shadier side of rationality, its tendency, however objectively academic, to see itself as the central discipline essential to all the others, to see itself as the key to the truth all others seek. Each discipline has an implicit imperialist urge only waiting for the chance to advance its claims on the others, as we theologians should know well. The ambiguity as well as the creativity of reason, even of objective reason, an ambiguity thoroughly discussed in the above text, thus reveals itself even within our present "objective" discussion of selfishness. Again, what is needed is not only brilliant and articulate defense of what one knows in one's discipline but also humility about the limited character of what one knows and about its cooperative place in the entire panorama of human understandings. Then what is called for is a synthesis of all these perspectives, each of which sheds its own light on the larger mystery.

Yet it is also true that all morality, even our own, remains ambiguous, even that of the most brilliant scientists and academic liberals (as of ecclesiastics and theologians). Ordinary morality is more creative than they seem to recognize in their theory; and probably their own morality is more ambiguous, self-deceptive, and manipulative than it seems to them to be. In fact all of human existence is ambiguous, at once creative and destructive, and this includes even intelligence and morals, even science and religion. All therefore depend upon the power beyond all human powers, on God, to renew what we have spoiled, to preserve what we destroy, and to temper and nurture what in us remains creative and lasting.

CHAPTER 14

THE CHRISTIAN UNDERSTANDING OF SUFFERING

ASSUMPTIONS ABOUT RELIGION AND SUFFERING

In addressing the Christian understanding of suffering, I will as in previous chapters also glance periodically at Buddhist understandings of suffering. I begin, however, by articulating some of the assumptions under which I address this subject and by offering some perspectives through which it can be seen.

RELIGIONS AS HOLISTIC VISIONS OF REALITY

First, it seems evident to me that each religion represents a unique overview or vision of all of reality, an overview that concentrates itself—although it does not confine itself to this—on the deepest problem of human existence as it sees it and on the answer to that problem as it has received or uncovered that answer. Each religious tradition also represents a unique access to that answer, to power, if you will, the power to receive, share, or embody that answer. In this sense each religion represents both truth and grace, to use Christian language. Clearly such a vision—and this is here our concern—is expressible in diverse ways: There are different interpretations of Buddhism, Judaism, Christianity. Nevertheless, each represents a version of or perspective on that unique vision or overview of the whole. In turn, this vision is expressed in and through the symbols (exodus, election, people, messiah, creation, incarnation, church, eschatology, to mention a few) that make up the ideational content of that religion; when formulated, this cluster of symbols becomes its truths, its teachings, its doctrine. This content can be delineated by those within and without the community; reflection on it and construction or reconstruction of it is the task, I would take it, of theology.

In such a cluster or gestalt of symbols, each symbol (for example, creation or revelation) is affected and shaped by its relation with other symbols within that gestalt. They form a relatively coherent unity and thus they serve in part to define one another. None can be understood in isolation, for part of the meaning of each comes to it as much from its role in the cluster that makes up the whole as it does from the character of relevant experience itself. Sin in Christian understanding cannot be understood except in relation to the Christian concepts of creation and redemption, just as it cannot be understood in exclusion from the experience of Christians. In this sense all of systematic theology is implicit in any responsible delineation of a part of it—as is even the case with Søren Kierkegaard!

If this disturbingly Hegelian introduction is correct, "the Christian understanding of suffering" cannot be articulated unless the other theological symbols significant to that understanding are also brought into view. Granting, then, that suffering represents a universally shared experienced but still one always received, experienced, and understood in a particular way, our question is the following: How does suffering appear, and what does it therefore mean, within the system of symbols that constitutes Christianity, within the Christian vision of existence (as the Buddhist understanding of suffering finds its place and its meaning in the total vision that constitutes Buddhism, with its cluster of dominant symbols)? An intelligible explication of this understanding requires a demonstration of the way the common and shared experience of suffering is shaped by and interpreted through the particular gestalt of Christian symbols, the way this symbol is given its character by its lodgment within that system. Since this is a large task, I can only begin here by drawing a rough map.

One may note that each cluster of symbols (each religious vision) pays a price yet also receives a reward for its particular emphases, for the unique shape of its dominant symbols. To those within a religious community, the benefits outweigh the price, and the balance comes across as true to experience and to the canons of intelligibility alike. Nevertheless, both debits and credits are there and can be seen by others and should thus be admitted. No cluster, I hazard, always wins—except to its most fanatical participants. This is why it is important, when examining another religion (or critically assessing one's own), to look at the religion as a whole rather than only at its debit points, as we are all apt to do when we point triumphantly either to the philosophical contradictions of theism or to the "world-denying" character of Buddhism. (A shared sense of where these debits or weak points are does indicate some sort of rough common ground!) In any case, it will be our effort here to understand the Christian view of suffering as that view appears within the gestalt of Christian symbols as a whole.

QUESTIONS ABOUT SUFFERING

The second comment concerns the richness, as well as the poignancy, of the question that here concerns us. To ask about the Christian (or the Buddhist) understanding of suffering is to ask several distinct yet related questions, not just one. Each is equally as important as the others because each of these distinct questions concerning suffering relates the issue of suffering to some particular symbol or symbols within the cluster as a whole. I will here list four questions (the clear debt to Aristotle's causes only occurred to me after listing them) involved in the understanding of suffering; there are no doubt many more.

1. The question of the source or cause of suffering: How does it arise and from what factors, in reality so viewed, in what Whitehead would call the metaphysical situation?
2. The question of what we may call the anatomy of suffering: What is its structure, or, if it has none, of what sort of healthy structure is it the disease, of what sort of order is it the experienced disorder, of what *telos* does it represent the deep frustration?
3. How is suffering overcome or conquered or redeemed in this gestalt: What are the conditions for this conquest? What are its limits? What are we called to be or do, if we are?
4. How does suffering relate—positively or negatively—to other symbols in the gestalt? For example: What is its role or purpose, if any? Does it clash with, contradict, or threaten any other symbol, for example, that of God?

As is evident from listing these various aspects of the Christian understanding, all of them are significant and all have functioned importantly in the tradition of Christian reflection, as I suspect they all do in other traditions as well. It seems clear that in certain religions (that is, in certain clusters of symbols) some of these questions are more pertinent, central, and thus worked out than others are—and possibly other questions than these four appear on the scene. Also, at certain times in a particular tradition, one or more will be emphasized. One may note that questions 2 and 3 are central to religious existence, to the piety of a faith—in fact very near its core. Correspondingly, questions 1 and 4 are more "speculative," more inferential from the existential center represented by 2 and 3, and thus more the result of theological or philosophical reflection on existential experience, religion, piety. For example, clearly Augustine's experience of sin as bondage and of grace (as an answer to questions 2 and 3) led to his articulation of the doctrine of original sin (question 1) as its explanation, that is, as the "cause" of suffering. Correspondingly, having experienced grace as rescue from sin and suffering by omnipotent divine power and unconditional love (questions 2 and 3), he was (and we are) then faced with the apparent contradiction of suffering in the same universe with an almighty and loving God.

My point is to emphasize that this subject, if we are to understand it aright, embraces more than one question, in this case more than the theodicy question, just as the Buddhist understanding of suffering embraces more than the blanket assertion "All existence is suffering." In fact most creative Christian reflection on suffering has concentrated far more on the first three questions than on the fourth; and it seems evident that the strengths or pluses of a Christian interpretation tend to lie in its answer to these three questions rather than in the fourth. One might even claim—although it is certainly controversial—that such concentration on question 4 and too coherent an answer to it may well subvert important answers to the other more religious and theological questions concerning the understanding of the anatomy of suffering and its possible redemption.

SUFFERING'S ROLE IN THE
CHRISTIAN VISION

The cluster of symbols within a religious vision forms, I have said, a rough unity. To understand how Christianity understands suffering, therefore, we must sketch out the most fundamental shape of that vision, the contour of that cluster, and locate there the place, possibly the role, of suffering within it. This contour is, so I believe, dominated by a dialectic, a sequence of affirmation, negation, and subsequent affirmation or reaffirmation, without which suffering cannot be understood in its Christian form. I shall therefore discuss suffering as it takes its shape within each moment of this fundamental dialectic.

SUFFERING IN THE MOMENT OF AFFIRMATION

Christianity, like Judaism, begins not with speculation about origins but with the historical experience of rescue or redemption. Nevertheless, logically and ontologically each begins with a fundamental affirmation of the divine creation and so with an affirmation of the essential goodness of the world: of the realm of nature and its order, of the body and its necessities, of the human spirit and its capacities (both made in the image of God), and, as a consequence, the goodness of family, community, society, and ultimately of history itself. Classically this goodness was expressed through conceiving the initial creation (at the temporal beginning) as perfect in all relevant respects. As a result, however, of the developments of science (natural science, social science, and history), new knowledge about the processes of development through which the present world, human being, and society as in history came to be, made incredible this story of a perfect beginning. As a consequence, this affirmation of the goodness of creaturely being has lost its temporal implications. The goodness of creation has come to mean the potential perfection of the world and human being (Hegel, Schleiermacher, and most of liberalism); or, as another example, the essential goodness of creaturely being (e.g., Paul Tillich and Reinhold Niebuhr). In each of these varieties of interpretation, however, the symbol of creation represents an affirmation of the structural goodness or potentiality of meaning and fulfillment of finite natural and human life.

Christianity, therefore, starts out with the assertion that it is good to be and to be alive: good to God who created and sustains life and good (at least potentially or normatively) to the creature who enjoys or might enjoy it. In epochs when the experience of suffering recedes rather than predominates (at least among the classes that reflect and write), this side of the dialectic tends to be emphasized: Christianity understands itself as affirming the divine creativity in existence, the goodness of finite being, and especially its potentialities of development and fulfillment, as has most of liberal theology. When the experience of suffering advances and dominates experience, this side (the emphasis on creation, development, and progressive fulfillment) tends itself to recede, and the other moments of the dialectic, the negative and the redemptive aspects, come to the fore — and a quite new perspective on suffering appears.

In addition to this initial assertion of creation, and so of a good finitude, we should note that Christianity adds that redemption also represents an affirmation or reaffirmation of this same point. Redemption constitutes either (in some versions) the reestablishment of created goodness (with some important additions) or (in other versions) the fulfillment of the potentialities of created goodness. The symbols of "the new creature" as one now initiated into redemption, of the people of God as a sociohistorical community now living or beginning to live a redeemed life, and of the resurrection of the body — all imply (as does the identity of God the Creator and God the Redeemer) the unity of creation and redemption, that is, on our theme, the reaffirmation of the essential goodness of creaturely life under God, of human and natural being within the conditions of finitude: space, time, the system of causes, and our physical-psychological substance. As the act of creation points, to be sure, backward and upward beyond the finite to the activity of the God transcendent to finitude, so redemption points beyond these conditions of finitude to what has been called, paradoxically, eternal life. Nevertheless, despite this wider transnatural context, it is well, in understanding suffering therein, to emphasize the forcefulness and the significance of this assertion of the potential, the essential, and the renewed goodness of finitude.

It is, I suggest, this strong and unequivocal assertion of the positive, the potential goodness of finite, and so of creaturely and historical existence that sets the stage for the peculiar character of the Christian understanding of suffering and so accounts for both its assets and liabilities. Clearly suffering, along with its elder sibling evil, enter this stage as aliens, anomalies, interlopers, and spoilers, in fact as enemies to what is — either to what is already there or to what essentially is. Were finite existence itself a "fall," an alienation from true being in the One (mystical monism), were it a union of good spiritual elements and evil material elements (dualism), or were it merely the unintended and so unvalued result of blind natural forces (naturalism), suffering and evil would not pose a contradiction as they do here. Also, if suffering finds its cause beyond this space and time in previous lives, according to the law of karma, so that this life expresses that inherited destiny, then again suffering is intelligibly explained and understood and hardly represents a contradiction. In each case the explanation for suffering within finitude is obvious: In the first, suffering is the result of the separation or alienation out of which finitude itself arises; in the second, it is the result of the mixture of good and evil elements that constitutes finitude; in the third, suffering is the consequence of the same natural and neutral forces of things that brought finite life into being in the first place; and, in the fourth, it arises from decisions made in earlier lives. In none of these cases is there a theoretical problem in understanding suffering (a theodicy problem), since suffering and finitude arise (and recede) together; this is surely a plus. In none of these cases, however, are there credible and valid grounds for hope for any redemption from suffering within our present finitude, since in each case to be finite as we are is to suffer. The very intelligibility of the explanation of evil and suffering reflects and depends upon a necessity for evil and suffering in this life that can be (if evil and suffering are taken seriously) spiritually stifling and lead only to an attitude of resignation.

I have pitched the dilemma of Christian understanding (How can existence be affirmed in the face of the obvious evil and suffering that penetrates that existence?) at a different point than it is usually (and wrongly) pitched. That point is generally taken to be the doctrine of God; thus, it is assumed that a rearrangement of that concept represents an answer to this peculiarly Christian dilemma. To be sure, the dilemma or contradiction I have outlined becomes more apparent when the two grounds for this affirmation of a good creation are clearly articulated: (1) that God's infinite power establishes finitude (thus are there no metaphysical or ultimate factors alien to God causing evil and suffering) and (2) that God's infinite love motivates the creation of finite being. These two, unconditional divine power and love, constitute the two elements of the classical doctrine of creation out of nothing, since they provide coherent grounds (and the only sufficient grounds) for the goodness of created finite beings.

My point is that it is not this doctrinal foundation (with which I agree) that creates the deeper problem of evil; rather the fault lies with the initial affirmation of the goodness of finite being. If any form of Christianity asserts this goodness, even the potential goodness, of finite actuality, evil and suffering pose a dilemma for that assertion, even if its God is finite or indifferent. Moreover, if the sense of evil and suffering rises to predominance, the finitude of God becomes an impotence unable to generate hope for salvation, and the indifference of God becomes unbearable. I suggest that such theoretical or philosophical solutions to the problem of evil reflect, therefore, a basic optimism about evil's ultimate conquest; and, further, that this solution to the problem of evil (namely, that God is finite) can neither explain nor ground that unexplicated optimism. Finally, such views (that

God is either finite or indifferent) will generate pessimism and resignation as we move into a more difficult epoch, one in which the consciousness of suffering rises.

In any case, I think it is fair to say that peculiar to the Christian understanding of suffering (and evil) is Christianity's initial sense of the antithesis that suffering poses to the essential nature of both God and finite existence, expressed vis-à-vis God in its symbol of God as Creator and vis-à-vis existence in its symbol of the good creation. Over against many forms of spirituality (mysticism, dualism, and naturalism), therefore, Christianity appears as fundamentally optimistic and affirmative about finite existence, about its ontological and metaphysical conditions, and about its prospects both individually and historically.

SUFFERING IN THE MOMENT OF NEGATION

Although the assertions concluding the last section are valid, it is also true that the Christian tradition has represented a strongly negative assessment of natural and historical life, especially of human existence. It has as frequently been called world denying as world affirming. Put in another way, despite its initial affirmation about creaturely life, Christianity has also seen that life as suffused with evil and suffering. In fact in classical Christian eyes, so permeated is human existence with both that it cannot extricate itself by its own natural powers from either one—that is, either from the bondage of its own evil or from the various forms of suffering that ravage its finitude and will conquer it in the end. Innumerable central symbols in the cluster that constitutes Christian understanding express this negative assessment of life as it is experienced, and so the emphasis on suffering and evil: on the human side, the Fall, being now captive to the devil, estrangement or alienation from our natural order or potentialities, enmity toward God and neighbor, the bondage of the will, inevitable death, captivity in death; and on the divine side, the judgment and wrath of God, the punishing righteousness of God, and condemnation. In optimistic epochs this emphasis recedes to that of a minor voice in the wider chorus of affirmation. At other times it comes to the fore as the pervasiveness of suffering challenges optimism. Correspondingly, an emphasis on fate, sin, and death as rulers of this age is then only balanced by a greater emphasis on the power and love of divine grace.

As noted, the sharpness of the contrast between creation and suffering stems essentially from the (apparent) antagonism between the initial affirmation of finite existence and its goodness, on the one hand, and the opposing affirmation of its evil propensities and the actuality of its suffering, on the other. This contradiction is accentuated but by no means created by the two classical doctrines of God's perfection of being and love and the original perfection of the creature. That these two must be reinterpreted and, so to speak, softened is evident. Yet however these two doctrines are softened, the contradiction remains in Christian understanding so long as finite existence continues to be affirmed theologically or metaphysically and the undeniable reality and the vast scope of suffering are admitted.

Granted, then, the reality of evil and suffering in a world affirmed by God, and to be affirmed by ourselves, how are we to understand this suffering that suffuses our existence? What can be its explanation, if God created and ruled our finite existence? That is to say, in such a universe, what are the ontological conditions under which suffering arises? This is the way the question of suffering — of comprehending why it is in the sense of its cause — arises in Christian understanding. For most of the tradition there was available, in fact provided authoritatively for them by both Scripture and tradition, a perfectly credible (to them) explanation, namely, the Fall. It is not because they believed in the Fall that Christians spoke about evil and suffering; on the contrary, it is because they knew and experienced the pervasive, universal, and conquering reality of evil and suffering that they found perfectly credible, and proceeded to emphasize, the authoritative explanation for it, the story of the Fall.

Thus, for generations, in fact from Irenaeus up to Schleiermacher, the explanation for suffering was the following: (1) Neither evil nor suffering was a necessary aspect of life since the latter had been created good. (2) Because of the temptations of freedom (and the lure of Satan), however, the first and representative man and woman misused this freedom and disobeyed God; thus they came under the dominant rule of Satan, lost their power of goodness (or potential goodness), inherited a propensity for evil (Augustine), and were confined to the limits of mortality. (3) As a further consequence, the vulnerabilities and the many sufferings of physical, psychological, and mental existence (natural evils, scarcity, drought, diseases, conflicts, injustice, and ultimately death) followed. To Irenaeus these, especially death, were "allowed to us" to prevent the everlasting continuation of sin and so represented gifts of grace; to Augustine they represented punishment for sin. In either case, suffering in all its forms was understood to be a consequence of human religious and moral disobedience to God. It was understood as stemming from the broken relationship (sin) between humans and God, however that brokenness in turn may ultimately have arisen in the Fall. Confidence and hope, therefore, despite this heavy estimation of the scope of suffering, rested on the fact that this brokenness could be mended by redemption.

For most of the tradition, therefore, the problem of evil and the problem of suffering did not represent problems of theodicy, of the theological justification of God, problems to be resolved by a new philosophical theology; such was to the tradition not to understand suffering aright. On the contrary, the problems of evil and suffering represented problems of the justification and redemption of men and women — that is, issues of how, in the face of the experience of massive suffering, interlaced with the experience of inward evil, God might reunite human beings to the divine self, heal the estrangement that has caused our suffering, and thus give us hope for its conquest both here and in eternity. In most of the Christian tradition, the understanding of suffering has meant understanding its ultimate cause in the Fall, its reappearance through our own freedom, and its cure in redemption. It has not, until after the Enlightenment, meant centrally understanding how to explain suffering so as to justify God's goodness. To those who find suffering mainly a philosophical or intellectual puzzle within a Christian universe, a puzzle to be resolved by a more coherent theological or metaphysical doctrine of God, such an existential or religious understanding of it seems strangely convoluted, perhaps even irrational. To those who have deeply experienced suffering, and especially its power to blot out coherence, such an understanding can make sense in its emphasis on the existential problem of suffering and its concentration on the divine cure for it.

I said "in most of the tradition" because a very significant change in the form of this understanding took place with the Enlightenment. At this point for a number of reasons — most but not all being new scientific and historical knowledge — this explanation of the human predicament became itself incredible. To explain the intractability and arbitrary character of nature, the conflicts within nature, the disease and death that permeate nature — as well as all the problems of universal history — in terms of that far-off event in Eden became impossible. New ways of understanding human evil and suffering were thus necessary, and Hegel and Schleiermacher were foremost in providing them. For the first time in dogmatic theology, Schleiermacher distinguished natural from moral evil and sought to explain the first under the rubric of creation and only the second under that of the Fall. Thus, the sufferings, he said, that arise from the condition of our finitude are aspects of our created goodness, not consequences of sin; they are therefore borne by faith, not eliminated by it. We can understand them (explain them) in a good world as setting the conditions necessary for our own moral development, for without them personality, decision, and virtue would be meaningless.

Most theologians, insofar as they use the symbol of the Fall at all, have followed Schleiermacher at this point and distinguished natural from moral, religious, or spiritual evil. Insofar as they explain the former, they do so in terms of the necessary conditions of a finite and good creation; insofar as they explain the latter, they do so in terms of the symbol of the Fall. Hegel and Schleiermacher interpreted the Fall as the symbol of the beginning stages of spiritual and moral growth, as in effect necessary to the development of a spiritual humanity. But more recently, because the sense of the enormity of suffering as a result of sin has been so profound, twentieth-century theologians have avoided this explanation or justification of sin. Rather they have been content with interpreting the symbol of the Fall as a description of our spiritual predicament rather than an explanation of it; and they have emphasized how spiritual renewal will transmute, even if it does not conquer, the sufferings caused by natural evils.

In its understanding of natural evil and the consequent sufferings, therefore, Christianity has almost certainly moved closer to Buddhism: suffering (of this sort) arises from the conditions of temporal existence themselves, not from any historical act of human moral or religious freedom. Yet Christianity has retained its traditional view that spiritual estrangement (sin) does not flow either from being finite or even from being appropriately attached to finitude; it flows from an inward separation or estrangement of the self from God, from itself, and from its neighbor, which it labels sin. As a consequence, when this estrangement is healed (or has begun to be healed) by faith and love, a proper attachment to and affirmation of the self, others, and the world are appropriate, and the ranges of suffering caused by want, disease, and death can be creatively borne. Whether or not, or how much, that view is different from contemporary Buddhism, especially those forms expressed in existentialist categories, remains an interesting question. In any case, certainly the strength of Christian interpretation rests on its dialectical understanding of suffering and evil, that is to say, as intelligible and bearable only when seen in relation to an affirmation of the goodness of creaturely and finite freedom, not in its grasp of the explanation or cause of evil and suffering.

One may put this point: (1) that present Christian theological reflection concentrates on understanding the anatomy of suffering and of evil rather than either its cause or its justification; and (2) that it seeks to describe this anatomy dialectically, in relation to the order and goodness of existence, on the one hand, and to the promise of redemption from suffering and evil, on the other. More concretely, this involves the understanding of suffering (a) in relation to the conditions of finite creatureliness as dependent and yet active within the wider system of finite creatures and (b) as in relation to the social and historical communities in which humans live, act, and suffer. Correspondingly, it understands human evil in relation to (a) finitude and freedom, on the one hand (possibility, anxiety, temptation, death), and (b) to redemption (the ideal of Christ, the judgment of God, and the mercy of God), on the other. How much of suffering is necessary, an inescapable aspect of finitude, and how much is ontologically "contingent" and so humanly generated, the result of ignorance, of lack of instruments or know-how, or sin (for example, exploitation or injustice) are important theoretical and practical questions for this view.

Further practical matters of great importance to a Christian interpretation depend on such questions. For example, how is suffering to be understood in relation to the possibility of redemption, to the possibility of individual health, renewed individual faith and courage, or renewed community between persons? How is suffering to be understood in relation to the possibilities of social redemption, the possibility of political or social renewal—that is, in relation to individual and social redemption as promised in the Christian gospel? How is suffering understood as the suffering of the victims of sin, those sinned against? How is suffering understood as that of the perpetuators, the suffering of the disintegrating and despairing sinner? How are these two related—as they are—in each one of us? Thus is suffering understood here dialectically: backward, so to speak, in relation to the affirmation of finitude and history and to the inexplicable appearance of estrangement; and forward in relation to the promises and the experienced realities of redemption.

As noted, the strength of a religious vision lies in large part in its understanding of what suffering is, how it arises, and what characteristics it manifests, on the one hand, and how it is to be overcome, on the other. Here Buddhist and Christian understandings are similar. A Christian understanding conducts this inquiry into the meaning and intelligibility of suffering in relation to (1) the affirmative symbols of creation and providence, (2) the negative ones of Fall and sin, fatedness and death, judgment and condemnation, and (3) the reaffirmative ones of individual and social redemption, the new creature and the kingdom of God. As noted, there are both pluses and minuses within such an understanding, as, I suspect, there are in others as well.

We have seen suffering, first, in its juxtaposition with creation, representing the affirmation of finite being as real and good; in this context suffering appears as a surd, an unwanted interloper, an irrational appearance in what is essentially a seamless, or at least a potentially meaningful, world. Next we considered suffering in relation to the actuality of that world, the way this essentially good structure appears in our actual experience, namely, as also estranged or fallen. Here suffering has, in the traditional understanding, taken a slightly different role, one as caused and so explained by the fallen character of the world. Later reflection has shifted this: Suffering is seen both as partly a function of the conditions of finitude, vulnerability, and mortality (that is, of creation) and as partly an effect of the estranged character of human being and so of its history (that is, of sin). So interpreted, suffering is by no means irrational or inexplicable, especially with regard to the suffering consequent upon estrangement. While itself without metaphysical cause, estrangement and the suffering it entails reveal an anatomy that can be understood, an anatomy articulated in terms of theological anthropology; that is, in terms of the structure of human being as creaturely, as image of God, as finite freedom, plus the temptations of anxiety and the role of self-constituting freedom — all this compounded in turn by the interdependence in space and in time of each person on the human communities in which we come to be and act.

These two moments (creation and Fall) were initially separated in time, the one temporally as well as logically and ontologically preceding the other. With the loss of this temporal precedence, their relation shifts. Now both are seen as characteristic of creaturely actuality, the one representing essential structure (or "real" or "original" nature), the other estranged actuality, as (to use Augustine's image) with an eye and its enfeebled or diseased state. Both are there: the first, its created goodness — essential, structural, and so necessary; the second, its estranged actuality — contingent, historical, inescapable, and yet removable because it represents the work of freedom. In somewhat similar fashion, in Mahayana Buddhism samsara is not only both fated and free but, even more, not separable from nirvana into two distinct realms; these two, samsara and nirvana, while distinguishable in analysis, nevertheless interpenetrate each other so that the enlightened eye sees both as characterizing present actuality.

SUFFERING IN THE MOMENT OF REAFFIRMATION

Now we move to the third moment of the dialectic, that of renewal, redemption, reunion. Here suffering is seen from still another perspective, since, in relation to the redemptive work of the divine, it takes on a quite new role. Here it is transfigured or transvalued into an aspect of redemption. This redemptive moment is different from the other two in that unlike the others, it *comes;* we are not thrown into (to use Heidegger's expression) redemption as we are into creaturely being and estranged existence, which are both already there. Rather Christians experience it as "coming to" them, and so they are, as they say, reborn (an interesting phrase in relation to Buddhism, underlining as it does the reemphasis on creation). For Christian understanding, redemption appears historically in a new dispensation of divine truth and grace in historical revelation; and it appears historically for each individual in personal rebirth in faith. Thus, while creation and fall are manifested in and through every historical moment, they do not begin "at a time"; yet redemption does so happen, and as a consequence history, both that of individuals and that of the race, is filled with unique, irreplaceable, and significant events. Once redemption appears, is accepted, and is experienced, however, redemption (grace and truth) joins the other two aspects of present actuality: created structure and alienated actuality, as a healing or renewing principle. Neither of these latter disappear (recall the contemporary presence of samsara and nirvana), although (hopefully) the new principles of renewal gain in strength and so predominance. Both the conditions of finitude and the temptations and ravages of alienation remain; but the sufferings, consequent on both finitude and sin, take on a different shape and a different role in this new redemptive context. It is to understanding suffering "Christianly" within this new context of redemption that my present remarks are devoted.

Because I am now of necessity dealing with each major doctrine in systematic theology, my remarks must be both brief and incomplete, intimating rather than spelling out varying aspects of the Christian meaning of suffering in light of the fact and the appearance of redemptive grace. In general, I can sum up this new perspective on suffering by giving it two names: the transvaluation of suffering, on the one hand , and the transcendence over suffering, on the other.

Transvaluation of Suffering

I begin with the new role of suffering as an aspect of the sacred, of the redemptive activity of the divine itself—a theme found in almost all religions but, in our tradition, starting explicitly with the Suffering Servant motif in Isaiah and reaching a crescendo in the earliest Christian interpretation of the cross and so of the atonement. Here suffering is seen to represent an essential, even necessary (see Anselm, *Cur Deus Homo*) condition, if not the sufficient condition (God's love is also necessary, for example), for redemption itself. In most although not all understandings of this unexpected union of suffering with redemption, the symbol of sin or estrangement plays a crucial role: Because of the separation and guilt of sin, the divine love as well as the repentant sinner must suffer if a reunion of human being with deity is to take place. Although few contemporary theologians wish to deny this relation of redemptive suffering to sin and its forgiveness, still a new emphasis has entered: the divine participation in our suffering as an aspect (rather than a cause) of our redemption. This has long been an implication of most doctrines of incarnation and atonement: "The immortal must take on mortality and suffer therein," as Irenaeus said.

This emphasis, however, has been given a new prominence in contemporary theology. (Is this because both the role of the devil and the problem of objective guilt have receded?). A hint of this new emphasis is in Whitehead's assertion that the consequent nature of God redeems the world through experiencing (prehending) and uniting in its own harmony the world in all its joy and suffering and so suffers along with the world through experiencing the suffering of the world.[1] It also represents the center of Tillich's understanding of the atonement, as the symbol of the divine participation and sharing in the suffering conditions of existence and so the divine redemption of them in the new being. Hence is the suffering of evil transmuted, made bearable, and so conquered by the divine presence within it.[2] It is even more prominent in Moltmann's view that the redemptive power of the cross lies in its witness to God's identification with those who suffer, the divine presence with them in their suffering, and so the promise of the ultimate victory of God over their suffering.[3] In all of these motifs, suffering is transmuted and transcended through the divine participation in it, expressed more literally in classical doctrine by the effectiveness of the atoning suffering of the Christ and more symbolically in present theology by the divine healing and redemptive presence within the suffering conditions of human existence, a healing presence manifested in, not effected by, the atoning suffering of Christ.

With regard to suffering as experienced by human beings, one may distinguish between inner forms of suffering and outer, historical causes of suffering. One may say that the existential tradition in modern theology has concentrated on the first and current political theologies on the second — both (to me) being essential to the understanding of this new role of and perspective on suffering. The beginning of the inner cure of suffering (an aspect of justification and sanctification) is the work of redemptive grace. Through grace and the new life (the new being), the inner ravages of doubt, despair, deep anxiety, meaninglessness, guilt, self-hatred, and subjection to

---

[1] Alfred North Whitehead, *Process and Reality: An Essay in Cosmology,* corrected ed., ed. David Ray Griffin and Donald W. Sherburne (New York: The Free Press, 1978), esp. 342–51.

[2] Paul Tillich, *Systematic Theology* (Chicago: University of Chicago Press, 1957), 2:132ff., 174–76.

[3] Jürgen Moltmann, *The Crucified God: The Cross of Christ as the Foundation and Criticism of Christian Theology,* trans. R. A. Wilson and John Bowden (New York: Harper & Row, 1974).

inordinate desires, unreal pride, and a sense of fatedness are lessened; with the growth of a humble or repentant self-awareness and of faith, grace, and confidence in one's new self, slowly courage, serenity, love, and hope appear as an inner balance over against the suffering that both one's contingency and one's own sin created.

Correspondingly, the outer causes of suffering that are rooted in sin—oppression, injustice, exploitation, hostility, and overt conflict—can be mitigated, if not removed, by creative political action. Although political action cannot remove estrangement and sin—rather historical change re-enacts estrangement in new forms—still political reforms can increasingly control and mitigate the consequences of continuing sin. Unjust institutions (slavery, colonialism, and so on) result from sin, encourage it, and give it ample room; in parallel fashion, more just institutions, for example, political, economic, and social equality, make the envy, hostility, and greed of persons of less effect, distribute power and goods more fairly, and thus reduce the vast amount of suffering that has been the consequence of sin if not of finiteness. As Metz has pointed out, the memory of suffering and identification with the history of sufferers function as radical forces in history, calling for the removal of unjust institutions and the beginning of more adequate ones.[4] This mitigation of the consequences of sin, along with its inward healing, represents in Christian understanding the purpose in historical life of God's redemptive providence. It is thus a deep faith in that providential power and meaning that gives to the Christian the ability to transmute and overcome the sufferings encountered in daily life. Thus, as Kierkegaard has said, it is in entering suffering voluntarily rather than in seeking to avoid it that we experience God's active presence with us and calling to us. Through sharing in suffering, then, the divine purposes are uncovered (one's vocation) and the transcendence over suffering is achieved, both in one's individual existence and in the social history of communities generally.

Transcendence over Suffering

Throughout the tradition of Christianity (and Buddhism) there has been a confidence in a final or eschatological transcendence over suffering, as well as the promise of its present transvaluation—that is the ability to deal creatively with its continuing actuality. This final or eschatological tran-scendence over suffering has been expressed in the symbols of resurrection and eternal life with regard to individual existence and that of the kingdom of God with regard to communal and historical existence. Needless to say, each of these symbols has received a wide variety of interpretations (Helle-nistic, medieval, Reformation, modern, and contemporary) and each tradi-tion within Christianity has seen these in significantly different ways. Some

---

[4] Johann Baptist Metz, *Faith in History and Society: Toward a Practical and Fundamental Theology*, trans. David Smith (New York: Seabury Press, 1980).

forms of Christianity—especially in the modern and contemporary periods—
have tended to deemphasize, if not ignore and deny, the transcendent meanings of these concepts (rejecting personal eternal life in an eschatological
fellowship or communion with God [cf. Charles Hartshorne and Schubert
Ogden] or rejecting a transhistorical meaning of the Kingdom, for instance).
But almost every other part of the Christian tradition (classical, Catholic,
Reformation, liberal, and neoorthodox) has viewed meaning as extending
beyond spatial and temporal life and so earthly suffering, and redemption as
therefore transcendent to the experience of suffering as we know it here.

Certainly it seems to be the case—at least to this interpreter—that the
Christian promise of the conquest of suffering, as well as its earthly mitigation, depends on this eschatological dimension of redemption, and that the
transcendence over suffering in terms of God's experience alone does not
exhaust the meaning of that traditional promise. It is commonly agreed
among modern theologians that the efforts of Augustine and Thomas
Aquinas to justify the presence of evil as forming creative "shadows" in the
total picture viewable from the divine perspective, if not from the finite, are
incredibly weak. In fact such arguments seem to make the suffering of finite
creatures mere means to a richer infinite harmony (shadows that add to the
total picture), an end experienced only by God. Ironically the same point can
be made, it seems to me, about Hartshorne's denial of eternal life. There the
enrichment of the divine experience by God's prehension of evil and suffering in the world may effect a redemption of the suffering but it hardly helps
redeem the sufferer, who, as a now-perished sentient being, remains an
instrumental means to that divine end, represented by the infinity and ever-
lastingness of the divine enjoyment. As I have indicated, however, in the
normative Christian understanding, both creatures and their suffering are
redeemed by the divine love, or, as Calvin felicitously put it, we are saved
alone for the glory of God, but the glory of God is conjoined with God's
love for us, with God's concern that we be saved. If this is egoism, it is of
a dialectical or transmuted sort; namely, one that first loses itself as the
condition of gaining itself and surrenders its own glory as the sole ground
of sharing in glory, a theme explicitly manifested for Christians in the
voluntary suffering of Christ through which he was accepted into glory.
This paradox of gaining the self through losing it expresses the dialectic I
have here outlined: of the affirming of our finitude, the surrender of it in
repentance and faith, and the gifts through grace of a new self united now
with the divine.

THE QUESTION OF ETERNAL
SUFFERING

What I have described above represents, I think, one defensible version or
survey (map, as I called it) of the modern Christian understanding of suffering. It would be irresponsible, even a bit shady, however, to stop with the

possibility of our eschatological transcendence of suffering and to omit entirely reference to the possibility of the opposite—namely, an eschatological continuation and even increment of suffering, as represented in the symbols of punishment in purgatory and condemnation in hell. Here some of the themes already rehearsed—suffering as punishment and suffering as purgation—reappear on a transmundane scale. Unpalatable as it may be to most of us today, it is simply a fact that in our tradition the final freedom from suffering promised in redemption has by no means represented the sole final Christian word about suffering. For those who remained unredeemed, untouched by the grace and truth represented in Christ, suffering had not only continued but increased, and—unlike systems of karma—classically no hope of redemption from it remain for those untouched. So much for the traditional Christian understanding.

Perhaps the most dramatic change in Christian doctrine in the modern period—more fundamental, I think, than issues of literalism, miracles, or even authority—has been what one author called "the decline of hell," namely, the dissipation of this concept of a transtemporal and eternal suffering as the punishment for unredeemed earthly sins. This development cannot be expounded here, but it must be mentioned. Few major theologians in the nineteenth century and, to my knowledge, even fewer major theologians in the twentieth century have wished to reaffirm, even to reconstruct in their own way, the concept of hell as a place of eternal suffering, a realm eternally beyond the reach of grace. Some hesitate to draw the universalist implication (as many who asserted divine election hesitated to draw the implication of double predestination), but none speak of eternal damnation, and all tend to regard eternal suffering as more a repudiation than a vindication of the divine justice. On this one point, interestingly, Schleiermacher, Ritschl, Barth, Tillich, the Niebuhrs, Brunner, and their many diverse followers since seem to agree: The traditional and eschatological dualism in the destiny of our race into damned and saved was a mistake. Insofar as it represents a picture of contemporary Christian understanding of suffering, therefore, our account has legitimately stopped before this epilogue and so before it reached the portals of that overheated netherworld.

In sum, suffering takes on quite different hues or colors as one moves through the Christian dialectic. It appears at first as the contradiction of creation, as its negative side or shadow, and as the consequence of creaturely estrangement. Then, as the drama moves toward redemption, suffering shifts to become itself an aspect of the divine redemption; our sufferings are shared in by God's presence among us, and they are mitigated, transfigured, and finally transcended by the power of grace, that is, by the divine being and the divine love. While, therefore, the Christian understanding of suffering includes the question of theodicy—how suffering and God can be understood coherently together—it far transcends that question and involves, if all that Christianity has to say about suffering is to be articulated, many other important understandings in terms of which it takes on its unique meaning, power, and peculiar difficulties. These understandings include (1) the affirmation of finite being and meaning; (2) the interpretation of the vulnerability, despite its goodness, of creaturely being; (3) the anatomy of the estrangement of finite freedom; and (4) the character and promise to redeem and transmute suffering. As I have tried to show, on each of these levels or facets of the Christian understanding of suffering, there are gains and losses, pluses and minuses. To some this understanding may at best be convoluted, bizarre, and contradictory. To others it may well appear to be the most profound and most experientially accurate understanding of evil and suffering available, for it sets suffering and evil against the background of affirmation and the promises of ultimate confidence and ultimate hope. Probably what is important in a discussion like this one is to gain a sure grasp of these pluses and minuses and so to understand a bit more clearly why each of us, in our different perspectives, see things in ordinary experience as we do.

CHAPTER 15

DEATH AND ITS
RELATION TO LIFE

I shall begin with a quotation from the contemporary Zen philosopher and master Abe Masao. "Why on earth does the West choose being rather than non-being, death rather than life?"[1]

The remarks of this chapter will at best form a meditation. Written abroad (in the Netherlands), sans well-marked and annotated books and accumulated notes, they will contain only random scholarly references and few analyses of the thought of others. But death is present, even abroad; the aura of death and its relation to religion and philosophy can be pondered anywhere and without the benefit of classical texts. In this meditation I am primarily interested in the meaning of death for our life, as opposed to any analysis — biological, physiological, medical, psychological, or metaphysical — of its structures. This chapter will provide no ontology of death, of dying, or of their possible conquest. However, if theology is concerned with the meaning of being, while philosophy is concerned with its structure, as Paul Tillich argued, this will be a theological discourse, a theological reflection, on the meaning for our being of our nonbeing.

As large sections of both our religious and philosophical traditions have seen, death and life have a strange dialectical relation to each other. Sometimes with beauty, sometimes with destructive terror, they perform a kind of intricate, interwoven dance with one another: in part a frenzied and

---

[1] Various reflections on this question may be found in the recent collection Masao Abe, *Zen and Western Thought*, ed. William R. LaFleur (Honolulu: University of Hawaii Press, 1985). See also Langdon Gilkey, review of *Zen and Western Thought*, by Masao Abe, *The Eastern Buddhist*, n.s., 19 (Autumn 1986): 109–21.

mortal duel, in part a courtship. Each seems essential to the other, as both an antithesis and as a necessary partner. For example, if, as in the modern West, personal life is valued ever more highly, death correspondingly, as the apparent negation of all of life's values, is feared, set aside, avoided, covered up, denied. But death is there, permeating our common existence, even that of modern men and women. The avoidance of death effects in turn a loss of life, a covering up and an eclipsing of life's depth, its risk, its meaning and so results in an ultimate loss of the courage to live. If, by contrast, life is negated or disvalued, and the reality of personal being not even uncovered, much less valued, then human death, too, loses its significance and becomes merely the removal from our common space of one more instance of the species. The perennial dilemma for religion and philosophy here manifests itself: How is life to be valued and loved and yet death accepted and faced? How is it possible to exist embodying a genuine dialectic or interplay between these two aspects of our existence rather than with a destructive concentration on and acceptance of only one of them?

This dialectic appears throughout the classical tradition of Christian theology. Preceded by the Israelite themes of the servant people and the Suffering Servant, the interweaving of suffering and death with victory and life dominates all of authentic Christian understanding. The self is to die if it would live; the death of the Christ is the principle of the possibility of his resurrection and of the eternal life of all others; and the death of each of us is or can be the entrance into eternal life. Nonbeing seems essentially interwoven with being in God's requirements for our existence, in the revelation of God's purposes and character and in the process through which reconciliation and redemption take place. Augustine sums all of this up in his meditation on the meaning of Christ's death: In dying himself, Jesus taught us not to fear the death of the body that is unavoidable but rather to fear the death of the soul (sin) that is avoidable. In running from death, which cannot be escaped, we fall more deeply into the sin that can be escaped; in accepting the possibility of death, we transcend ourselves and at last can begin to live as we ought.[2]

One theme within this classical tradition seems to qualify this interdependent dialectic of life and death, however: the insistence that our common human death is the punishment for and the result of Eve and Adam's sin. The deeper theological themes at work here are surely that our finitude, as the result of the loving God's good creation, is itself good and not evil and, as a consequence, that life's evident and pervasive evils (weakness, disease, suffering, and death) are not natural and so necessary to our existence as created. Rather, in God's good world, evils are unnatural, the result, as Augustine argued, not of the necessities of our nature but of a contingent historical event. They are thus susceptible to being overcome by

---

[2] Augustine, *De Trinitate* 4.

the further historical yet divine event of the resurrection. Thus is creation despite its obvious ambiguity, unequivocally affirmed; redemption from death, as well as from sin, is made credible; and God's goodness is thoroughly justified.

One of the most significant changes modern experience and reflection have effected in the classical tradition of theology is with regard to the status of death. More specifically, almost universally since Schleiermacher, death has been interpreted as an aspect, a necessary and essential aspect, of our finitude rather than as the result of an original sin by the two progenitors of the race. There are innumerable grounds for this changed understanding of death and, along with death, all so-called natural evils. These grounds include: (1) our increased awareness of the continuity between our own organic structures and those of all living creatures, and so the continuity between our death and the death of all natural creatures everywhere; (2) the intricate relatedness of the physiological structure of our life with the structure of our dying; (3) the present impossibility of identifying the origin of either death or sin with the actions of a primordial pair of ancestors; and (4) the difficulty of conceiving of God as punishing the subsequent race for the misdeeds, however spectacular, of their progenitors. For most contemporary theologians, the story of Adam, Eve, and their fall remains the most profound and illuminating symbolic account of the predicament participated in by each of us: "In each the work of all, and in all the work of each," as Schleiermacher put it.[3] It has ceased to represent a historical report of a definite action or a definite event in the past, an event causative of our present inner estrangement, of our present miseries, or of our having to die. With the evaporation of the historical Adam and Eve and the historical event of the Fall has vanished the explanation of death as the result of a primal act of sin.

This shift in the relation of suffering and death to finitude and sin has been one of the major factors that has made the problem of evil, the theodicy question, such a forceful, disturbing one for modern times. Prior to the Enlightenment, when the disease, suffering, vulnerability, and death characteristic of our existence could be ascribed to Eve and Adam's sin—and our participation in that sin—the presence of these "negativities" could be easily comprehended in terms of Christian belief; God had not willed or created them, and life is good because real life, authentic life, life as created by God, is free of them. When once, however, our finite existence has been seen inescapably to be characterized by suffering, disease, vulnerability, and ultimately death, the question of the value or worth of life suffused with death, of a being permeated with nonbeing, and the question of the loving goodness of a God responsible for them suddenly have gained force, and

---

[3] Friedrich Schleiermacher, *The Christian Faith,* trans. and ed. H. R. Mackintosh and J. S. Stewart (Philadelphia: Fortress Press, 1976), 288.

theism has subsequently had a much more difficult time defending itself against modern criticism.

The eighteenth and nineteenth centuries, which uncovered this nest of worms, quickly covered them over again for themselves through their faith in the progress of the race. Individual life, they said, might in truth be beset with weakness, vulnerability, and death, but the ongoing life of the species is not. On the microscopic scale, growth is balanced by decay, life by death. But on the macroscopic scale of the race and its history, growth appears without decay, life unfolds without death, because human history represents a continual progressive fulfillment. Thus is creation justified, existence affirmed, and (if a God was desired) God acquitted. Our century has come to disbelieve in historical progress almost as thoroughly as the eighteenth and nineteenth centuries came to disbelieve in original sin. Thus, the macroscopic answer to the fact of suffering and death—that a deathless race will in the end achieve in history a perfectly meaningful, unambiguous, and "happy" mode of life—is no longer a possible answer for us. Death has returned now with a renewed force as a threat to the goodness of life, to be countered neither by the older, orthodox Christian answer nor by the modern progressivist one. The dilemma for our reflection, theistic and non-theistic alike, is therefore both real and significant: How can we understand the goodness of finite existence, if vulnerability and death are essential and ineradicable aspects of that existence? For theists the issue is even sharper: How can we understand the purposes and goodness of God if death as well as life, nonbeing as well as being, seem to characterize the finitude that God has so graciously created?

I make no claim to be able to answer these questions, either by the end of this chapter or by the end of my own life. Some initial clarity, however, is perhaps possible. My theme will be twofold: On the one hand, I will suggest that the dialectic with which I began—that finite existence must participate in an interweaving of life and death if it is to be authentic—is one clue to the understanding of the role of death in life; on the other hand, I will suggest that this dialectic is possible only if death and life are understood theonomously and not autonomously, as characterizing a finitude grounded in the divine and not in itself. This will lead to the final question, which for the moment I will not pursue further: Does this dialectic of life and death in finitude, if it is true, imply a similar dialectic in God?

DEATH'S AFFIRMATIVE ROLE IN LIFE

I shall begin with the positive role of death in life, a theme uncovered and emphasized in modern times by Kierkegaard and by the existentialist tradition that has followed him, much as it was sounded earlier by the Socratic and the Stoic traditions. Here death, like our temporality and spatiality, is understood as an essential part of the structure of finite life itself. As setting the limit or boundary of the self's life, it is the condition, as are all limits in finite life, for the reality and meaning of the self and for the possibility of its *aretē* or spiritual and moral fulfillment.

CONDITION FOR THE SELF'S REALITY AND VALUE

The presence of death as the terminus for life, and its reflected presence "backward" in awareness in each moment of life, is the condition for a real self; it establishes the possibility of the seriousness of life and thus for its inner reality and depth. Only if the series of moments of life is finite does each one of the moments in the series count as the locus of a significant decision, of a serious either/or, a turning point decisive for subsequent moments. (Note how here death functions on the microscopic level as a terminus, of history and even of time, to give the moments of time decisiveness, only orthodoxy failed to see this positive role and to draw this conclusion in its assessment of death!) Only if this creative presence of death is made conscious by reflection is this seriousness realized and the possibility of decision, of the ethical, open. A life lived only from moment to moment, a life that continually evades the presence of death, one whose attention is averted from death and so is unaware of the limit and the seriousness of its moments, dissipates into the abstracted unreality of the spectator or the dilettante in life; thus, it fails to achieve either unity, meaning, or selfhood; and it culminates in the despair of emptiness and boredom characteristic of the aesthetic mode. As Kierkegaard remarks, such a cipher "dies and leaves the scene and nothing of him remains; or rather, he himself remains like a ticket in the hands of the usher, an indication that the spectator has gone."[4]

Death uncovers backward the ineradicable individuality of human existence, the fact that we each must achieve seriousness, decision, selfhood, commitment, and obedience—the ethical and the religious that constitute human existing. No one can be a self for us; nor can we become a self through dependence on the selfhood of others; here we are alone and alone responsible. Self-constitution is something each self must do for and by itself. In its loneliness death uncovers this for us. In this ultimate apex of life's seriousness, we are absolutely alone. No one else's courage or faith will avail us. As Luther said, "The priest can shout in your ear from the edge of the bed, but each of us welcomes death alone, and only our own faith will avail." Kierkegaard repeats this theme: "When those closest to you quietly leave and the stillness grows because only the most intimate ones remain, and when the last one is gone—then there still remains one by the deathbed, he who

---

4 Søren Kierkegaard, *Concluding Unscientific Postscript,* trans. David F. Swenson and Walter Lowrie (Princeton: Princeton University Press, 1968). I wish here to record my indebtedness to a former student, Marcia Bunge, whose paper "Kierkegaard's Examination of Death" for a seminar on Kierkegaard helped me, far from my own books, immensely with these Kierkegaard references.

was the first — God."[5] The presence and awareness of death in life is the condition, the sign, of individual selfhood and thus the condition for the reality and value of the self.

Finally, death can express, give form to, and so seal the meaning of a person's life. To face the risk of death, as we have noted, is a condition for the reality of commitment and so for the meaning that commitment gives to human existence. No one who loves, who is loyal, who believes in a cause, who stands for a principle — however deeply that commitment may be felt — is assured of the reality and power of that love, loyalty, or belief until it is tested, so slippery is the character of our inner intentionality. Nor is that inward seriousness shaped, defined, and sealed until that test comes. The only fail-proof test is, however, the willingness to face death, which, ironically enough, will bring that commitment to its temporal end. Thus can the meaning of a life be sealed finally in death and only in death. Every tradition recognizes this in the status given to the martyr. Japan has made it the awesome center of its understanding of human excellence (*aretē*): to "enjoy" a noble death is everything that a finite creature might ask, for here is sealed in eternity all the meaning (that is, all the loyalty and courage) that such a life might contain. Again, death functions as the condition for a full life, as the structure or frame within which deep meaning is possible.

PARADIGM OF THE AUTHENTIC SELF

The second positive role of death in life is as the paradigm of the authentic self. Only the self that is willing to die can truly live; or, as Augustine put this, only the self that is willing to die can escape sin and live. Mortality (having to die, being about to die) is the ever-present sign of our finitude. To recognize our own finitude and live within its bounds — and so to live creatively — is therefore synonymous with the recognition and acceptance of our death, our own having to die, as Kierkegaard reminds us, not the "having to die" of the race. But one of the conditions for a relation to eternity, a relation to God, is the recognition of, better, the appropriation of our finitude. Unless we experience and affirm the relativity of all we are and do, we are, say Augustine and Kierkegaard together, mired among the transient things of the world and among the crowd. We never achieve either personal integrity or a relation with God. Thus, "resignation of all that is finite," established by recognizing our mortality, is the first step to spiritual health.

One mode already explored for escaping the presence of death is to avert the eyes, pretend it is not there, thus losing all seriousness and inner reality. The other is to resist our finitude, our having to die, to seek to make ourselves transcendent to the finitude and the death that is ours. More often than

---

[5] Kierkegaard, *Søren Kierkegaard's Journals and Papers*, trans. and ed. Howard V. Hong and Edna H. Hong (Bloomington: Indiana University Press, 1975), 3:39, entry 2407.

we are wont to think, a choice is given us between security and justice. To be just—in personal, business, political, social, and international matters—all too often represents and requires a risk, a new and deeper openness to vulnerability, if we are to further the cause of justice, to create community, to establish or preserve peace. Those who cannot bear to face insecurity, who cannot face the possibility of their own death, will consistently refuse that risk. On the contrary, they will seek to amass property, annihilate the competitor, overwhelm their rivals, pile up more armaments, grasp and hold more territory, lest they themselves be overcome by the enemy "over there." The insecurity of finitude (represented quintessentially by the threat of death) can lead to an anxiety that drives us into the sin of injustice: imperialism, oppression, violence, and conflict. In this way finitude and anxiety, death and sin are related, sin being precisely the refusal to recognize and live with the limit, the vulnerability, the terminus, represented by death. Thus, if "resignation," recognition of our finitude and partiality and the acceptance of both, is the beginning of inner spiritual health and true self-understanding, acceptance of death is also the possibility of the ethical, a just relation to the other, and the possibility of creative community. The community that loves itself exclusively, said Augustine, cannot but serve itself and its own interests; and thus it cannot but end in the self-destruction of injustice and conflict; to refuse to face one's own death is to fall ever more deeply into sin. Only if we or our group are in the end willing to be nothing can we escape the demonic absolutization of what we are and then creatively affirm the partial values that we do represent. Death, like seasickness, deals "justly," chortled Kierkegaard; neither one recognizes distinctions of rank, wealth, power, or brilliance. Death, the recognition of having to die, also is the condition for our earthly justice: Only if each accepts the possibility of insecurity can humans be just to one another. Strangely enough, the aura of death is one of the elements necessary for the establishment of the kingdom of God, at least on earth as it is in heaven.

In two distinct modes, I have outlined the dialectical dependence of life—a meaningful, personal, and communal life—on the presence of death: as the condition of seriousness and so of decision within the moments of time and as the condition of justice through the recognition and appropriation of our finitude and so of our essential insecurity. Let us note that precisely these two arguments, posed, to be sure, in slightly different terms, have formed the substance of a major naturalistic attack upon religion, at least insofar as the latter has been concerned with the ultimate transcendence over death. Religion, it is said—and in many respects this argument, let us admit, has been quite correct—promises a solution to the problem of death, namely, a life after death. In so doing, so the argument runs, it essentially removes the sting of death; the seriousness and finality of death are reduced; death becomes for faith merely the anteroom of a better world. As a result of this dilution of death, this removal of life's terminus, the argument continues, there is also the removal of the possibility of an authentic and creative life. How can we be serious about our own present temporality, if we are promised an eternity later? How can we be ultimately concerned with justice here and now, if our "real home" is somewhere else, in a life beyond death? For this reason the powerful critics of religion—from Feuerbach through Marx and Nietzsche to Camus—have repeated, in varying ways, these same themes. Certainly, we may remark, if Augustine and Kierkegaard could also echo (in fact, devise) this understanding of the positive role of death in authentic life, then these arguments against religion become a bit more problematic. Nevertheless, one obligation for us in seeking to give a religious interpretation of death will be to show how such an interpretation incorporates and deepens this understanding of the positive role of death outlined in the preceding pages.

DEATH'S NEGATIVE ROLE IN LIFE

The positive role of death in the achievement of an authentic and creative life is unquestioned once one is made aware of it by the profound insight of religious and philosophical reflection. Much more obvious—in fact the very first article of any summation of human "common sense"—is the negative role of death in relation to authentic life, the threat (a mortal threat, as we say) that death poses to life on all its levels and in all its facets. In this role death is the concrete and effective sign of the nonbeing that permeates our finitude, that erodes and finally disintegrates our being. One may say that since in and through it the unconditioned power of nonbeing manifests itself, death is the medium or vehicle of a negative revelation, the locus of a negative theophany, the archenemy of being and so of our being.

This is certainly the way death has been understood in most cultures ancient and modern (as in the Gilgamesh epic) and in most religions. Patristic Christianity interpreted the gospel almost entirely as the effective divine answer to death (not to sin). For almost every patristic theologian, the ultimate purpose of the incarnation was that here the incorruptible (immortal) divine being had united itself with corruptible (mortal) human being to rescue the latter from death. As Irenaeus said, "He became what we are, corruptible, that we might become what He is, incorruptible." Athanasius added, "Had our problem been merely sin, the incarnation would not have been necessary; but since it was corruption and mortality, a union of the divine with the human was essential in order that God's will to save might be realized."[6]

This attitude of fear, loathing, and horror toward death is felt universally; and it is expressed universally in myths, symbols, and rites. It hardly needs philosophical or theological explication to give it force. Nevertheless, such explication can help us to understand what we are otherwise aware of; it may make theoretically intelligible the character of the mood we find inescapably

---

[6] Irenaeus, *Against Heresies;* Athanasius, *On the Incarnation of the Word of God.*

in ourselves whenever death enters our scene. There may be said to be three dimensions of human existence that are subject to the negative force of death: (1) our life, being, or existence in the ordinary sense of those words; (2) the meaning of our life; and (3) the issue of the justice or righteousness of our life, the problem of guilt. Death is intimately related as a powerful negative force to each of these dimensions; let me briefly discuss them in turn.

NEGATION OF BEING'S CATEGORIES

Death, I said, was the vehicle or medium of a negative theophany. Through it is manifested, with unconditioned force and effect, the apparently almighty power of nonbeing over us. This is the source both of its numinous character and of its final terror for all that yet lives. This role as the decisive sign of unconditioned nonbeing can be thematized and so understood in terms of death's interrelatedness with the categories of being—those structures of existence and our thought about existence that constitute finitude: time, space, causality, and substance. As Tillich has shown us, each of these categories expresses the presence of being: We are in time and in space; we are as caused and as causes; and we are as continuing entities.[7] Yet each of the categories, as a category of finitude, carries with it the presence of nonbeing, the boundedness of finite being by nonbeing, and, in principle, the final conquest of being by nonbeing. Death both symbolizes and effects, in the case of each category, that final victory of nonbeing.

Time passes by and vanishes, and ultimately that time has an end when there is no more time for us—in death. Our space, which is only precariously and barely ours and can each day be lost so that we "have no place," is in the end finally lost—in death. A tomb is the symbol of the attempt to preserve for ourselves and our own a continuing place, but as every myth and ghost story, every joke about worms, and our own visceral feelings tell us, even our tomb is hardly ours. Similarly our power to be a cause and to maintain ourselves, even though caused, comes to an end; we are finally only caused, determined, impotent at death. Our own reality, preserved precariously throughout life amid an essential vulnerability, comes to an end; our reality, our substance, becomes totally vulnerable in death. The radical insecurity and nothingness that are felt in connection with death, our descent into nonbeing, is uncovered theoretically here. Each of the categories of finitude, insofar as it expresses the nonbeing as well as the being characteristic of our existence, culminates in death when that nonbeing totally engulfs our precarious being. One may remark as an aside that what is apparently called for in death is the presence of an unconditioned being in which we may participate both in life and death.

---

[7] Paul Tillich, *Systematic Theology* (Chicago: University of Chicago Press, 1951), 1:192–98.

NEGATION OF LIFE'S MEANING

As I noted earlier, death can become the shaping force, the guarantee, and the seal of a life's meaning, of that value to which a life gives itself and from which in turn it receives worth. I do not have space to give here an adequate analysis of this conception of meaning. Suffice it to say that the giving of the self to a person or a relation, to a task, a community, a cause, is the condition for the reality, vitality, power, and fulfillment of the self; and that death, or the acceptance of death, can effect and seal that commitment and that meaning. But meaningful martyrdom is rare; far more frequently death has a negative role with regard to meaning. It may intervene before such meaning appears in life and cut off that life's possibilities; it may prevent the giving of the self for the other or for a cause; it may so permeate and dissolve the courage and the *eros* of a life that no such commitment can arise. In all these cases, death prevents or cuts off the meaning of a life, renders that life by its own standards empty and useless, and thus represents an unconditioned threat to its fulfillment. This strange dialectical relation of death to meaning is perfectly expressed in the classical Japanese fear of being prevented, by an untimely or an ill-prepared death, from enacting a noble and worthy death. What is apparently called for — to continue my aside — in death's threat to our finite meanings is the presence of an unconditioned meaning in which we may participate both in life and death.

NEGATION OF LIFE'S AUTHENTICITY

The close relation of death to guilt has always been sharply realized. This relation is expressed in countless religious myths and rites: At death the soul is finally and decisively judged for the sins of its whole life; at death it "pays for" its sins; by death the soul is separated from any further opportunity to attain reconciliation, forgiveness, and peace. In each of these themes the negativity of death includes, enforces, and increases the negativity of guilt. The reason for this close relation between the terminus of life in death and the moral or immoral quality of life is again death's role in providing a boundary and a shape or form to a life. Death defines the extent and the quality of a life's span. Thus does death function positively in giving a life character and meaning; thus, as we have just noted, does it function negatively in preventing any meaning in a given life. In this case thus does it function negatively in defining, shaping, and summing up the moral ambiguity of a life.

The moral quality of a life is related to that life's temporal extent, but it is not identical to it. The termination of the life does not terminate its moral ambiguity. Like the positive meaning of a life, this moral ambiguity remains as the character that life has had, a character not only undissolved by death but even more made definitive thereby. Of course, if neither meaning nor integrity is considered important, death poses little threat. Then, however, we have returned to the case of a lifespan characterized precisely by the absence of life from the beginning, or, better put, to the fact that a self and so a human existence were never achieved at all, symbolized by the ticket stub in the hands of the usher.

To any life, therefore, for which authenticity or integrity are significant, death remains an ultimate negativity. Whatever inauthenticity or lack of integrity that life incarnates will be summed up, shaped, made definitive and permanent in death, as when a text or a work of art is completed, its contents for good or evil also completed and given their final, permanent form. Since no life is free of the dark shadow of bad faith, death brings with it for all of us the negativity of guilt. What is apparently called for in the alliance death makes with guilt is an unconditioned forgiveness and acceptance in which we can participate alike in life and death.

On every level, then, death poses an ultimate threat to human existence: to its being, its meaning, its authenticity. Death brings with it nonbeing, meaninglessness, and guilt — the three primary enemies of human reality and fulfillment. No wonder it is feared and hated; no wonder that welcoming it, however it comes to us, is an act of supreme courage, self-control, and self-transcendence. No wonder the avoidance of it permeates and mummifies our daily life. Insofar as to be is to be good (the seat and source of value), insofar as creativity and love are of ultimate worth, insofar as authenticity and integrity represent human worth — in precisely that far is death always able to represent an unconditioned negativity, the annihilation of all that is of worth, the ultimate sign of nonbeing.

THE NOTION OF THEONOMOUS DEATH

This last part is very tentative, although I am too far along in years for it to remain much longer too tentative. Our dilemma stems from the dialectical relation of death to life, the appearance of death in vastly different guises: as partner or lover to life in a strange yet intensely meaningful courtship, and as the enemy, and the destroyer of life and so, apparently, of all. Because of that dual role, seemingly each of the classical resolutions is wanting. The ordinary religious answer sees death in this latter, sheerly negative role as the unique and decisive sign of nonbeing; it defines the self and God precisely over and against death, the first as finite being and the second as absolute being. Thus does religion hope to overcome the enemy death through the absolute power of God. Naturalism has rightly criticized this as removing from life the conditions for the possibility of life's depth, integrity, meaning, and justice, as we noted. Yet, having no answer itself to death, naturalism hopefully (if uncertainly) views death as the misunderstood courtier, as easily acceptable if not adored by a cool, transcending reason and a resolute will, and thus as posing no real threat to life, its meaning, or its integrity. Against this the facts also speak: Death is more terrible than this, more annihilating to our finitude, our rationality, our will, and more destructive of the personal relations and the communal tasks that make life meaningful.

Left alone, our frail being and precarious meanings crumble before its mighty nonbeing, and so again we are unable to be in the face of this shadow falling over our estranged and fleeting life.

My tentative suggestion is that we consider the notion of a theonomous death. Theonomy is a category used to describe an essential and creative finite being and thus a creative culture.[8] Contrasted as it is with both autonomy and heteronomy, theonomy points to finite being as essentially dependent on an unconditioned depth or ground beyond itself. In separation from this ground, the autonomous (rational, emotive, aesthetic, and moral) powers of the creature go awry, come into conflict with one another, and dissipate into nothingness. Thus, an autonomous (naturalistic or merely humanistic) understanding of human being and an autonomous (secular) culture ultimately lose their spiritual power and meaning. In such a situation of separation or estrangement, the unconditioned, the transcendent, and the holy do not go away; rather they now appear as heteronomy, as that which as transcendent is alien to the powers of autonomy and to the freedom and creativity of culture; they appear outside of and over against rational and moral autonomy, as oppressive, dogmatic, moralistic, and intolerant, and as ultimately irrational and demonic. The twentieth century has witnessed innumerable examples of the appearance of a demonic heteronomy, expressed in myths and cults, claiming to speak a transcendent message with a divine voice, moving with power against all autonomous freedom and creativity (in politics, art, thought, speech, and social existence), and harnessing to its own irrational ends the entire autonomous powers of reason, science, technology, and law created by an autonomous culture that had lost its depth, meaning, and power. Theonomy thus represents, over against both autonomy and heteronomy, a self-transcending finite being, dependent on a ground beyond itself yet in such a way that its own creative powers, its own standards, goals, and projects, its own *aretē* and fulfillment, are realized and not crushed. A theonomous finitude, in being fully its creative self, is at the same time a medium or vehicle — or symbol — of the infinite power and unconditioned meaning, an infinite power and meaning that is communicated through that medium and manifested or revealed within it. Such a manifestation of the ultimate and the sacred is expressed, of course, through its own particular historical and individual style; nonetheless it is this relation to an unconditioned meaning that gives to that "creaturely reality" (be it a person, a work of art, a system of laws, a religious text, a culture) its own finite spiritual power and meaning. A theonomous finitude is thus at once real, significant, free, and creative; but it also points beyond itself. It is a self-transcending symbol or theophany of the unconditioned, the infinite, and the sacred, of the divine.

---

[8] Tillich, *Systematic Theology* 1:83–86, 147–50; Tillich, *Systematic Theology* (Chicago: University of Chicago Press, 1963), 3:249–65.

Although, to my knowledge, Tillich never used this concept in connection with death, nevertheless I suggest that such use can help to clarify and make comprehensible what occurs in the creative dialectic of life and death — or when their inevitable interrelation is creative. Then death (not finite being but, in this case, finite nonbeing) is itself theonomous; it represents a theonomous nonbeing, the nonbeing within our own finitude as pointing beyond itself to its own deeper ground and so manifesting that ground in and through itself. On the one hand, death appears as real and full of power, the power of definition and meaning, as we have seen, and the power of destruction or annihilation. Here death is and must be confronted and accepted as an autonomous power with its own negative and positive reality. That positive role cannot be separated from its negative, annihilating power, as we have seen. But taken fully autonomously, as a negative reality on its own, as the enemy of our finite being, death is victorious. Because of its infinite power, its creative role turns into a heteronomous role, oppressing and crushing the value of life. Taken theonomously, however, death shows its reality, power, and meaning; but in pointing beyond itself to its own infinite ground, it is itself transcended, and its negative annihilating power is withdrawn. Through death we transcend both life and death. Death can, therefore, be transparent to the transcendent, to a divine power and meaning that is neither simply life nor simply death.

This view of death as theonomous provides, I take it, the ontological and theological framework for understanding that final ethical message of the gospel, and of many another religious tradition: They who would live, let them first die; they who would save their life, let them give it for another. To die to the self is to begin truly to live. Here death is more than a mere negation; it is itself a vehicle or medium of the transcendent, a medium that must be accepted, approved, and willed (justified, as Luther would say) if life is to be found. I am not at all sure that the tradition has seen precisely this point in this, one of its central motifs.

Finally, one may well ask, If death is theonomous, if it itself can become a medium or vehicle of revelation, what does this mean about the divine that is thus manifested through death? Does this mean that negation, nonbeing — the opposite seemingly of finitude and life — are in God and not, as we were always sure, God's antithesis, God's enemy? Is not God, on the contrary, pure being, absolute *esse,* pure actuality, being itself, and thus ipso facto the opposite of nonbeing? These are interesting questions but far too complex to discuss adequately at the end of a chapter.

Surely, however, it is not too much to say that if a Christian takes the cross and the atonement as revealing God's nature and purposes (and not merely of Jesus' own human fidelity and courage), then in some strange way death has already become a medium of revelation, a mode of the divine action, and even a symbol of the divine through which the divine is itself manifested to us. Through this death, according to all Christian piety and theology, God manifests the divine power, purposes, and love to us. This we have also found appropriate and true for our own death: For a self that is willing to die to itself, death is an aspect of our existence to be accepted and embraced as itself a step, a medium, a symbol of the transcendent ground on which we are dependent. Quite possibly this, if true, means that the divine, revealed in this way through both life and death, shares in both being and nonbeing. In the Christ figure and in our own existence, the divine power and meaning are manifested through both life and death. In a Christian way this perhaps approximates the sense of the Buddhist quotation with which this chapter began.

INDEX